Love
Was Not
Enough

By Peter Edward Baumann

Founder and President of
PROBE GOLF, Inc. and Reciprocal Golf, Inc.

Order this book online at www.trafford.com
or email orders@trafford.com

Most Trafford titles are also available at major online book retailers.

Printed in the United States of America.

ISBN: 978-1-4269-2837-6 (sc)
ISBN: 978-1-4269-2838-3 (hc)
ISBN: 978-1-4269-2839-0 (e)

Library of Congress Control Number: 2010905018

Trafford rev. 04/07/2011

 **www.trafford.com**

North America & international
toll-free: 1 888 232 4444 (USA & Canada)
phone: 250 383 6864 ♦ fax: 812 355 4082

Based on a True Story

Watch for LOVE WAS NOT ENOUGH, the movie!

2ND EDITION

Dedication

This book is dedicated to my two sons, Pete (a.k.a. Rio Veradonir) and Bobby. They are a testament to what will happen when parents lift up their children, and never put them down; what will happen when parents educate their children, and encourage them to believe in themselves and achieve their dreams.

Foreward

This story is based on actual events. The names of the family characters have been changed to protect the identities of those involved. The names of the PGA Tour professionals involved in this story are real. The places are real, and the dates are as accurate as memory allows.

Two weeks out of college after majoring in Business Management, in 1970, I started my first company, Intertel, Inc. We invented, manufactured and marketed worldwide the world's first cordless telephone, and the first "touchpad dialer", used worldwide on rotary dial telephone systems when touchtone service was only available in 19% of the United States, and nowhere overseas!

I have been self-employed ever since, as the President of six businesses I founded. After taking a Dale Carnegie sales training class in 1970, my motto for the next 40 years has been, **"You will get everything you want out of life if you help enough other people get what they want!"**

I have followed that motto in the real estate industry, my golf equipment business, Probe (www.probegolf.com), and my current golf service company, Reciprocal Golf (www.reciprocalgolf.com). I followed that motto while producing my son's independent film, SPIN OF FABRICATIONS (www.spinoffabrications.com) at our Film Production company, Veradonir (www.veradonir.com).

I decided to write this story for several reasons. First, when I lost Patti for the fifth time in 15 years, the fifth time to a heart attack, I was tremendously depressed. I was so depressed, I considered suicide. Finally, I decided that if I could tell my story, a story many people think is shocking, appalling, and unbelievable, it would be good therapy for me. I figured I could get some feedback from readers to find out if I am way off base in my opinion of several members of her family, and also if Patti's family is out of their collective minds!

Secondly, I am writing this true story because I have never read a fictional love story that approached the twists and turns, the ups and downs, and the shocking ending of my real life experiences I lay down in this book.

Thirdly, the life lessons I learned from my own experiences the last 16 years are lessons I want to share with others. First of all, millions of married couples may learn why marriages fail because the wives insist their husbands put them ahead of their careers. Secondly, many parents fail to follow two simple rules of parenting when raising their children and their childrens' futures suffer as a result.

> *Men and women who hope to marry and raise*
> *children successfully should take heed and learn*
> *from my story how to avoid the mistakes that were*
> *made in this story.*

A word of caution: this book is a true and accurate love story, the story of the last 31 years of my life, and as such contains adult content. Only mature readers should read this book!

Contents

PROLOGUE

October 19, 2009

One hour ago I was driving my 2000 Chevy Blazer S-10 SUV along Highway 3, north of Yreka, California. The road wound left and right, with the Shasta River to my left, two hundred feet below, only a thin metal barricade between me and the end! All it would take is a quick jerk of the wheel to the left, a brief fall of about three seconds, and the pain would stop forever!

I never knew depression could be such a strong force! Obviously there are different levels of depression, but to be so depressed to think of ending your life? I never understood how that could be a reality, until now.

My best friend, my soul mate, was gone. I would have given my life for her at any time over the 16 years I wanted her. I loved her with all my heart and soul. Unfortunately, love was not enough!

PART ONE – The Beginning

Saturday, May 5, 1979

Her name was Patti. Her sister, also behind the bar, was Katy. I couldn't decide which one was prettier. I had just driven 752 miles from Newport Beach, California, to the Lake Shastina Golf Resort outside Weed, California with my brother, Brian, in my 1978 light blue Chevy Camaro and I needed a drink. We planned to play some golf for a week, then return to Newport Beach to get back to work.

"Jack and water", I ordered from Katy. She was pretty with her long, brown hair down to her shoulders. Brian ordered a red wine by the glass. Patti, pretty and cuter than Katy with a look of mischief in her eyes, barely covered by her short blond hair, watched us from the other end of the bar.

Brian and I whispered about which of the two sisters was hotter! After Katy walked to her sister, it looked like the sisters were talking about Brian and me as well, sizing us up.

We learned that night that both sisters were married. One had two children, the other, none.

Brian and I asked Katy for a deck of playing cards and we started playing gin rummy while sipping our drinks at the bar. Katy asked if she could join us, so we played three ways.

By the end of the night, Brian and I would get into a fight over Katy, who was flirting with both of us.

Within three days, both sisters would come on to me. It looked to me at the time that neither sister was satisfied being married. Within ten days, I would respond back positively to one of them and end up breaking up her marriage.

Within two years I would be married to one of the sisters, the oldest sister. Within fourteen years I would have an affair with the other sister, the younger one, and end our marriage.

If I had known that by 2004 I would be living with the younger sister, for four years, and then lose her to a heart attack on her 55th birthday in 2008, I probably would have finished my Jack and Water and driven back to Newport Beach that night, in 1979.

I wonder every day how my life would have been different if I had done just that.

I also wonder what would have happened if I had responded back positively to the other sister that first week, instead of the one I did respond to, and ended up marrying.

I can only speculate how my life would have changed.

THIS IS MY (TRUE) STORY:

May 6, 1979

I woke up in my waterfront townhouse at Lake Shastina that I had bought as an investment five years earlier. My head was throbbing. The first Jack had turned into several more the night before. I looked around for Brian and then remembered he had found a townhouse the night before right next to the golf club. I couldn't remember exactly what the fight was about, except that it was about the sisters.

Women will do that to men, mess up their heads. But try to remember what it was all about the next day, forget it.

I drove back to the club for breakfast. Katy was serving. I ordered a western omelet with two eggs, rye toast, and coffee, black. The omelet was delicious.

After serving two other tables of golfers, complete with their golf spikes snagging on the carpet, Katy came over to my table and asked if she could sit down and visit. I said, "Sure".

She asked me where I was from. I told her my brother and I were from Newport Beach, California and were up to play some golf. She asked where my brother was, and I told her.

"You and he seemed mad at each other last night," she said.

"He'll get over it," I said. "I'm over it already," I added.

"What was the argument about," she asked. "Nothing important," I replied. "Forget about it."

She asked me if I had ever been to Lake Shastina before, or was this my first time. I told her I used to sell the golf lots around the course eight years earlier, and had played the golf course many times before.

We chatted for a while, as she jumped up a few times to refill the coffee at the nearby tables. I was on my third cup myself and was getting light-headed. If I didn't stop with the coffee, I was going to have to switch to Jack soon, and I didn't want to do that! I had golf to play!

During our conversation, she learned that I was 31, had been married once, divorced about a year ago and that Brian, two years and a day younger than me, was never married. I learned she was married, for ten years and had two kids, a girl, nine and a boy, six. I asked about Patti and learned that Patti was married, about four years, to the club manager, Mick, with no children. Katy was 28, and Patti three years younger. As Katy was getting up again to refill coffee at the next table, Brian walked in.

"Morning!"

"Morning," he replied. "Sorry about last night!"

"Forget it. Too much Jack after an eleven hour drive."

"OK. What's good for breakfast?"

"The western omelet is good."

He waved Katy over and ordered. Over breakfast we talked about relaxing for a full week and playing golf. Brian was left-handed; in everything he did, including golf, and was a pretty good player. A scratch golfer, he had played on the Florida Space Coast Tour in 1973 and 1974. I was his sponsor and covered his expenses for those two years. He was my major write-off from my real estate income. I played right-handed.

I was a pretty good player myself, so we always played even; no strokes either way. He finished his omelet and coffee and we headed to the parking lot to change into our golf shoes.

Four hours later we were back in the clubhouse having lunch, big juicy hamburgers! Brian had a beer, Budweiser, and I had a Coors Light. We were eating at a round, walnut table for six, in the bar, and the twosome we had played with joined us and ordered drinks. Tom had red wine and Bill ordered a coke.

As they waited for their drinks to arrive, Bill took out his scorecard and started computing our bets. Brian and I had won all three Nassau bets, at $25 each, plus one press. Brian and I were buying lunch! As Tom and Bill ordered their sandwiches, with Patti taking their orders, we collected our winnings.

I looked around for Katy, but she had gone home, having opened the restaurant at 5:00 A.M. Patti, I learned, was closing at 6:00 P.M. I had noticed their hours on the sign out front, with the summer hours not starting until Memorial Weekend.

We finished our lunch and were on our third drinks, watching the PGA Tour event on the wall-mounted television, when Patti walked by. Tom flagged her down and asked for the dice!

"Do we get a chance to win our money back?" asked Tom.

"Of course you do. Bring on the dice!"

An hour later I was up another $50 on each of them, including Brian. Then I noticed Patti sitting across the table from me. I asked if she was still working.

"Yes, but I'm on a break. Mind if I get in on the next game?"

"We're playing Boss Dice, $10.00 each. Winner takes the pot."

"Great! Count me in."

We were on the third time around the table when I felt something smooth rubbing my leg below the knee. I was wearing shorts already, a little early for the season. I looked down and saw a very sexy bare foot rubbing up and down my leg.

I looked over at Patti and her eyes met mine with a slight grin. I pushed my leg against her foot, so she would know I wanted her to continue. She responded by raising her foot toward my crotch. I felt aroused and immediately lost it on my next call, "three sixes!" Tom called, "Bull Shit", and picked up the box.

I was done playing dice. Tom won that game.

When I got back from the bathroom, Patti had gone back to work. I saw her behind the bar as Brian and I walked out. I glanced back and was glad to see Patti following me out the door with her eyes. Then she winked!

Brian and I went into Weed for dinner that night. I told him I was not feeling very well, and wanted to call it an early night. We drove back to the course and Brian said he was staying at the townhouse for another two nights.

"I met a pretty girl earlier, and might get lucky," he told me.

"OK, I'll see you in the morning for breakfast."

I drove back to my townhouse and hit the sheets within thirty seconds. I was feeling a chill, and didn't want to catch a cold, or worse yet, the flu. I took a shot of Nyquil just to help me sleep.

May 7, 1979

Around 8:00 A.M. I heard a knocking on the front door. I always sleep in the nude, so I threw my robe on and answered the door. Every bone in my body hurt and I was a little dizzy. It was Katy.

"Hi," I said. "What are you doing here?"

"I thought I'd bring you some fresh coffee!"

"Thanks, but I think I need to sleep some more. I hurt all over and my head is stuffed up. Hope I'm not catching a cold!"

"Can I come in and make you some breakfast?"

"Seriously, I need to sleep some more. Thanks for the offer, but I better get back to bed."

"OK, I'll leave the coffee so you can heat it up when you get up."

"Thanks! Talk to you later."

She turned around after she handed me the coffee and headed for her van, a dark blue Dodge.

I closed the door, took the coffee into the kitchen and went back to bed, leaving the robe on the nightstand.

Just as I was dozing off again, the phone rang. It was Brian, calling from the club. I told him I was feeling badly, and needed to sleep some more.

"OK, I'll find someone else to play with. I'll call you around lunch time."

"Perfect." I hung up the phone and went to sleep, wondering about Katy's motivation for bringing me the coffee.

The phone rang again around 1:00 P.M. It was Brian, wondering if I was ready to join him for his second 18 holes.

"I don't feel very good and I'm stuffed up! I think I'll make some chicken soup, then sleep some more."

He said, "OK, see you later," then hung up.

I heated some soup in the microwave, then chugged some more Nyquil, and hit the sheets again.

The Nyquil knocked me out. It seemed late when I heard knocking on the door! I looked at my watch and it was almost six. I threw my robe on again and walked to the front door.

"Who is it?" I yelled.

"It's Katy."

"Wow, I thought, what's with this woman?"

I opened the front door and saw that she was standing there with a tray of something that smelled really good.

"Brian told me at the club that you weren't feeling very well, so I brought you some dinner."

"Wow, come on in."

Katy walked past me and headed for the kitchen, with a smell of steak mixed with a strong perfume permeating the air.

"Sit down at the dining room table and I'll serve dinner."

"Yes, ma-am."

"Do you like red wine? She held an unopened bottle of Merlot in front of me. "Red wine is supposed to help kill viruses, you know, so I brought this along."

"Sure. Let me open it," I said as I started to get up and look for a corkscrew.

"You just sit there and let me do it."

I resigned myself to letting Katy take care of me. She opened the wine and poured me a glass in one of my crystal wine glasses, then poured herself a glass. Without saying anything else, she set the table from the cupboards and drawers and then served the food from her tray.

There was top sirloin steak, medium rare, with mashed potatoes, and a Caesar salad. She must have asked Brian at the club what I liked. It smelled delicious.

We ate in silence for a while, while I tried to think of something to say to this stranger who seemed to want to help me and see me, even though we had just met.

Finally, I thought of something to say.

"Aren't you married?"

She looked up from her food, then said, "Yes, but we've been fighting a lot lately, so I come and go as I please."

"What about your kids? Don't they need you to fix them dinner?"

"Rob is taking them to McDonald's tonight. They'll be fine."

"Rob, that's your husband?"

"Yes."

"What does Rob do?" I asked, trying to make conversation.

"He's a butcher at the supermarket in Yreka."

"Does he know you are here with me?"

"No. Like I said, I come and go as I please."

We finished dinner with very little to say after that. I was getting a headache, probably from the wine, so I rubbed my temples lightly.

"Do you have any cold medicine to take?"

"Just some Nyquil, mostly to help me sleep. Thanks for the dinner," I said as we put the dishes in the sink.

"My pleasure," she answered.

"I don't mean to be rude, but I'm not very good company right now. My head is killing me."

"No problem, I'll let you get back to sleep."

I escorted her to the door and said goodnight.

"Goodnight. I hope you are feeling better by tomorrow."

I locked the door and headed back to bed. It wasn't ten minutes before I heard a knock at the door.

I jumped up, put my robe on, and yelled, "Who is it?"

"It's me again, Katy. I brought you some Tylenol Cold Medicine from the store!"

"You didn't have to do that," I replied as I opened the door.

"Thanks," I said as I took the medicine. "See you tomorrow."

I closed the door before she could start up another conversation.

I heard her drive off and then went back to bed. I hoped I could get to sleep before she came back again!

May 8, 1979

I woke up around 9:00 A.M., surprised that Katy had not knocked on my door already that morning! I was feeling better, so I called Brian in his room and told him I'd be up for breakfast and then some golf.

When I walked into the club's restaurant, Brian was ordering food while sipping on his coffee. Katy was waiting on Brian and the other six or seven golfers sitting nearby. She looked at me and before she could ask I told her I'd have the same omelet as before.

We ate quickly because Brian informed me we were on the tee within twenty-five minutes! I paid the bill, leaving a twenty-five percent tip on the table, and we walked out to our cart.

We were paired with a different twosome this morning, so we introduced ourselves and teed off.

We decided to play eighteen holes without stopping for an early lunch. When we finally finished around 2:00 P.M., we were starving!

The restaurant was pretty quiet when we showed up and Patti was standing at the counter. She handed us menus and showed us to a large round table where the other half of our foursome was sitting. Brian and I had taken $50 each off of Fred and Roger this time, so they paid up as we ordered lunch.

Burgers all around was the choice of the day, with beers as well.

When we finished our burgers and had ordered more drinks, we were about to ask Patti for the dice cup when she walked up to the table with the cup in her hands.

"I thought you boys might like these," She said as she placed the cup in front of me.

"Thanks," I replied, then told the table to put up $10 each in the pot. "Liar's dice OK with you guys?"

"Sounds good to me," responded Fred, the same from Roger. Brian didn't have to respond. He and I always played Liar's!

After two games, both of which were won by Brian, Patti once again came up to the table and asked if she could join us. "Are you on another break?" I asked.

"Nope, I'm off for the day. Dinner shift is coming on."

She threw a ten in the pot, as did the rest of us, and sat across the table from me, between Fred and Roger. I wondered to myself if she was getting ready to give me the foot again! Patti ordered a White Russian from another cocktail waitress. I switched to Jack and Brian switched to Merlot. Fred and Roger stuck with Budweiser.

We were passing the cup around the table for the third time when, sure enough, I felt cold skin against the inside of my right leg. I looked up, instead of down, and saw a slight smile on Patti's lips. I smiled back and felt the increased pressure from her foot.

I immediately felt a rise in my groin and tried to concentrate on the dice box and the bets to get rid of the bulge beginning to grow in my crotch. It didn't help. As Patti's toe touched my crotch and felt the bulge between my legs, she had a startled look on her face, followed by the smile, bigger than before.

I felt an embarrassed look come over my face and shifted my left leg toward the right one, pushing her foot away under the table. I looked back at Patti and she was smiling and lightly licking her lips!

I was afraid I'd shoot a load right in my pants, and frantically tried to think about the game. I also looked at the others at the table to see if they knew what was going on under the table right in front of them. Luckily for me, they were concentrating on the dice.

May 9, 1979

I woke up the next morning with a hangover and tried to remember the night before. All I could remember was Patti's foot in my crotch and the thought made my crotch start to rise!

I jumped out of bed, with my manhood jumping up as I did, and headed for the bathroom. I opened the medicine cabinet and took out five Bayer aspirins, washing them down with a glass of water.

I got back in bed and tried to go back to sleep, but images of the look on Patti's face while she stroked my manhood with her toes kept going through my head. I decided there was no getting around it. I knew I couldn't play golf with a set of blue balls, so I relieved myself.

I took a hot shower, got dressed in light blue shorts with a white golf shirt and tennis shoes with short white golf socks, and headed to my car.

Brian was waiting in the restaurant when I arrived, Katy serving him pancakes and coffee. I ordered the same omelet for the fourth morning in a row, with coffee, black.

Brian informed me that he had called his office in Newport Beach that morning, and that he was going to have to cut his vacation short. A big client was flying in from the east coast and wanted to discuss with Brian his making a large purchase of gold!

Brian had the gift of gab on the phone and talked to clients all over the country about investing in precious metals. This client, according to Brian, had a large sum to invest and he didn't want to discuss it over any telephone line. Thus the meeting in person.

He said he had time to play eighteen holes and then he had to get to the Medford (Oregon) airport by 3:00 P.M.

I told him I could drive him there.

We headed for the first tee, this time being paired with Tom and Bill again from two days earlier.

Brian and I were feeling a little guilty about taking $100 each off of Tom and Bill previously, so we went easy on them and lost back $25 each.

We paid up in the parking lot, then told Tom and Bill we had to get on the road to Medford, a drive of about an hour and a half.

We made it in 65 minutes in my Camaro!

I told Brian at the gate that I'd see him in about four days and wished him good luck with his client.

As I drove south on Interstate 5, I wondered to myself if I'd get lucky that night with one of the sisters and if so, which one?

But by the time I got to the club, it was after 5:00, and I learned from Judy, one of the waitresses, that Katy and Patti were off that night. Even if I had both of their phone numbers, I wasn't about to call either of them at home! Just as well, I thought to myself. I needed to get a good night's sleep!

May 10, 1979

I got to the golf course and ordered breakfast from Judy. Patti and Katy were nowhere in sight! I had scrambled eggs this time, and coffee, black.

Then I walked into the pro shop and asked if they had anyone I could join for 18 holes. Mick, Patti's husband and the club manager, walked in and introduced himself. He said they had a foursome and had room for me in their group!

I asked the pro behind the counter if we could play five and he said to go ahead, since play was slow.

I grabbed a cart, threw my bag on the back, and headed for the first tee. Mick was there with three others and I introduced myself.

I asked what we were playing that day. Everyone said almost simultaneously, "We're playing Wolf."

I informed them that I was familiar with the game. "How much per point?"

"Five dollars," said Ted, an older guy in his late forties wearing blue jeans and a red golf shirt.

Everyone decided to start teeing off by handicap, highest handicap first. That meant I was last, since I was a scratch! But it also meant I was the first wolf, since we started with the lowest handicap, then the second lowest handicap on the second hole, and so on.

After everyone teed off, I chose who would be my partner on that hole, to play our best ball against the best ball of the other three. I chose Ted as my partner. My birdie on the first hole tied the par, net birdie, Mick scored on the hole. Ted made bogie, net par, but it didn't matter. No blood, and we moved to the second hole.

I was elected to keep track of all bets, which I did on the score card. We were just walking off the eighth green when a golf cart pulled up. It was Patti. She had arrived early for work and decided to come out and watch us play a few holes before work.

Mick was the wolf on the ninth tee. Nine was a long par-5, with a lake to cross on the second or third shot, depending upon how well you hit the tee shot. I didn't catch my drive very well and knew I'd have to lay up short of the lake before going for the green. No one else could go for the green in two, so I was at a disadvantage, since all four of the others got a stroke on the hole.

After we all teed off, Mick said, "I'll take Pete."

"You want to take me? I didn't hit my drive well, so I'll have to lay up just like the rest of you. Why would you want me?"

"I have a feeling, that's why!"

"OK. I'll do my best."

I was the only one who wasn't sharing a cart, other than Patti, and she pulled her cart alongside mine. We chatted about the nice weather as we drove.

The other four all hit their second shots short of the lake and I advanced to my drive. I had a carry over the lake of 245 yards, so I laid up with a seven iron and drove forward.

The other four hit their third shots across the lake to the green. Mick, my partner on the hole, hit the green about fifteen feet from the hole, putting for birdie, net eagle. Ted did the same and the other two were on the fringe.

It was my turn to hit. As I took a pitching wedge out of my bag, Patti drove up and said, "Good luck. Get it close!"

I pured the wedge and it rose directly at the pin, then headed down. Then the ball disappeared!

"It flew in the hole," yelled Mick. "I told you I had a feeling!"

I turned to Patti and said, "Stick around girl; you're good luck!"

"How long do you want me to stick around?" Patti asked, with glint in her eye.

"As long as you can," I replied with a wink.

My eagle won the hole for Mick and me, and another $5.00 each, from each of the other three!

We decided to catch a snack at the turn and Patti announced she had to go to work.

We all grabbed candy bars and drinks, just soda this time, and headed for the tenth tee.

All I could think about during the back nine was whether Patti would be there when we finished and I wondered if her bare foot would be in my crotch again!

She was, and it was.

When we got back to the clubhouse, Mick had to get back to work. That worked for me. After all, how could his wife play footsie with a cock if he was at the table? We had lunch and drinks and played some dice, again! Patti joined us for about 30 minutes, and her foot joined my crotch for about ten of those minutes, again!

Judy, the other waitress, asked us if we would take a table outside, since they needed the indoor tables for the lunch crowd. We said, "Sure."

We took a round table on the veranda, overlooking Lake Shastina, and ordered a new round of drinks. This time Katy joined us on a break. After two Jacks, I told everyone I had to run into Weed for a haircut, and started to get up.

Katy said, "Wait a minute." She got up and then came back in about five minutes with a set of hair cutting scissors in her hand!

"I'll cut your hair for you!"

"I don't think so!"

"Why not? I've been training for two years."

I thought about it for a minute, then said, "Get me another Jack and Water and I'll let you cut my hair!"

She brought me another Jack, then told me to sit in another chair and put a table cloth over my shoulders, pinning it in place with a safety pin. I chugged the Jack and then sat back and waited.

I have to admit she did a great job cutting my hair that day!

I drove back to my townhouse and passed out! Too many Jacks, too much excitement!

May 11, 1979

I didn't play golf on Saturday. I actually relaxed that day, went down to the lake, and fished for some bass. I used a purple artificial worm lure, with a light weight in front of it, Texas style. I knocked them dead down by the cove on the 13th hole, par-3. I took a lunch with me in a cooler, with three beers.

At the end of the day I went up to the club for dinner. "New York steak, medium rare, with a baker and dinner salad, Ranch dressing, and vinegar and oil on the side!

Katy took my order and then came back with a Jack, without my asking for it! She was getting to know me!

"You didn't play golf today?"

"Nope! Went fishing instead."

"Catch anything?"

"Six largemouth bass, the limit."

"What did you do with them?"

"Gave them to a kid who was fishing next to me. He didn't have any luck!"

"Aren't you nice?"

"I've been told that."

"Are you golfing tomorrow?"

"Nope! Driving back to Newport Beach."

She looked at me with disappointment in her eyes and then walked away. I noticed she got on the phone and talked for quite a while.

When I finished dinner, I headed for the door, when Katy ran up to me and announced, "I just talked to my Mom in San Diego and told her I was flying down to San Diego the day after tomorrow to visit her. Can we carpool as far as Redding tomorrow?"

"Tomorrow? Aren't you going the day after tomorrow?"

"I thought we could maybe drive to Redding tomorrow, and have dinner together, then you could continue south the next day, and I'll jump on a plane from Redding to San Diego the next day!"

"And what about tomorrow night?"

"She looked at me sheepishly and said, "I thought we could stay somewhere tomorrow night!"

"Together?"

"Together, if you promise to be a gentleman."

"I can't promise that!"

"I'll take my chances. Meet me in the golf course parking lot at nine tomorrow morning."

"How about at the Chevron station in Weed tomorrow morning at nine?"

"OK! I'll be there."

May 12, 1979

At 9:00 A.M., I drove into the Chevron station in Weed, and saw Katy's blue Dodge van. I parked next to her, opened the door, and walked up to her window. She rolled her window down.

"I've decided I am staying up here for another two or three days," I told her.

A disappointed look came over her face. "But I am all excited about having dinner with you in Redding tonight!"

"Really? Or are you excited about staying in a motel with me tonight?"

"That, too!"

"Shame on you. A married woman!"

"I told you, it's over between me and Rob."

"I'll tell you what. I'll follow you to Redding, we'll spend the day, have dinner, and spend the night. Then you drive to the airport to fly to San Diego and I'll drive back up here for a few more days of golf. Follow me to Redding."

"That sounds good."

"OK, let's go!"

As I walked back to my Camaro, I had a feeling that Katy wore the pants in her family and that Rob was not the strong one. I hadn't met him yet, so I was not positive, but the feeling lingered!

It took an hour and twenty minutes to reach Redding. Driving across the bridge over Shasta Lake at Bridge bay showed how little rain the area had received that winter. The lake was down about 50 feet from the full level.

I took the Market Street exit at North Redding and looked for a nice motel. I spotted a Best Western on the right and pulled in. Katy parked in the space on my right.

"Can you get the room while I wait out here?" she asked through the open window.

"Sure."

I checked in as a single, queen bed, non-smoking, one night. The clerk said the room wouldn't be ready until noon, but their restaurant was open for a late breakfast or lunch.

I walked up to Katy, who was taking a suitcase out of her van and gave her the info. She put the suitcase back and locked the door.

We walked to the restaurant, sat down at the nearest table, and asked for menus. She was nervous.

"Have you ever done this before?" I asked her.

"Done what?"

"Spent the night with another man while being married."

"No."

I dropped the subject, and asked, "What looks good?"

After we moved into the room, we changed into bathing suits and went out to the pool. The sun was out, but it was a little cool, about 66 degrees Fahrenheit. We relaxed on lounges by the pool. I asked Katy about her kids.

"Kandi is nine, and Willie is six. Kandi takes after me and Willie takes after his Dad. They both like to fish."

We talked and enjoyed the direct sunlight for about three hours, then went to the room. I walked up to Katy and kissed her. She kissed me back.

"Let's get into bed," I suggested.

She crawled under the covers, then took off her bathing suit and tossed it to the floor. I took off my suit in front of her and joined her under the covers.

We kissed, and then I moved to her neck, kissing it and smelling her perfume. My manhood started getting aroused. Katy was stiff, and I told her to relax. I moved to her left breast and rolled her nipple around with my tongue, then sucked on it hard.

"Ouch!"

"Sorry!" I moved to the other breast.

"Then I started to move down her stomach and she stopped me with a firm grip.

"Relax."

I moved lower, and she exclaimed, "What are you doing?"

"I want to taste you."

"No. Don't. I've never done that before."

"You've been married for ten years and your husband never licked you there?"

"Yes."

"Yes, he licked you there before, or Yes, he never licked you there before?"

"Never!"

And no other guy has ever licked you there either?"

"No. Rob is the only man I have ever been with."

"Just relax. You'll enjoy it."

My tongue got to work and I heard her moan. After her orgasm, I told her to relax again, and enjoy.

As I continued, I remembered what a golfing buddy had told me years ago. Jack said, "Show me a man who won't go down on his wife, and I'll eat him out of house and home!"

She came again, and then I got on top. I was excited about being her first in a number of ways, and I came quickly!

I lay down beside her and gave her a chance to relax and calm down. I suggested she do something for me, but she said, "No. I've never done that before."

I thought to myself, who has she been married to all these years?

She got her first lesson that day on how to do several things. The rest of the night we made love, slept, made love again, and slept again. We didn't get a lot of sleep.

May 13, 1979

Katy got into her van and I loaded her suitcase in the back. I kissed her goodbye and told her to drive safely the short trip to the airport. She drove off and then I got back in my Camaro and headed back to Lake Shastina.

I played 18 holes with three guys I had just met from Medford, Oregon and then hit the bar. Patti brought me a Jack and we rolled dice. Patti didn't join us this time, probably because her husband, Mick was working in the restaurant, and too close to our table.

Around 7:00 P.M. I went into the dining room to have dinner. I was just ordering, Salmon with Hollandaise sauce, asparagus, and a wedge salad with blue cheese dressing, when some guy walked up to my table.

"Pete?"

"Yes?"

"I'm Rob, Katy's husband."

"Oh, shit." I thought to myself.

"Hi, Rob."

"I owe you an apology"

"Why is that? Have we ever met?"

"No, but I knew you were spending time with Katy, and I thought for sure you were going south with her when she told me she was going to San Diego to visit her Mom. Now I see I was wrong!"

I felt like shit! "No, she told me she was leaving to visit her Mom, but I'm not going home for a few more days."

"Listen, I want to buy your dinner for assuming you were going with her,"

"That's not necessary."

"Really. Let me buy your dinner."

"Rob, I'm going to say this one more time. You do not need to buy me dinner!"

"OK, but again, I apologize for being suspicious."

"No problem! See you later." Rob got up and left. Whew, that was weird!

I finished my dinner and got out of there, back to my townhouse.

I stayed another two days, playing golf and fishing a little, then drove 12 hours back to Newport Beach. I needed a rest.

May 21, 1979

I opened my mailbox and saw a letter addressed to me in a woman's handwriting. I opened it and saw it was from Katy.

"I expected God to strike me down for sleeping with you........!" She spilled her feelings in the letter and I read it three times. I reread it again, at least once a day for the next week.

Business was going smoothly in the office, so I planned to drive to Lake Shastina again. I had to see her. I left the next morning.

May 29, 1979

I walked into the bar at the club and waved to a few friends shaking dice in the corner. Katy was behind the bar. She noticed me and seemed pleased. I sat down and said, "Hi."

"Hi."

"I thought you were going to visit your Mom for a couple of weeks."

"I visited her for a week and then flew back to Redding yesterday. I drove up yesterday afternoon."

Then I heard a scuffle behind the bar, in the kitchen. I glanced through the door and saw Patti and her husband arguing. Mick told her to "Do it!", and Patti ran out of the kitchen, crying. Interesting, I thought. Katy obviously wore the pants in her family, the dominant one over her husband, and Patti was just the opposite. Mick ruled that twosome, and it looked to me like Patti needed some self-respect!

I chatted with Katy for about an hour and then drove to my townhouse. I was in the middle of a salmon, mashed potatoes and green salad dinner when I heard a knock at the front door.

Katy was standing there, with a bottle of red wine in her hand.
"Hi. Come on in!"

She walked up to me and kissed me hard on the lips! Dinner would have to wait. We barely got to my bed before I was inside her! She was voracious!

She spent the night after calling her home phone and telling her baby-sitter where she was and that she'd be home in the morning.

She was warm lying next to me, or I should say, lying on top of me.

The next morning she cooked bacon and eggs in the kitchen, not saying much in the process.

"Still nervous about being with me?"

"No, not any more. But I feel guilty about being here."

"Then why are you here?"

"Because I want to be here."

June 21, 1979

Things happened fairly quickly from that day onward. I went back to Newport Beach to put most of my personal property into storage there and then drove back to Lake Shastina.

I didn't see much of Patti, because her husband, Mick, had gotten together with a few investors and bought a restaurant and bar in Montague, CA, six miles east of Yreka, and about 25 miles north of Lake Shastina. It was called the Corner Club, and was across the street from one of the area's oldest hotels, the Montague Hotel, often referred to as the Montague Hilton by the locals. I had stayed there many Saturday nights when I sold Lake Shastina golf lots to clients flying in from southern California in 1971 and 1972.

Our salesmen could relax at the Hilton after taking our Saturday clients back to our Boeing 737 nearby; get a steak dinner, a room for the night, and steak and eggs for breakfast, all for about $12.00!

Mick and Patti virtually lived at the Corner Club for weeks at a time, so Katy and I didn't see much of them during this period.

Katy and I had looked around for a house to rent at Lake Shastina, and found a three-bedroom, two bath, single story house across the street from the seventh hole on Lake Shastina's Championship Course. We moved in with Kandi and Willie in August of 1979.

My folks had moved to Lake Shastina back around 1971, and had three homes in the development by 1979. I put my California real estate license with my Dad's office, right next door to the country club clubhouse.

After I was living with Katy and her kids for about six months, my Dad started asking me if I was going to marry Katy. I told him I probably would be doing just that, as soon as her divorce was final from Rob.

October 1, 1980

We finally set a date of December 21, 1980 to get married. In October of 1980 we moved into a brand new house on a hill to the north, still within the Lake Shastina community. It was a much larger house than the house across from the seventh fairway and the architect had just won some award from Architecture Magazine for his design of the house.

As it turned out, the house was not very well designed for the cold weather that was about to begin in November! The front entrance was at the top of some long stairs, with a single garage to the left of the stairs and a two-car garage to the right of the stairs.

A huge deck covered both garages, with the stairs breaking up the deck in the middle.

As you entered the front door, a left turn took you to the living room, with a high ceiling. The living room had an Earth wood stove. The ceiling dropped to a flat eight feet in the hallway passing the front door and entering the main part of the house, with three bedrooms upstairs and a dining room and kitchen downstairs.

It was pretty, but not practical. When we started a fire in the Earth stove in the living room, the temperature reached 90 degrees Fahrenheit in the living room, but the low ceiling in the hallway did not let the heat get to the rest of the house and that half of the house was freezing!

So much for Architectural awards!

The three days we took to move into the new house took its toll on my right shoulder. I tore the rotor cuff in my shoulder and my golfing buddy, Dr. Will Lilly, an orthopedic surgeon, told me the shoulder would never heal by itself.

That was not good, because we teed it up for 18 holes the next morning. Will and I played with Dr. Bob Bayou, the County Medical Examiner, and Fay Pemberthy, owner of Pine Mountain Lumber Company in Yreka.

I shot 86, grabbing my right shoulder and cringing after every swing.

At lunch, I had a burger and a Jack and water. Then another Jack and another. By the time the guys asked me if I was going to play another 18 holes, my right should was feeling no pain, so I said I'd play.

I shot 66. A twenty shot improvement! I couldn't remember ever doing that before. Believe it or not, my shoulder improved on its own, so Will never had to operate.

Katy was not the easiest woman to live with. I remember she and I getting into a big knockdown drag out fight about one week before the wedding.

But we made up and the wedding proceeded as planned. It was at the Arrow Lodge about half a mile from the house and the reception was also there.

Katy's Mom, Margaret, was there, as were Mick and Patti, my folks and a lot of our friends from Lake Shastina.

I was officially married for the second time, having been married in 1974 to the Siskiyou County Maid of the County Fair, and divorced in 1978.

Not being very happy with the design of the house we lived in, we moved a year later into a one-story house on the 1st fairway of the Scottish Nine hole Course.

July 6, 1984

That is where we lived when our first child was born, a boy, and we named him Peter Alan Baumann. Katy had been bouncing around Lake Shastina on our jet ski on July 4, and must have knocked him loose! The evening of July 5, Katy and I drove our 260-Z to the Rogue Community Hospital in Medford, OR, and Pete was born early the next morning.

Kandi and Willie loved playing with Pete. We lived in that house for about one year, finding our first and only winter in the house quite exciting! Lake Shastina is known for having the lightest snow load factor in the building codes, but the highest wind factors of any place in Siskiyou County.

During December of 1984, high winds knocked out our power, leveling about six power poles in the process. We not only lost power, but bolts of electricity shot out of the TV screen and the microwave, scaring the heck out of the kids!

We spent the next three days replacing appliances, which fortunately were covered by insurance.

Our real estate office at the country club was doing fairly well reselling golf course lots to visitors to Lake Shastina, but I wanted to do something else as well. I started researching how to manufacture golf clubs, primarily custom fit iron sets.

July 15, 1985

Pete was about one year old when I noticed the Katy was not feeling very well. She had stayed in bed for several days, complaining about an upset stomach.

One morning I got out of bed and as I walked to the bathroom, Katy said, "Honey, can we talk?"

I had visions of being married to Phyllis Diller!

I climbed back into bed and said, "What's up?"

"You know how I haven't been feeling very good, lately? I called the doctor's office and made an appointment for yesterday. I went to his office and had some tests done."

Katy continued talking about tests at the doctor's office and I started thinking the doctor had found something seriously wrong with her.

Then she said, "I'm pregnant!"

I looked at her and then I laughed! "Is that all? What's the problem?"

"I thought you might be mad about having another child so soon after Pete."

"Not at all. That's great!"

We talked for a while and then got up and had some breakfast with the kids. Kandi and Willie already had Pete in his high chair, feeding him some cereal.

A few months later, Dr. Will Lilly told me during 18 holes that he needed someone to rent his big house up on a hill overlooking Mt. Shasta and the back nine holes of the Championship course. You might say, he "made me an offer I couldn't refuse", so we moved again.

Christmas of 1985 was spent in our new home, and we had Patti and her husband, Mick, visit us for Christmas, along with their new son, Mick. Mick and Patti seemed to be happy together, but it was still clear to me who ran the show. Patti was usually subdued when Mick was around, and only seemed to come out of her shell with Katy when Mick was out of the house.

Katy was showing her six month's pregnancy by this time, and we were excited about having another baby. As with Pete, we did not want to know if it was going to be a boy or a girl.

March 21, 1986

We found out on March 21, 1986, when Robert Andrew Baumann was born at the Yreka General Hospital. I now had two sons.

Will's house had a three-car garage and I had set up a work station in the garage to start experimenting with putting golf clubs together. I had acquired a number of golf equipment manuals and was learning the difference between the major golf companies and how they differed in their methods of assembling sets of irons. Most importantly, I was learning the differences between the many steel iron shafts manufactured worldwide.

I spent the next year learning all I could about how to make the best performing golf clubs in the world, which basically requires that each set be custom fit to each customer. I also learned that specific golf companies that claimed to custom fit did not, in fact, custom fit! I knew, therefore, that it would be easy to make a better set of golf clubs for each and every future customer. All I had to do now was find customers who wanted to play better golf. I was on my way to a new career.

In the spring of 1987, Dr. Lilly informed me he had sold his house, so we were moving once again!

A friend of mine, Jim Klein, lived on the 15th fairway of the Championship course at Lake Shastina and Jim was planning to move his family back to southern California.

We agreed on a monthly rental price and moved into his two story, four bedroom home on the golf course. The house had a two-car garage and I immediately set up my workshop in the garage for assembling golf clubs.

I needed a name for my golf company. I wanted something that denoted "to search", or "to search for" perfection. I thought of "Quest", and then settled on PROBE Golf.

I located a foundry in China that made golf components and ordered my first iron heads from them, 1-iron through 9-iron, pitching wedge, and sand wedge. I ordered myself a set of steel iron shafts called Apollo AP 44, so I could make myself a stiff-flexed set of irons with a high flex point. That is what the best golfers play.

Within two weeks I was assembling my own personal set of irons for the first time, ever.

May, 1987

I had been a 6 handicap golfer at the Lake Shastina Men's Club. Within three months of making and playing my own assembled set of PROBE irons, I dropped to a "0" (scratch) handicap and got my first hole-in-one on the eighth hole, a 195-yard Par 3, with a 5-iron! I had been playing for 25 years and had never had a hole-in-one! Now, three months after make a set of golf clubs that were custom made for me, by me, I had my first one!

To show how playing with a custom fit set of clubs can make a difference, I made my second hole-in-one two months later, on the 11th hole, 222 yards with my 2-iron. Furthermore, my handicap dropped another two points, to a "+2" and I won the Lake Shastina Men's Amateur Championship that August with a 70-70-140, four under par.

I knew thousands of golfers would give their eye teeth to get hold of golf clubs that would make them better golfers. I was excited about what I had learned about the differences in golf shafts. I knew the leading seller of "custom" iron sets in the country was PING, and now I knew they really did not custom fit like I did, because they used one type of iron shaft for all of their customers, and that one shaft was a compromise, not a custom fit!

I was excited about a possible promising new career, selling a better custom fit set of golf clubs, with a potential 25,000,000 customers in the United States alone!

We lived in the Klein's house for three years, Bobby and Pete growing up with a big back yard on the golf course and my golf company, Probe Golf, was taking off. I had set up a distributor program that offered avid golfers a chance to buy my Probe iron heads, shaft, and grips, and assemble custom fit iron sets for golfers in their own exclusive territories. I had created a Probe Custom Fitting Questionnaire for my distributors to have their customers fill out and then I could advise each distributor which shaft to use for the customer, to achieve each customer's goals.

One day Katy came to me and said the boys were feeling sick and seemed to be losing weight. We took them into Yreka to the hospital for blood tests. We learned they had caught some kind of bug, called giardia, bacteria that are found in contaminated water! The boys had been playing in some stagnant water in our back yard, caused by a leaking sprinkler head and caught the bug. They were each losing one pound per day. A trip to the pharmacy and their taking pills for ten days and they were back to normal.

We saw my folks often, since my dad was my real estate broker and they had four houses by this time at Lake Shastina. They lived in the largest home and had tenants renting the other three.

We seldom saw any of Katy's family during this time. Mick and Patti had not made it with the Corner Club in Montague, so they had moved to Burbank, California. Mick had worked in Hollywood before in food and beverage and had gotten a job running the cafeteria at Universal Studios. Patti was waiting tables. The girls' mother lived in San Diego, and their sister, Muriel, was working at a McDonalds south of San Francisco.

In early 1990 I decided my garage was not big enough for my golf club production, so I started looking around Yreka for some manufacturing space. I came across a city program that was trying to bring businesses to Yreka, and they offered me about 6,000 square feet of manufacturing space, with a receptionist out front. I took it.

Katy and I started looking for a house in or near Yreka, and found a two-story, five bedroom, three bathroom, circular house on top of a hill in town, on 25 acres. What a retreat it would make at the end of each working day. The only problem was the horse stables and fencing that was everywhere. I had tried to support 16 quarter horses with my first wife and had been ripped off by every horse person she ever introduced to me. I hated horse people, so the horse shit had to go.

There were also hundreds of piles of brush and branches on the 25 acres. I was told by the realtor that they were rat's nests. I had visions of cleaning up all of the acreage and building my own small golf course! The boys loved the house, or more importantly, they loved the woods surrounding the house.

October 20, 1990

As soon as we closed escrow on the house, I rented a D-6 caterpillar at $85 an hour and went to work playing Demolition Man. First to go was the four stall barn. In two hours it was gone, demolished and buried under dirt. Then I ripped down all of the horse fencing. Katy videotaped the job, but I don't know where the video tape might be today.

I took a week cleaning up our property. I had pushed most of the debris into piles that would later be burned and left many of the scrub oak trees standing, so we could pick and choose which ones we wanted to keep and which ones we would cut down later for firewood. Winter was coming and we had hundreds of scrub oaks available to burn.

We had been in the house for about two months when Katy came to me and told me she had just received a phone call from Patti. Mick's job in Burbank was not going well and Patti asked Katy if they could move up to Yreka, stay with us for a while, and Mick would look for a job in Yreka. Katy also said that Patti had hinted that Mick was dealing drugs again and she wanted to get away from that area.

I remembered that Mick had dealt drugs in Palm Springs when they lived there a few years earlier. Patti had evidently gotten so mad at Mick that she dumped his stash of cocaine down the toilet and flushed it! I remembered the fight I had witnessed between them behind the bar at the Lake Shastina Golf Resort back in 1979, and wondered how often they got in serious fights. I also wondered if Mick had ever hit Patti, causing physical harm. It was already obvious just by looking into Patti's eyes that she was harmed mentally by her husband!

I told Katy that Patti and her family were welcome to move in with us. I also told her that I would find a place in Probe Golf for both Mick and Patti. My Probe distributorship program was working well and Mick could sell distributorships over the phone when inquiries came in from our Wall Street Journal Ads. To date, only my brother, Brian, had responded to those leads and he could use some help. I was sure Patti would work well in our office. I told Katy everything was going to be fine.

The Thomas family moved into our house on the hill just in time for Thanksgiving that year.

Our first year at our house on the hill went fairly well. Probe Golf was flourishing in town and my spare time was spent cleaning up the 25 acres. Mick Thomas, Patti's husband, was a big help clearing the acreage. Together, we burned much of the star thistle that grew on the left and right of the long driveway, which ran at least 400 yards inside our gate and up to the house.

I had about six truckloads of gravel delivered to improve the driveway, which was all dirt when we moved in. I bought the largest Sears driving mower that was available at the time, as well as the large blade accessory. With it I was able to move quite a bit of dirt and cleared what was going to be my nine greens on my short golf course.

After six months, working through the winter, the area around the house was looking pretty nice. I bought large sheets of Astroturf and cut it in 15 foot by 15 foot squares for the putting greens on the course. Each hole was between 80 yards and 150 yards long. I bought small Astroturf tees for each of the nine holes. I had my own golf course!

The first tee, sitting next to the portable hot tub we had delivered from Medford, Oregon, was used as our driving range tee. We could hit full drivers over 250 yards down the hill, with a landing area about 100 feet by 100 feet in dimension.

Mick, Patti and their son Mick, and daughter Carol, stayed with us for about four months. Everyone was feeling a little tense in the house from the lack of privacy after that time, so they started looking for a house in town. Mick was making some pretty good money working as my sales director, so money wasn't a problem.

They found a nice three bedroom, two bath house on Turre Street in town, less than a mile from the Probe Golf offices and assembly facility on South Oregon Street. All of their spirits seemed to rise after the move. I especially noticed the improved spirits when in my office. Patti enjoyed working as my personal assistant. Kandi, Katy's daughter, was our bookkeeper. Katy seldom worked in the office herself, preferring to stay at home and keep the house and property looking nice. That was a big chore, considering we had 25 acres.

She informed me that she was running out of water quite often when cleaning, so I investigated the problem. The realtor had told me that we did not connect with the city water system and had our own well about 100 yards down the hill from the house. The pump system pumped the water up the hill to a 1,200 gallon underground cement holding tank. I drove into Yreka and started shopping for a larger tank.

I found an above-ground 2,500 gallon round rubber water tank for sale and then found a contractor who could install it across the driveway from the existing tank. The contractor took three days to install the new tank and the pump system that would connect to the original tank. We now had an additional 2,500 gallons of water, basically tripling our total capacity. We also had a much larger hot water heater installed under the house.

We were finally getting settled and enjoyed our privacy on top of the world, as it seemed. We could sit on the deck outside the living room and watch the sun rise to the east, view the entire city of Yreka to the north and west, and watch the sunsets to the west!

We had a pellet stove installed in the living room, to replace the wood burning stove, so having to cut down oak trees on the property for heat was no longer necessary. I actually had oak to sell, which brought about $185 per cord at that time, so we had an added source of income for over a year.

July, 1991

Probe Golf was flourishing. Katy enjoyed shopping for the house and surrounding 25 acres. She ordered new furniture from Redding, California, 100 miles to the south. The hot tub from Medford, situated right outside the door from the kitchen, was used at least twice a day by Bobby and me. Even in winter, with a foot of snow on the ground, Bobby and I would get in the tub every morning and every evening. He'd love to open one of my golf umbrellas when it snowed, so we could sit in 102 degree water and watch the snow fall from under the umbrella.

Business in the office and manufacturing was going great. My production manager, a retired Navy Chief, took care of everything in the facility and I was able to play a lot of golf at Lake Shastina, 25 miles to the south. I won the Men's Club Championship for the third year in a row. Bobby was playing golf by now. He was five years old, and growing like a weed. Pete wasn't interested in golf and spent most of his time on his computer. Katy played after I had made her a custom set of clubs and had a pretty good swing.

The rest of 1991 was spent enjoying our house on the hill and developing new golf products for Probe Golf to manufacture. The most important golf club to most golfers is the driver. If a golfer can hit his drives long and straight, the rest of the hole is set up for him to attack.

I remembered my early days as a kid and young man playing baseball. A fungo bat was used, usually one-handed, to hit fly balls to the outfield during practice, with very little effort. The fungo bat had a much smaller radius than a regular bat.

I decided to experiment with a metal driver head that had a smaller radius on its face than drivers that were on the market at that time. I discovered that most of the major driver brands measured a radius from toe to heel of 16 inches of radius. That meant that the curvature on the face was the same as a circle having a radius of 16 inches, or a diameter of 32 inches. As a circle got smaller, its radius got shorter. I also discovered that the major brand drivers had a perfectly flat face from top to bottom, with virtually no curvature at all.

I figured that if I could make a driver with more curvature than 16 inches of radius from toe to heel and a curvature from top to bottom, compared to being flat, my driver would impact more power to a golf ball and drive the ball farther.

I contacted the owner of the foundry in China that we had been purchasing components from for over a year by email, and asked him if he could manufacture exclusively for Probe Golf a new metal driver head with 10 inches of radius from toe to heel, and 10 inches of radius from top to bottom. He replied that he could and would do so and sent me a box of 50 such heads with which to experiment.

The driver heads arrived about a month later, and I glued several different shafts to three of them and went to the driving range. I was amazed at how much farther the new Probe driver heads carried each drive! Tests showed that our new driver heads carried an average of 30 yards farther than any of the competition and kept the ball in the air about 2 and ½ seconds longer!

I contacted my patent attorney and told him about my invention. He told me that, unfortunately, curving the face on a driver more than other manufacturers was not a patentable invention.

He suggested we simply advertise that Probe drivers were longer than anyone else in the marketplace and not mention why, just let customers learn for themselves.

I had been to a number of PGA Tour events, demonstrating my Probe drivers. One of the first tour players to give me some advice on how to ask players to try my driver was Johnny Miller. He had tried it on the driving range and could not believe how much farther my driver carried the ball than the driver he was using at the time. In fact, Johnny asked me if I would ship him a dozen Probe driver heads every month or two so he and his sons could try it on different shafts. I agreed to do so.

Since PGA Tour pros were offered a tremendous amount of money by the major manufacturers to play their drivers and other equipment, I decided to spend most of my time following the Senior PGA Tour. I figured the seniors would be more inclined to play a driver that gave them 30 added yards off the tee than simply the money offered to them to play another driver.

One day one of my tour representatives, Tom Spessard, called me from Naples, Florida and said that Chi Chi Rodriguez had broken his driver shaft. Chi Chi had played the same driver since early 1983. It was a Thursday, a practice day for the Senior Tour event in Naples. Tom had asked Chi Chi about the specifications Chi Chi liked on his driver. Tom informed me that Chi Chi liked a 45 ½ inch driver, 9.5 degrees loft, stiff flex, standard grip.

I told Ron Weber, my assembly manager, to make one up with a new True Temper graphite shaft that had just come out, with Chi Chi's specs. Ron used some quick-glue on Chi Chi's driver, so we could ship it that afternoon Red Label, UPS.

Tom called me the next afternoon, and said the driver had just arrived. He had given it to Chi Chi on the driving range. Chi Chi had just shot a 78 the first day of the tournament, using another major manufacturer's driver. He was in last place for the tournament!

He tried the Probe driver on the range, then told Tom it was perfect and would be in his bag the next day. He shot 66-66 on the weekend and almost won the tournament after being in last place the first day!

I decided to drive from Yreka to Ojai, CA the next day to see Chi Chi personally and bring him a matching Probe 3-wood and 5-wood to match his driver. Katy wanted to come with me, so we hit the road. It was a 474 mile drive!

Chi Chi had the flu when we got to the GTE Western Classic in Ojai. Fortunately, it rained all day Friday, so that day's play was cancelled. If the Senior Tour had played that day, Chi Chi would have had to withdraw. As it was, he shot 66 on Saturday and was leading the tournament. He shot 66 on Sunday and won the tournament! He told the press his new Probe driver and its 30 added yards off the tee won the tournament for him.

Back in Yreka, we started receiving phone calls from golfers from all over the country asking if this was the company that manufactured Chi Chi's new driver.

At the same time, one of my golfing buddies, Terry Wiens, a Canadian golf pro, was experimenting with a novel new idea pertaining to a golf putter.

He mentioned that the putter was the only golf club that was never swung hard, like the woods or irons, yet it was made basically the same as the other clubs, with a thick end of the shaft in the grip and the thin, flexible end in the head. He said that reversing the shaft, thin end in the grip and fat end in the putter head, might work better! That made sense to me, since putting more weight in the head would make the putter more like a pendulum and encourage a pure, pendulum stroke.

Terry had found a broken driver shaft in a garbage can at a nearby golf course, removed the grip, and put a home-made putter head shaped like a hotdog with flat sides onto the fat end of the driver shaft. Then he built up the thin end of the shaft with duct tape and put a grip over the tape.

It was a flimsy grip, but stroking the putter head on the fat end of the shaft felt great! All a golfer had to do was to slowly take the putter head back, then swing it forward. The shaft did all the work!

Terry and I headed for Lake Shastina to play nine holes with his crude invention. He made almost every putt he stroked! He shot 31 on the par 36 front nine. I called my patent attorney in New York early the next morning. I told Mick Striker about Terry's invention and Mick told me not to mention the putter to anyone until he could start a patent application.

January, 1992

It took Mick, my patent attorney, about two weeks to submit our patent application to the United States Patent Office for our inverted-shafted putter. We received approval from the office about three months later. Terry and I now owned three patents on our "Inverted-shafted" putter, the Probe 20/20!

I called in our production manager and told Alan to start figuring out how to make a prototype of our new putter head. At the same time I called around to several aluminum putter shaft companies and gave them the specs for an inverted-shafted putter shaft.

Within ten days we had three prototype Probe 20/20 putters made and ready to test. My next Senior PGA Tour event I had planned to attend was the GTE Western Classic in Portland, Oregon, in the fall.

During the summer of 1992, I spent more time than usual at the Lake Shastina Golf Resort. I was determined to win my Men's Club Championship for the fourth year in a row.

One reason I spent less time in the office was the fact that Katy had decided to work more and more in my office, and to be honest, she was driving me crazy! It seemed that I could not make a decision about the business without her finding fault with that decision. And rather than ask me about each decision in private, she would express her doubts out loud, for everyone in the office to hear.

Ten years earlier, when I was getting my real estate license and was training at the Dale Carnegie sales seminar, we were taught the importance of a wife believing in her husband's career and backing him up in his decisions. We also learned that a wife's arguing with her husband about his decisions and her insisting that he place her wants ahead of his career, was one of the major causes of divorce.

It was around this time period that I was becoming aware of my feelings for Patti. She would anticipate my needs in the office and would take care of problems before they became apparent to me. At the same time Katy was questioning my every move. Patti would get me aside and ask me why I put up with Katy's arguments, why I let her talk to me the way she did.

So, playing more golf and working less was my answer to the problem. One subject that Katy kept bringing up was our getting a dog for the boys. I don't remember the boys asking me more than once or twice if we could get a dog. When I explained to them that I was too busy to take care of a dog and that their Mom and I traveled too often to care for a pet, the boys seemed to understand, and stopped asking. But not Katy.

She kept bringing up the subject, saying it would be good for the boys to have some responsibilities, taking care of a pet. I kept telling her that I did not want additional responsibilities at home, when that was my place to relax.

One day things came to a head. I was driving home from the country club on Highway A-12 around 5:00 P.M. I called Katy from my Ford F 150 and asked what time I should be home for dinner. She said around six. Then she asked me, "Guess what I did with the boys today?"

"What?"

I took the boys to Medford, and we bought a dog, a pure bred basset hound puppy!"

"You did what?"

"He's so cute! You will love him."

I hung up the phone. I was fuming. At the next intersection, in Grenada, instead of continuing toward Interstate 5 and Yreka, I turned right toward Montague. I needed a drink. My cell phone rang. I noticed it was Katy, and ignored it.

I drove to the Corner Club, the restaurant and bar Mick and Patti used to own, and walked up to the bar. An old friend was bartending, Nancy Brown. Eight years earlier, when I sold golf lots at Lake Shastina, Nancy and I dated. She was a doll and still had long, straight, brown hair. I remember hearing rumors about six years earlier that Nancy had a two-year-old son who looked just like me!

"Hi, stranger."

"Hi, I haven't seen you in years!"

"I've been married and divorced since I last saw you."

"Anyone I know?"

"Terry Hittson, former 1973 Miss Siskiyou County."

"Yeah, I know her. I just heard she got married again."

"Wouldn't surprise me."

"What can I get you?"

"Jack and water."

Nancy brought my drink and then waited on another guy who had just walked in. I chugged my drink, then ordered another.

"Wow, slow down big guy."

"OK, I just needed a quick one."

"Problems?"

I told her the whole story about the dog, my wife's arguing with me in my office, everything that was bothering me. I was getting stressed just talking about it.

Nancy had always been a good listener. My cell phone rang. I noticed again that it was Katy, so I ignored it.

I sat there at the bar getting smashed and talking to Nancy. She was relieved at 6:30, then came around the bar and sat in the stool next to me. I bought her a drink and we talked some more. Her left hand moved to the inside of my right leg, and slowly rubbed me. I responded and she noticed and smiled. I learned she had also been married and divorced since we dated. She had a seven-year-old son and when I hinted that he might be mine, she laughed and said, "No."

Nancy asked me if I wanted to give her a ride home, just a mile away. I said, "Sure."

I was mad at Katy and didn't want to go home.

We were just inside her front door when Nancy was all over me, and I responded. I remembered the sex with Nancy had always been great and learned that afternoon that she had learned a few new things in the last ten years.

In twelve years of marriage, this was the first time I had ever cheated on Katy, but enough was enough. I thought again of the concept that had been taught to our salesmen when taking the Dale Carnegie sales course. Not only did a wife's arguing with her husband about his business decisions lead to divorce; so did a wife demanding that her husband put her first, ahead of his career. The lesson, basically, was that a husband would put his wife ahead of everything else if she put his career ahead of herself. That's a lesson most women who go through a divorce never learn in time.

Two hours later I was on the road home. The house was dark when I drove up our long driveway. I wasn't interested in a confrontation that night, so I kicked off my shoes and tried to sleep on the couch. Katy must have heard me come in, because within five minutes she was in the living room looking for me.

"Where have you been? I've been worried."

"After the news about the dog, I was mad and didn't want to come home, so I went to a bar."

"What bar? I called all over town."

"I don't want to talk about it right now. Go to bed."

"Are you coming to bed with me?"

"Not now. I want to be alone."

She went upstairs. I slept on the couch.

The next morning I awoke to a wet nose on my face. I opened my eyes to see big brown eyes and a black nose and a long tongue.

"Look Dad, we have a dog."

"That's nice, Pete, but take him outside."

"Pet him, Dad. He's friendly."

"I'm sure he is, Pete, but I'm allergic to dogs and have trouble breathing around them."

Pete said, "Come on, Bogie. Let's go outside."

"Bogie?" I asked of Katy, who was making coffee as I went into the kitchen."

"His legal, certified name is Beauregard. The boys call him Bogie. You'll love him, Honey."

"I'm sure I will, but that's not the point, is it? I told you I'm allergic to dogs and cats and that's one reason I didn't want you to get a dog. The other reason is because we are gone so much on business and can't get someone to take care of him easily. I wish just once you'd listen to me."

Katy started to argue and I told her I was tired of arguing and was going to the office. I went upstairs, showered, changed and drove into town. Katy did not come into the office that day.

Patti asked me where she was, so I told her the whole story about driving home the previous night, learning about the purchase of the dog, and driving to the Corner Club. I left out any mention of Nancy!

Patti once again commented about Katy's refusal to back me up in my decisions. I was getting to like Patti more and more and I was becoming more upset with Katy as the days went by.

October, 1992

I drove to Portland, Oregon by myself on Wednesday, to the GTE Western Classic. I brought a total of ten of the Probe 20/20 putters with me, several of each weight. On Thursday, a practice day for the Senior Tour pros, the first pro I saw on the putting green was Arnold Palmer. I walked through the ropes surrounding the green, holding back over 500 viewers, and went to Arnie.

"Hey, Arnie, mind if I show you something new?"

"What do you have, Pete?"

"We invented a new putter that has the thin end of the shaft in the grip, and the fatter, heavier end in the head. It gives you a pure pendulum stroke each and every time and keeps the putter head moving toward the hole."

"Let me try it."

I handed the #3 Probe putter to Arnie, explaining it was the lightest one.

"It's pretty heavy!"

"It's made that way to keep any jerkiness out of the stroke."

Arnie stroked a ten foot putt uphill and it went right in the center of the hole.

"It feels pretty nice."

"Now try this one. It is 50 grams heavier."

"It feels even better."

"We found the heavier putters give you more control on faster greens. Now try this one. It's the heaviest model at 450 grams in the head."

"I think I like this one the best."

"Let me show you something I incorporated into the putter."

I placed the ball about three feet from the hole, with a slope from the left to the right.

"Arnie, this putt normally breaks from left to right about three inches. With any other putter, you'd have to aim outside the hole to the left and hope you hit it the proper speed so it breaks three inches and you make the putt. But with this putter, you can hit the ball with the mark at the heel, and it will put left-hand spin on the ball, reducing the break to the right so you can aim the ball at the inside of the left side of the hole and it will only break about an inch. The putter actually straightens out the putt and you make it without aiming outside the hole."

Arnie tried it and the ball went into the center of the hole. "That's amazing!"

"Now put the ball on the other side of the hole, so the putt will normally break about three inches from right to left. Then aim the putt inside the right side of the hole and hit the ball off the mark on the toe of the putter. The putter will put right-hand spin on the ball and the putt will only break about an inch, into the center of the hole."

Arnie tried the putt, placing the ball off the toe of the putter and the ball went into the center of the hole.

"Whoa, that is nice. So I can hit short breaking putts off the toe or heel when appropriate, and take the break out of the putt?"

"Exactly. You can take the guesswork out of making short breaking putts."

"OK, may I take this putter out for a practice round right now?"

"Of course, but let me show you one more thing you can do with this putter."

"There's more?"

"Yep." We walked to the edge of the putting green, toward the first tee. "Let's say your ball landed on the green, but up against the fringe line. You can't putt it easily with your putter, because of the two-inch taller grass behind the ball. Some players try to use a wedge and blade the ball in the center. But with the Probe 20/20, you can turn the putter to the left 90 degrees and hit the ball with the toe of the putter, like this."

I demonstrated, and Arnie was shocked!

"OK, I'm looking forward to trying it on the course."

As Arnie headed for the first tee with his caddie, I looked around for my associate, who had a video camera with him. I wanted to follow Arnie with the video.

I found Steve and told him to come with me. We followed Arnie play the first hole, a par-4. He hit driver, then 8-iron about ten feet from the hole. He took one practice stroke with his Probe 20/20 and then holed the putt for birdie.

On the second hole, a par-3, he hit the green and then holed the 15-foot birdie putt. He was two under par for two holes.

He hit the third, a par-5, in three and then sank the 18-foot birdie putt. He was three under after three. As he walked off the green, he dropped his ball against the fringe, turned the putter to the left, to play the ball off the toe as I had demonstrated on the putting green, and then stroked the ball into the hole about 25 feet away!

"I can't miss with this putter," he told his caddie as he retrieved his ball from the hole and walked to the next tee.

Steve and I were pretty excited while walking back to the clubhouse. I wanted to show the putter to some more players before they teed off. I ran into Jim Kelley from ESPN and told him the story about Arnie. Then I explained to him the major benefits of our Probe 20/20 putter and the inverted shaft. He said he'd try to mention it during the telecast.

I called my office and asked my receptionist to tape the tournament that week on ESPN.

By Sunday night, Arnie had played his best tournament of the year, and finished seventh!

That night I met Katy and Patti at my hotel. They had driven from Yreka to Portland to watch the Fred Meyer best-ball tournament nearby, an annual tournament sponsored by Peter Jacobsen and Fred Meyer. Jacobson always teamed up with Arnie as his partner and we were looking forward to watching Arnie with his new Probe putter.

The hotel was full due to the two tournaments in town, so Katy, Patti and I had to share one room and one queen-size bed! That was interesting!

The next morning we drove to Portland Country Club, site of the Fred Meyer. I led the girls out to the driving range and headed for the biggest crowd, figuring they were watching Arnie. I was right.

I showed my Tour Manufacturer's badge and the security guard let me through. I indicated to him that the girls were with me, but the guard said, "No." Then we heard Arnie's distinctive voice tell the guard that it was OK, that the girls were friends of his!

I heard Patti exclaim, "Wow, I didn't realize Pete was so important!"

We all three walked up to Arnie and I introduced Katy and Patti to him. Arnie's eyes smiled. He always liked pretty women around him. I asked Arnie how the putter was working, and he turned to his bag and pointed. "It's still in my bag," he exclaimed.

I asked him if I could get a picture of the girls and him on the putting green before he teed off and he said, "Sure. Let's get Pete in the shot also."

As we walked to the putting green, he called Jacobson over. I arranged Pete on the left, then Patti, then Arnie, and then Katy, for the picture. Arnie told Pete, "Pete, stay away from my women," as I took the picture. "OK, Arnie."

The girls laughed.

As Arnie and Pete headed for the first tee, the girls and I started walking around, watching the players. It was a long day.

That night we partied at a local bar and ran into Jim Kelley from ESPN. He was putting the moves on Patti, but somehow he and Katy ended up drinking together and Patti and I danced together. Then the three of us, pretty well lubricated from the cocktails, headed back to our room and our one bed. Like before, I felt it was best for me to sleep in the middle. That was a night I'll never forget! Not that anything happened, but just the thoughts running through my head were enough.

The next day we watched the tournament again, then drove back all night to Yreka. I should say I drove, and the girls slept.

By Wednesday morning, when we three got to the office, my receptionist told me she had taped the Fred Meyer tournament too, and Jim Kelley had mentioned Arnold Palmer and his new inverted-shafted Probe putter 19 times during the two-day telecast!

By the end of the week, we had received at least one phone call in the office from every state, asking "is this was the company that made Arnold Palmer's new putter?"

It was an exciting ten days, to say the least.

By the end of that year, a golfing buddy of mine, Jim Harrison, called me and told me he had obtained the interest of a marketing company in Florida regarding my putter. They wanted to fly out and talk to me about doing an infomercial on the putter. We set a date for that meeting in Yreka a few days later. Needless to say, our whole office was excited about the prospects.

January, 1993

I met with a Marketing Resources of America (MRA) representative, Bill Seidell, in Yreka, and discussed how we could make some money together marketing my putter.

I liked Bill and we roughed out an agreement whereby MRA would loan Probe Golf $250,000 to manufacture the 20/20 putter in quantity for MRA and MRA would spend about $750,000 producing an infomercial on the putter and airing it nationally. We would share the proceeds according to a formula Bill and I came up with.

A month later his partners flew to Yreka and I met the President and Vice President for the first time. I liked Bill much better and learned 18 months later that my first impressions were right!

We increased production capability of the 20/20 putter drastically in the next 30 days, buying six used milling machines, each one serving one function in the production process. We also bought one $125,000 new computerized CNC machine, financed over five years. By March 1, 1993, we were making about 780 putters per day.

By April of 1993, Katy was starting to drive me crazy again, increasing her criticism of how I was running Probe Golf. With the

MRA contract, she was spending more time in the office, criticizing my decisions more and more.

Our cash flow was slowing at Probe Golf and I had to do something to improve the situation. My brother, Brian, and Mick Thomas, Patti's husband, were making substantial commissions selling our Probe Distributorships over the phone and I figured we needed to reduce those sales commissions if we were to survive. I decided to reduce the commissions from 20% to 15%.

Brian was tremendously upset with the reduction, and gave me a lot of grief over the phone. Mick also complained, threatening to quit. I was pleasantly surprised to see Patti argue my point and take my side, against Mick. Mick did quit over the cutback in commissions. He went home and then called Patti at the office, and told her to quit also and come home. Patti told him, "No. I like my job, and I want to stay!"

She hung up the phone, then turned to me and told me what Mick had demanded she do. I told her I was glad she chose to stay, because I valued her work and her loyalty. That was the beginning of the end to their marriage.

Patti was her usual self during the next few weeks, helping me and encouraging me in my decisions and once again asking why I put up with Katy's criticisms. That can have a huge effect on a man, especially one who has been self-employed all his life and welcoming all the enthusiasm and encouragement he can get.

One night I called Patti at her home. Her daughter answered the phone, and I asked to talk to her Mom. Patti came on, and I told her I had something I wanted to talk to her about outside the office. She hesitantly said, "OK. When and where?"

I asked her if I could pick her up the next morning and take her out for coffee, so we could talk. She said, "Sure. What time?"

"I'll be there at 8:00 A.M."

"OK. I'll be ready."

I picked up Patti at her house in my new 1993 Ford Probe GT the next morning. Instead of going for coffee, I drove north of Yreka and then stopped on the side of the road. I was nervous, and I could tell Patti was also.

I started with small talk, telling her I wanted her to know how much I appreciated her giving me encouragement in the office and that I appreciated the job she was doing at Probe.

Then I blurted it out. "Do you want to have an affair with me?"

Patti just sat there, shocked. "You're married to my sister! I couldn't do that to her."

"I understand. I just want you to know how I feel. I'm having a hard time being married to someone who criticizes me all the time and having you around all the time giving me encouragement. That attracts me to you."

"I can understand that, but I love my sister and could not do that to her, ever!"

"OK. I just had to tell you how I feel. Let's get to the office."

We drove to the office and didn't say much to each other the rest of the day.

It was obvious that my relationship with Patti had to be different after that morning in the car before work. Even though she had turned down my proposal, she actually became a close friend to me. We talked more openly about her sister and she even suggested a few things I could do to improve my relationship and my marriage to Katy!

MRA had scheduled their infomercial shoot for three days the end of June, the 29th and 30th. I had some business in New York with a stock brokerage firm, so I scheduled it for a few days before the shoot. Katy wanted to come along, so we both flew out of Medford, Oregon on the 26th.

We arrived in Orlando on the 28th and met with two MRA officials. MRA had paid Gary Player $100,000 to spend two days in front of the camera at his club, Alaqua Country Club near Orlando. Gary was quite a gentleman and I enjoyed our conversations between shoots.

I could never live in Florida. The humidity was awful. We'd get dressed in the air conditioned clubhouse before each shoot and have make-up applied just before going outside to the putting green. Within five minutes I felt as if I had jumped into a lake. My clothes were soaking wet!

We shot the infomercial in two days, with another hour thrown in the third morning to reshoot a few takes.

Katy and I flew back to New York for another quick meeting with the stock broker. While Katy took a tour of New York with one of the brokers, I caught up on some sleep in the hotel; at least that was my excuse for not taking the tour. I actually wanted to check in with my office in California and hopefully talk to Patti. That day, you might say, was the start of our affair!

Patti answered the phone at the office when I called from the hotel room. She gave me my latest business messages and then we talked about the infomercial shoot. The discussion turned to sex. I asked what she was wearing and she told me. I told her I was looking forward to seeing her the next day when we flew into Medford and drove to Yreka. She said she looked forward to seeing me also.

The next day, Saturday, July 1, I called Patti at her house and asked her if she would meet me in the Wal-Mart parking lot at 9:00 A.M. the following day, Sunday. She asked, "What for?"

"I just want to see you and talk."

"OK, see you then."

I was nervous about the meeting, because I wanted her.

July 2, 1993

At 8:30 the next morning, I walked into the Food For Less to pick up a few things and walked right into Patti and her daughter, Carol, coming down the aisle. I said, "Hi." They said, "Hi," back! It was awkward.

"What are you girls shopping for?"

"Just a few food items for lunch. What are you getting?"

"Just some shampoo and toothpaste."

"OK, well, have a nice day!"

"Thanks, you too." I walked to the cashier, and checked out. I walked outside, looking back, glad to see Patti's eyes were following me with a smile.

At 9:00, I drove into the Wal-Mart parking lot and saw her van. I pulled up next to her and signaled for her to get in my Ford F-150 truck. She opened the door and got in.

I said, "Hi. That was awkward. Does Carol suspect anything?

"She does and she's excited. She likes you."

"I like her, too. Want to go for a drive?"

"OK."

We drove off and I turned left on Highway 3, south out of town. I said, "I can't wait any longer. I need to make love to you."

She looked at me and smiled. "I want you too."

I drove half way up the hill toward Fort Jones, then turned left behind a huge pile of dirt and rocks. I parked, turned off the engine, then turned around and opened the window into the back of the truck, which was covered with a custom made red canopy.

"Climb through," I told her. She climbed through the window into the back compartment, and I followed her. I cut my leg on the frame of the window as I climbed through and said, "Ouch!"

She looked at the cut, which was starting to bleed, and asked, "Can I help with that?"

"Later." I started to get undressed and she did the same. In a minute we were naked. She had very tiny breasts, which surprised me, because I had always thought she had a great figure. The magic of the bra I guess.

We hugged and kissed, and then I was inside her. I was too anxious and nervous, and so was she. We both came almost immediately! I was embarrassed and said so. She said not to worry, that it was natural that we were excited the first time. We were also afraid someone would drive up at any time, so we dressed quickly, and climbed back through the window into the cab.

I started the engine and then pulled onto the road back toward Yreka. I reached over and held her hand as we drove the four miles back into town and she responded with a firm grip and smiled.

I dropped her off at her van in the parking lot, and said, "Thanks for the quickie, I needed it."

"So did I."

"We'll have to take more time the next time."

"OK,"

"See you later." I drove off, looking around to see if anyone I knew had seen us together. I could see Patti was also looking around for anyone she knew.

Monday morning I walked into the office and the first person I ran into was Patti. We said, "Hi" to each other and smiled. Kandi was just inside the front door and I said, "Good morning."

"Good morning!"

I went to my desk and got busy with messages. The rest of the day Patti and I didn't say much to each other, but exchanged looks and smiles, each enjoying the feelings and excitement that come with a new love.

Two days later I met Patti in front of the supermarket at the north end of town, and we drove in my F-150 north on Interstate-5 to the Klamath River off ramp. We then drove along the river on its dirt frontage road about five miles, to one of my favorite fishing spots. I didn't see any other vehicles around, so I drove down by the river and stopped the truck. We got out, then opened the back of the cab, climbed inside, and closed the door. We took our time that afternoon, and thoroughly enjoyed each other.

It was the second time we were intimate together.

Business at Probe Golf was good that summer. With our inventory of 20/20 putters growing in preparation for the release of MRA's Probe 20/20 infomercial in December, I was able to spend some time with Patti almost every afternoon, sometimes with Katy joining us at local bars for a relaxing drink after work.

Both women were my best friends. That may sound strange, but it was the truth. Patti loved her sister and in many ways she wanted our marriage to work. Patti even made a comment to me one afternoon that it was too bad our laws only allowed a man to have one wife! She asked me if it was still legal for a man to have two wives if he were a Mormon in Utah. I told her I honestly did not know for sure, but that I didn't think so.

That night I even went online and investigated the Mormon laws in Utah. I learned that Utah had changed the law in 1899, forbidding such practices any longer. I told Patti the next morning about my research. She was disappointed and so was I.

I had some crazy ideas running through my head that summer. I thought about marriage, divorce, what made some marriages work and many end in divorce. I didn't want to divorce Katy, mostly because she was the mother of my sons, and my sons were the most important thing in my life. I thought of what it would be like to be married to Patti, a woman who always supported me in my business and my personal life. I never heard her raise her voice to anyone, except for her husband.

It seemed to me that she had definitely married the wrong man. Mick was about twelve years older than she and had been affiliated with people in Hollywood. I'm sure that had impressed her and was the main reason she married him. But it also seemed to me that Mick was always putting her down, telling her she was only good for one thing, waiting on tables in his restaurants. Patti definitely had a self-confidence problem. It seemed to me that Mick was tough on his kids as well, especially his son, Mick. Years later that criticism of the son by his father would show up when Mick was older.

November 3, 1993

I called Patti at her home in the afternoon and asked her if she'd like to drive down to the south fork of the Salmon River with me the next morning and keep me company while I fished for steelhead.

"Sure. Sounds like fun."

"OK, but we have to leave very early, before dawn. Can you be ready at 5:00 A.M.?"

"I'll be ready. Can I bring anything?"

"A couple of sandwiches and a thermos of coffee would be great."

"I'll do that, and I'll be ready at 5:00."

"See you then."

I drove up to her house at 5:03 A.M. I could see her looking out the front living room window and then the front door opened. She was carrying a bag, probably food and coffee.

"Good morning," I said as she opened the right-hand door.

"Good morning."

I drove off as Patti poured me a cup of coffee from a thermos into one of my travel mugs. I headed south on Highway 3 out of Yreka toward Scott Valley. It would be a two-hour drive to Cecilville on the south fork of the Salmon River. I told Patti she might want to sleep during the drive, but she said she wanted to keep me company. She was like that, always thinking of what I needed and put me before what she wanted.

I drove through Etna, California, then 18 miles to Callahan, a small old mining town of one bar and one market. The old motel from the 1850's was closed.

I turned right at Callahan as Patti commented how much farther we had to drive.

"Thirty miles. It will take another hour."

"Ready for a tuna sandwich?"

"Half of one would be perfect."

In another 55 minutes we drove into Cecilville, more of a logging camp rather than a town. It had one gas pump in front of a small market and bar. There were about 15 small cabins that loggers used as motel rooms sprinkled among the tall pines.

We picked up a few food items, then continued west along the one-lane forest service road. Just as we followed the road to the right, a large brown and red tail appeared right in front of the hood of my F-150 pickup!

"What is that?" yelled Patti.

I looked to the left of the truck to see an adult mountain lion jump into the bushes to our left. "Cougar."

"A cougar? Is that like a mountain lion?"

"It is a mountain lion."

"Wow! I'm never seen one outside of a zoo. Is he dangerous?"

"I wouldn't want to run into him outside the truck."

We both watched as the tail disappeared into the woods.

"I'm planning to stop at the river in another two miles. We probably should wait a few minutes before getting out of the truck, just in case the cougar is still around."

"That sounds just perfect to me."

I parked the truck at one of my favorite fishing spots. I took advantage of the wait to explain to Patti what I was fishing for. "The steelhead in this river are rainbow trout that hatched in this same river about six years ago, and then migrated to the ocean, spent about five years in the ocean and then returned to the exact same river to lay their eggs. They get tired swimming up the river against the current, so they stop to rest. They stop at parts of the river where the current is not as fast, such as just below waterfalls, in the slow moving pools. Do you see that ten foot drop into the slow moving water just above that big rock?"

"I see it."

"The steelhead would be lying just above that rock. I'll throw my bait, a chunk of shrimp, in the fast water at the top of that drop. It will fall the ten feet down to the pool, where I'll wait to feel a steelhead pick it up. If the line feels like it stopped in the current, I'll assume a steelhead picked it up and set the hook."

"You mean pull back on the rod?"

"Yep. If the bait is in the steelhead's mouth, the hook will sink into its mouth and I'll start fighting the fish."

"That sounds exciting!"

"It is. Trying to land a six or seven pound steelhead in this narrow river with a fast current running could be tough. The odds are actually in favor of the steelhead. He could head down river with the current and I could break my line before landing him."

"Why don't you use stronger line?"

"Excellent question, Honey."

"If I use line that is too strong and too easy for the fish to see, they would never bite the bait! And the water here is from melted snow and is very clear. I have to use no bigger than six pound monofilament or else they will see it and not bite."

"OK. Do you think we can get out safely? Or is the cougar still around?"

"He's probably gone by now."

We got out of the truck and I started pulling my chest waders over my jeans. Patti walked down by the stream and sat on a rock. The "river" was no more than ten feet wide at this spot, but it was amazing how big the steelhead were in this small stream!

I put a small piece of shrimp I had bought at the supermarket on my size 10 hook. Any larger hook would have scared the fish away.

A foot above the hook I had placed a ¼ inch piece of rubber tubing, with a 3/8 inch piece of 1/8 inch wide lead weight, to give the bait a little weight.

I tossed the bait in the middle of the stream above the drop-off into the pool and watched the bait drop over the ledge. I saw the line stop just before the rock and felt a tiny tap on the line with my fingertips.

I held the reel and line with my left hand and jerked back on the rod with my right. Something pulled back for a split second, but then was gone!

"Missed him!"

"You had one?"

"He picked up the bait, but not all the way in his mouth. The hook didn't sink in when I tried to set it. Let's go to the next spot."

"You don't want to try again here?"

"Steelhead protect their territory. Once you lose one, he is spooked for a while and you have to move to find another spot."

As we walked back to the truck, I glanced at Patti, and she smiled.

"Want to have some fun before we move?"

"I thought you'd never ask."

I put my arms around her and pulled her close for a kiss. Without saying a word, I dropped my hands to her belt and slipped open the buckle. She pulled her jeans down and turned around while I dropped my waders down around my boots and unbuckled my jeans. Then I slid up behind her.

Five minutes later we pulled up our jeans.

"That was fun."

"It was," she added with a sigh.

We got into the truck and I started driving down river again to the next fishing hole. Patti sure was fun. We could just look at each other and know what the other was thinking. We were like an old couple that had lived together for 40 years and knew exactly what we both felt without having to say a word.

I hooked two more steelhead that day, but did not land one. The longest I had one on the line was about three minutes before he got into the current and broke my line! Around 3:00 P.M. the sun was behind the hills and it was getting dark down in the crevasse by the river.

"Hungry?"

"I could eat something."

Heading back up river the way we had come, we stopped in at the bar in Cecilville and said, "Hi" to Bob, the bartender. We ordered two hamburgers with everything and two Jacks. Patti had always ordered White Russians before the affair, but switched to Jack after it started. I always wondered why that was.

"Bob, we almost ran over a cougar this morning when we drove in from Callahan."

"That must have been Old Tom. He's getting on in years and has lost half his teeth and his mind is going. Not as quick as he used to be."

"That explains why he almost got run over."

"See you next time, Bob. We have a two hour drive back to Yreka and it's getting dark. Don't want to run over Old Tom in the dark!"

"See you next trip, Pete."

I paid the bill and walked Patti out the door.

"Nice to meet you, Bob."

"You, too, Patti."

Patti asked me a lot of questions about that part of the country on the ride back. She asked what the big piles of smooth rocks were on the side of the rive, and I explained they were left over by the gold miners back in the 1850's after dredging the river for gold.

"Look out," she yelled as a black bear jumped in front of the truck. I almost hit the bear, but he ran off into the woods.

"Wow, there's more wildlife than other fishermen in this area."

"That's why it's called the Marble Mountain Wilderness Area."

We drove into Yreka around 6:00 P.M., just as it was getting dark. I pulled up in front of Patti's house and kissed her goodnight. I squeezed her left breast with my left hand, then the right.

"She giggled, and said, "Goodnight."

"See you in the morning at the office."

"OK."

Christmas that year was held at our house on the hill and Katy and Patti's family all came up to enjoy the festivities. The younger sister, Muriel, was putting on weight, which surprised me because Katy and Patti had such nice bodies. I remember asking their Mom, Margaret, about Muriel a year earlier and whether she had a boyfriend. Margaret had told me that Muriel had one date when she was younger. When her date came to the front door to pick her up, she had run to her room and told her Mom to tell the boy to leave, that she wasn't feeling well! That was the only date Muriel (almost) had in her entire life. Now food was taking the place of any man in her life.

Christmas Eve, Muriel announced that she was going to wake everyone up at 4:00 A.M. to open presents. I said, "No way. We'll wake up when we wake up!"

"Oh, come on. Where's your Christmas spirit?"

"I stopped getting up early on Christmas morning when I was eight."

"So let your sons have some fun."

"They can have fun opening presents at 6:00 just as easily as they can at 4:00. Good night."

The next morning I had Muriel's face in my face at 4:00 A.M., insisting we get up to open presents. Fifteen years later Muriel would become the most wicked, self-serving, smart-ass know-it-all I would ever know personally! All 400 pounds of her!

Among other things, she would ruin Patti's life!

December 28, 1993

I received a phone call from my attorney in Minneapolis, suggesting that I move Probe Golf to Nevada for tax purposes. He knew that MRA was about to air our new infomercial and that our gross income was about to take a huge jump upward. I told him I'd investigate the possibilities in Nevada and get back to him.

Katy did not suspect anything about the affair and did not object when I told her about possibly moving our head offices to Nevada, and transferring Patti there to run the office. Patti was ecstatic, mostly because no one had ever trusted her with such a responsibility!

She and I made plans to go to Las Vegas and look around for a location for the new offices and production facility. When Katy learned I was planning to take Patti with me to Las Vegas, she became upset and we argued. I had not been feeling very well for several days. I felt run down and the added stress of the argument caused me to come down with the flu. I also got hives all over my legs and torso.

There I was sick in bed, and both my wife and mistress were waiting on me, bringing me soup, crackers, aspirin, whatever I needed. It took me three days to get up and around again.

Finally, Patti and I flew out of Medford, OR, for Las Vegas. I had gotten a room at the Stardust Hotel and Casino, which we hid from Katy. I had told her that Patti and I had separate rooms. I still had hives all over my legs, so Patti prepared an oatmeal bath for me in the tub in the room. She babied me for another two days with the oatmeal baths and lots of rest. I was finally up and around the third day.

I didn't want an office and assembly facility in downtown Las Vegas, so we drove toward Henderson and Boulder City, close to Lake Meade. We found a 4,500 square foot facility in Boulder City. We both loved the town. It had gotten its name from the fact that it had sprung up in the 1930's when Boulder Dam was constructed. The work camp of 10,000 construction workers became Boulder City later on. The dam was later named Hoover Dam.

We signed a one-year lease on the building and then made plans to fly back to Medford and then drive to Yreka.

The 1994 PGA Merchandise Show was scheduled for the end of January in Orlando, Florida. Patti reserved airline tickets and two hotel rooms for the four days for herself, Patti, and me.

We had reserved a booth at the show six months earlier and were going to show our new line of custom fit golf clubs in our booth.

The first two days of the show went well. Larry Laoretti, who had won the 1992 Senior United States Open using a Probe custom fit driver, came by the booth the second day and hung around for three hours, telling visitors to our booth about the amazing advantages of playing a Probe driver over any other driver! The girls had fun posing for pictures with Larry for the visitors.

The night of the second day at the show, the fun ended!

January 31, 1994

Patti had been approached by a tall blond guy at our booth toward the end of the second day of the show and asked out to dinner. She had glanced at me before politely declining. But the guy was persistent and she finally said, "OK."

Katy and I enjoyed dinner alone and then went back to our room. We turned in at 10:00. I didn't sleep well and glanced at my watch at 1:00 A.M. Patti, who was in the adjoining room, had not come in yet and I knew she was still out with tall Blondie.

At 1:30 A.M., I heard them enter her room. I heard her say, "Goodnight", but Blondie was once again persistent. I could tell from the voices and other sounds that he was on her bed and she was trying to politely get him to leave.

Katy woke up and sensed my discomfort. "What's wrong?"

"It sounds like your sister is having trouble getting rid of her date."

"Don't worry about it. She's a big girl. She can take care of herself."

I couldn't stop worrying about it and the more I heard next door, the more upset I became. Finally, I got up, walked across the room and knocked on the door.

"Hey," I yelled. "If she wants you to leave, then leave!"

I heard some movement, voices arguing, then the front door to Patti's room opened and closed. There was silence.

I looked back at Katy, now sitting up in bed. She had a look of surprise and understanding on her face. "You bastard!"

"What?"

"You're having an affair with my sister!"

I was speechless. Katy got up, then and knocked on the door to Patti's room. Patti opened the door and was standing in her nightgown looking guilty. The next ten minutes were not pleasant.

Katy accused Patti of having an affair with me and all Patti could do was apologize.

Then Katy slammed the door, came to bed and started crying. I could hear Patti crying next door. What a mess!

The next morning we three met for breakfast in the hotel, with no conversation at all. We got through the day with the girls giving each other the cold shoulder. When the show closed for the day, we all went back to our rooms, changed into bathing suits, and went to the pool. Again, there was no conversation.

I tried to make small talk, to no avail. It took the girls another 24 hours before they talked to each other.

The flight back to California the next day was still awkward, with Katy and I sitting together in First Class, me at the window, with Patti at the window right behind me.

Patti and Ron Weber, my production manager, and Ron's wife were scheduled to make the trip to Nevada two days later, driving a large U-Haul truck with machining equipment and 40,000 Probe putters. Mick, Patti's husband, had left town in his Chevy Blazer, pulling a small travel trailer behind it. Patti had already seen a divorce lawyer.

February 6, 1994

The next morning was cold and foggy. Ron had had the U-Haul loaded the day before by several of our employees. Katy, Patti, Patti's daughter, Carol, Ron, Ron's wife, and I met outside our building in Yreka to say goodbye. They would be driving part of the distance to Boulder City that day and finish the drive the next day.

Katy and Patti were more civil to each other at the departure. We waved goodbye.

Katy and I walked back into our offices, to see Kandi behind her desk. I could feel a chill in the air as I walked past her. We got to work for the day.

MRA had started airing our 30-minute infomercial, starring Gary Player and ESPN's Jim Kandi. The first day we had received $22,000 in orders! Our employees were busy that day boxing and shipping putters via UPS.

By the end of March, we had sold $1,240,000 in putters! Most of the profit was wired into MRA's bank account.

I was on the phone with Patti and Ron at least three times per day the next week, following their success in getting the Nevada operation going. Everything was moving smoothly. Back at home things were different. Katy wanted to take the boys and move elsewhere in town. We were not getting along at all. She found a small house in town about two blocks from where she was working for a CPA, doing accounting work for his clients.

I was alone on top of our hill, on the 25 acres. Patti had asked me to move to Nevada, to leave Katy, and I was not sure what I wanted to do. My heart told me to move to Nevada with Patti, but my common sense told me to stay in Yreka because of my sons.

The spring of 1994 was probably the most important time for me from 1979 to the present; because it is the time I made one of the most important decisions of my life!

Should I move to the woman who seemed perfect for me? Patti supported me in my business, in my decisions, never argued with me, and loved sex and exiting surroundings as much as I did.

Or should I stay near my sons? I knew the importance of properly raising children. Mick and Patti had always put their restaurants and bars ahead of Mick and Carol, leaving them with various babysitters while working and playing until all hours of the morning. It showed in their kids. Even at this early stage of their development, both of the kids were wild and undisciplined.

Pete and Bob were very bright and knew how to behave. I often wonder how things would have changed if I had decided to follow Patti to Nevada.

Other than visiting the offices in Nevada every few months, I stayed and lived in Yreka. During one visit to Nevada in May, 1994, I asked Patti if she would like breast implants! She said, "Of course!"

I set aside $4,000 for Patti, and she scheduled a flight to Phoenix, AZ with Carol during the month of July to have her surgery.

There were minor complications with the surgery later on, but being the trooper she was, she handled them professionally and unemotionally. The implants were magnificent and Patti was very proud of them! They seemed to help her self-esteem, which was the major reason I wanted to get them for her. Ever since I had come to the conclusion that her husband had always put her down and told her she could not get any job other than waiting on tables, I had promised myself I would do everything I could do to build her feelings about herself. She had done a great job at Probe Golf as my assistant and I made sure she knew I appreciated it. For years after the implant surgery, she told me stories about how men and women complimented her about her figure. It's too bad I couldn't do more to build her son's and daughter's self-esteem over the years!

One night in August I took Patti out to dinner in Las Vegas. On our way home, we drove by the Pioneer Club and Patti suggested we go in for a drink. That sounded good to me, so we stopped. I had never been to such a fancy strip club and neither had Patti. We ordered drinks and then watched one of the strippers walk down the runway. She was naked.

Patti loved to dance, so I was not surprised when she got up and started dancing herself at our table. Within a minute, most of the men near our table were watching Patti instead of the pro on the runway! The bouncers did not appreciate Patti taking the limelight, so they asked her to sit down. I grabbed her arm and we walked out to the parking lot, jumped in the car, and drove home. I couldn't wait to get her in bed. She was so-o-o-o-o-o-o sexy!

In September of 1994, I learned that MRA was not complying with its contract with Probe, and I had to hire an attorney to try to work things out. Some of my stockholders back in Minnesota had learned about my affair with Patti, and wanted new management to take over in the legal conflict with MRA. I made the mistake of trusting one of my original stockholders, who lived in Chico, CA to take over. He basically ran the company into bankruptcy, failed to reply to specific legal papers submitted to the court by MRA in the time allowed, and put Probe in jeopardy, then resigned in December, 1994.

I was forced to come back as President and rescue the company. My last act as president while the company was still in Boulder City was to arrange to sell 18,000 individually-boxed Probe 20/20 putters to a company in England, Regal Group International.

I had asked Patti to help me meet and entertain the President of Regal Group International in Las Vegas to close the deal. She not only helped me at our first meeting at Caesar's Palace, she was so entertaining and professional at that dinner meeting that Richard, the President, complimented me over the phone three days after he returned to England for having such a professional and charming assistant.

After that meeting and closing that sale, we moved the company back to Yreka, and Patti and Carol moved back into Yreka at the same time.

I helped Patti put some of her personal property into storage in Yreka, and helped her find a small apartment in town. She was able to find a job bartending at Wah Lee's Chinese Restaurant, while I downsized Probe Golf and operated it out of my house on the hill, with production in the three-car garage.

It was about that time when I received a letter in the mail from my Dad. He had learned about the affair with Patti and I was surprised to learn that he understood why it happened!

The point in his letter that he wanted to make perfectly clear was that I should get a divorce from Katy before starting a relationship with another woman. Then he wished me well.

Winter of 1994 / 1995

With Patti working at night at Wah Lee's, she usually came up to the house during the day to help me in the garage with putter orders. As the weather warmed up, she loved to sunbathe naked on my deck; she loved to run around naked as much as possible! Katy had told me that when the girls were young, living in San Diego, the family had a problem keeping clothes on Patti in the house. When the front doorbell rang, they had to intercept Patti before she would answer the door in the nude!

During the summer of 1995, I had a project going on down the hill from the house of installing gravel over dirt while building a garden. Patti offered to help. I'd work in my office in the house, and glance out the window at Patti walking up and down the hill in nothing but tennis shoes!

In July, the two of us drove down to Lake Shasta for a few days on my 27-foot Bayliner and she didn't put any clothes on for two days!

In August, I went by her apartment in Yreka to go over some business letters I needed her to mail and before I left, I asked her if she wanted to have some fun. She said, "Sure!"

I told her to take off all of her clothes, which she did immediately. Then I tied her hands together and told her to stand on a chair I had moved to the center of the room, under an overhead light. Then I stood on another chair and tied her hands to the light fixture in the ceiling. I left her standing on the chair, naked, with her hands tied over her head. I told her I'd be back in a couple of hours to check on her. She asked, "What if Carol comes in with a friend?"

"Then, won't you be embarrassed?"

I kissed both breasts, and then both cheeks. I locked the front door and walked down to my car. I ran a few errands around town and then stopped to call her apartment. She answered on the first ring.

"You got loose!"

"Yes, and just in time. Carol came in with her boyfriend about two minutes after I got the ropes untied."

"Too bad. That would have been interesting."

She laughed.

"Have a nice day with Carol, Honey. I love you."

"I love you, too."

Patti and I used to have fun like that whenever one of us wanted to shock the other. We have many such stories we could tell, but I can't take up too much room in this book at this time. Maybe in the sequel, if there is one?

August 16, 1995

I opened a new Probe Golf facility in a commercial business park in Yreka, and Katy moved back into the house on the hill with the boys. I used the upstairs of Probe's new facility as an apartment. Patti often stayed with me in that apartment at night.

That month we were filling an order for my Probe 20/20 putters for Japan. We had to box 1,200 Probe putters for delivery to Japan, where our buyer was going to air our PUTT LIKE A PRO Gary Player infomercial nationwide, but dubbed in Japanese. I had Patti help with that order, along with two other young local ladies, and my son. Pete helped with the assembly and boxing the order. It took us two weeks to assemble the 1,200 putters, and then box them up for the trucking company that would ship them to Japan.

The night of August 20, Patti and I went out for dinner and dancing in my red Ford F-250 4X4 truck. On the way back to my apartment above Probe's facility, I pulled over and turned to Patti.

"Want to have some fun, Honey?"

"What do you have in mind?"

"Take off all your clothes, then get out of the truck. Find your way back to the apartment on your own, hopefully without being seen and picked up by the police. I'll meet you at the apartment."

"Wow! That sounds like it would be exciting. What if I get caught by the police?"

"Then give me a call. You're allowed one phone call. I'll come down and pick you up."

"OK"

Patti stripped in the truck, then leaned over and gave me a kiss. Then she was out the door. She had over four blocks to run and hide, and hopefully find her way to the back door to the apartment, where I told her to knock on the door, and I'd let her in. I watched her fantastic ass disappear into an alley, then drove back to the apartment.

I parked in the back of the apartment, then unlocked the side door and entered. I fixed myself a Jack and water and then put on a Righteous Brothers CD. I sat down, looked at my watch, and waited. It was 1:33 A.M.

I was getting concerned around 1:50 A.M. Patti should have made it to the apartment in less than fifteen minutes. I had dropped her off naked at 1:27 A.M., so I figured she'd be at the apartment by no later than 1:42 A.M. At 2:00 A.M. exactly I heard a soft knock at the back door.

I went to the door and asked, "Who's there?"

"It's me, open the door."

"What's the password?"

"Sex!"

"That works." I opened the door, and Patti was in my arms immediately. She kissed me hard on the lips, then tore my pants off and climbed onto my already hard member while I was still standing. She came almost immediately, and then continued riding me for another orgasm. Then I came in her, and we fell to the couch.

"My goodness. Weren't you horny?"

"Pete, I have never been so horny in my life. I had to hide behind a car for almost five minutes while a police car drove by slowly, and then stopped. I was afraid they had seen me. I had an orgasm right there, kneeling down, when they finally drove away. I wasn't even touching myself or anything."

"So you had fun?"

"Fun? I have never experienced anything like that. Thanks for making me do it."

"Any time, Baby, any time."

September 2, 1995

Patti and I drove down to Lake Shasta for a few days. The second morning she was lying naked on the stern couch when a young man rode by on a wave runner about thirty feet from the boat. I thought Patti would hide from the young man, but instead she stood up and waved to him. He almost fell off the wave runner when he saw her standing there naked.

He did not ride away, but sat there gawking while Patti said good morning to him. The young man couldn't say anything at all. I guessed he was around twelve years old, and Patti might have been the first nude woman he had ever seen. I walked up on deck and said, "Hi. How are you doing?"

"OK" is all he could manage, so I gave him an out and started the engine. We slowly moved away from him, with Patti still standing and waving at him, proud of her attributes that made this young man speechless. We were almost a quarter of a mile from him when he finally came out of his trance and started up his wave runner. He sped up and rode away, possibly because he could not wait to tell his friends about the nude goddess he had seen that morning, only thirty feet away!

December 14, 1995

Patti and I were out having dinner at the local Mexican restaurant until about 10:45 that night. We each had had two margaritas with dinner, but then we stopped at Wah Lee's and I had three Jacks and water. I was a little inebriated, so I suggested to Patti that she drive us back to my apartment in my big Ford F-250 4X4 truck.

"I've never driven a big truck like that!"

"You can do it, Honey. Just take it slow and easy."

"OK."

She climbed up to the driver's side and got in. I got in on the passenger side. The truck, fortunately, was an automatic. So she was doing just fine until we were half a mile from the apartment. She pulled over to a stop.

"Anything wrong, Honey?"

"It's your turn. Take off your clothes and get out."

"Honey, it's freezing outside. Not like last summer when I told you to do it."

"You heard me, get naked and get out."

I could tell she was having fun as the "master", so I took off my clothes until I was naked.

"Now give me a kiss, then get out."

I leaned over and kissed her on the mouth. She grabbed my penis and stroked it until it was hard, which was in three seconds.

"Now run back to the apartment with a hard-on, and I expect it to be hard when you get there."

"I don't know. It's freezing outside."

"Do it."

"Yes, Master."

I got out of the truck and closed the door. She drove off immediately, heading for the south end of Yreka. I had about seven blocks to find my way to the apartment. It felt like I would freeze to death before I got halfway.

I looked at my watch, the only thing I had on my body. It was almost midnight. I started running down a back alley.

I made it two blocks when a car came around the corner in front of me. Its headlights almost hit me from the front on when I ducked behind a parked car. I squatted down into a snow bank with my genitals finding the freezing ice. I could hear the car's studs hitting the road while the car drove past. I could vaguely see a young blond girl behind the wheel as she glanced in my direction. If my hard on was losing its stiffness due to the cold, it was back with a vengeance!

Before the car was twenty feet past me, I was on the run again. My feet were beginning to freeze, and I couldn't feel them when they hit the frozen ice. I had to throw caution to the wind and get to the apartment as quickly as possible or I might be found frozen, and naked, the next morning.

I finally got to the back of the apartment having no idea of how long it had taken me. I looked at my watch. It was 12:16 A.M. My truck was parked right where I had told Patti to park it, but she had parked it back end in first, not front end in first as I had instructed. I was afraid to let her back in, and my reasons were obvious as I approached the truck. She had backed into the corner of the Probe unit, and had bent the frame of the building!

I had lost all feelings in my feet, hands, legs, everything, so I decided to worry about the building and my truck the next day. Just as I was about to knock on the door, I remembered Patti's instructions. "Make sure your hard on is still there when you reach the apartment."

I looked down and could barely find myself in the cold. I stroked myself, but it took a while to get hard due to my having no feeling at all.

When I thought I had given it the old college try, I knocked on the door.

"Who's there?"

"It's me, Honey. I am freezing. Please open the door now."

"What's the password?"

"It's co-o-o-o-o-l-l-l-d!"

"That's not the password."

"S-E-X," I screamed.

"That's the one." She opened the door, and I ran in as fast as my frozen feet would move.

Patti had a warm blanket ready for me, and she wrapped it around my shoulders.

"You poor boy. Let me give you what you need."

She knelt in front of me and wrapped her warm hands around my semi-hard member.

"It's not fully hard, but I know you did your best in the cold. I forgive you."

She put me in her mouth and stroked me hard. Then she took all of me into her mouth. As the feeling returned, her hands and mouth felt fantastic, and it didn't take me long to reach climax.

As Patti gulped down the last drop, she smiled as her lips reached mine. For the first time since I got through the door I noticed she was naked underneath her own blanket. Our bodies entwined, and I carried her upstairs to my bed in the apartment. I began to tell her about my run to the apartment in the freezing snow, but her body wanted more than just words from me, so I shut up and enjoyed the moment.

February 19, 1996

Patti and Carol drove out of Yreka toward Palm Springs, Patti in the large U-Haul truck and Carol in their 1992 blue Ford van. Patti had given up trying to get me to move to Palm Springs and out of Yreka to be with her. She had decided that if she moved, I would have to make a decision to be with her, or be with my sons. She was my best friend, and I had decided she was my soul mate as well. But I could not bring myself to abandon my sons.

Every day I wonder if Patti and I would still be together if I had chosen to follow her to Palm Springs that year.

I had given both Patti and Carol two of my radios, or walkie-talkies, to keep in touch while they drove south. I had also suggested they turn toward the east once they got west of Bakersfield and take the back roads through the high desert, instead of staying on Interstate 5. I had heard that there was snow across the Grapevine.

As it turned out, high winds closed I-5 south of Bakersfield that week and they could not have gotten through if they had stayed on I-5!

As soon as Patti and Carol got settled into an apartment in Palm Springs, Patti called me and told me about the apartment. They had moved into a one-bedroom on Riverside Avenue. The complex had about 24 units, with a nice pool just below their second-story unit.

March 2, 1996

I called Patti and told her that I missed her so much I had to drive down to visit Carol and her. She said she missed me, too.

I made the 752 mile trip in ten and a half hours the next day and drove up to her apartment building around 8:30 p.m. I knocked on her door and Patti answered. We hugged and kissed and then she invited me in.

She had leftover pizza and heated it up in the microwave while she brought out a bottle of Jack Daniels and poured us a drink. We adjourned to the bedroom, where we embraced, took each other's clothes off, and got into bed.

"Where is Carol?

"She's out with a friend for the night. We have the whole apartment to ourselves."

We stopped talking and got busy!

The next morning was beautiful, about 75 degrees by 9:00 A.M. We put our bathing suits on and went down to the pool. Patti introduced me to her neighbor, Mick Kaufmann, who walked down about ten minutes after we got there. We took in the warm sun for about an hour, when Mick went back to his apartment.

Patti and I talked for a while, when I noticed a difference in her attitude.

"What's wrong?"

"When are you going to move down here?"

"I want to move right away, Honey, because I miss you terribly. But I'm trying to sell the house in Yreka and the market is slow. I need to sell the house and get a divorce from Katy before I can move down."

"Have you filed for the divorce?"

"Not yet."

"Pete, you promised me that once you moved Probe to Nevada, you would be following me there right away! That was two years ago!"

"I know, Honey. But I didn't think with my head at the time, only with my heart. I didn't realize all the things I needed to do before I left Yreka."

"Did you know that I took a lover in Boulder City after we moved Probe there?'

"No, I didn't know, but I can understand why."

"You know how much I missed you and yet you stayed with my sister for two more years!"

"Honey, I stayed because of my sons. I didn't want them hurt by having to grow up without a father around."

"Why didn't you think of that before getting me to move to Boulder City and telling me you would join me there?"

"Like I said, Honey, I was thinking with my heart and not my head."

She got up and went upstairs to her apartment. I sat by the pool for another ten to fifteen minutes and then went up. I drove back to Yreka the next day.

We kept in touch by phone, but our relationship was obviously strained.

March 30, 1996

I called Patti on the cell phone I had given her before she and Carol moved to Palm Springs.

"Hi, Honey."

"Hi. How are you?"

"I miss you. I need to see you."

"I miss you, too. Are you driving down here?"

"I'm pulling the boat down to Lake Havasu south of Las Vegas, on the Colorado River. I was wondering if Carol could drive you over there, or someplace where I can meet you can pick you up, so we could continue to Lake Havasu together. Barstow, California would probably be a good place to meet."

"When are you pulling the boat down?"

"In a few days, if you and Carol can tell me when you can drive over."

"Let me talk to her, and I'll call you back."

"OK, Honey. I'll wait to hear from you."

Patti called me later that night. "Hi, Baby. I talked to Carol and she can drive me to Barstow with her boyfriend tomorrow. Where should we meet?"

"Let's both try to get into Barstow around dinner time and then coordinate by cell phones to find a place to meet. If I get into town first, I'll find a place and call you with directions. If you get there first, you find a place and call me. OK?"

"OK, Baby. I miss you. We'll wait for your call tomorrow evening."

"I'll call you tomorrow afternoon around 4:00 P.M., OK?"

"OK. I love you!"

"I love you, too, Honey. Talk to you then."

PART TWO – The Separation

APRIL 1, 1996

I left Yreka at around 7:30 that morning, pulling my 27-foot Bayliner Cierra 2655. My new Ford F-250 had plenty of power to maintain the 70 MPH speed limit through the mountains.

I stopped in Sacramento for lunch and then continued driving south. I pulled off I-5 at the Highway 58 turnoff and drove east toward Bakersfield. In Bakersfield I drove four miles south on Highway 99 and then turned east again toward the high desert. It took me another three hours to get to the outskirts of Barstow.

I called Patti's cell phone around 4:15 P.M., and she answered on the third ring.

"Hi, Honey!"

"Hi. I just got into Barstow. Where are you?"

"Rick drove like a maniac and we're already at Joe's Bar on First Street in Barstow."

"What's the address on First?"

I heard her ask the bartender for the address. "925 First Street. It's in the shopping center two doors down from Safeway."

"OK. I should be there within fifteen minutes."

"OK, Honey. Drive safely."

"I will. See you in a little bit."

"Bye!"

I knew where Safeway was, and slowly pulled out, the Bayliner bouncing in its trailer as I drove over a slight curb. I was parked in front of Safeway within ten minutes. I took up two parking spaces in a row at a distance from the entrance so I could pull out easily. I walked into Joe's, and immediately heard Patti's laugh.

I walked up behind her at the bar, where Carol and some guy were sitting beside her. I put my arms around her and gave her a hug. "Hi, Baby."

She turned around and smiled. "Hi. You got here fast."

"I missed you. I need a kiss."

We kissed long and hard. I could smell the White Diamonds perfume on her. My favorite scent!

Carol introduced me to her boyfriend, Rick. We shook hands, and then Patti moved over one stool so I could sit by her.

"I already ordered you a Jack and Water."

"Thanks, Honey. Why don't we get a booth?"

"OK."

We got up and entered a booth next to four nice-looking young ladies against the far wall. A waitress came over and asked if we were ready for a round of drinks. I signaled "all around" to her, and she walked away.

"How long have you three been here?"

"Long enough. One more and I'm switching to a Kioki Coffee," replied Patti.

We talked for about an hour and then ordered some appetizers from the waitress; buffalo wings, stuffed mushrooms, stuffed potato skins, French fries, and pork ribs. We were hungry.

Around 6:00 Carol said, "Rick and I should probably order some coffee to go and get on the road back to Palm Springs."

"OK, you two drive safely. I'll get the check."

All three got up and hugged. Carol walked to the bar and asked the waitress for two large coffees with cream to go. I waved to the waitress and asked her to add the coffees to the ticket.

After Carol and Rick were out the door, Patti sat down next to me and we hugged again. "Ready for some dinner?" I asked.

"After all the appetizers?"

"You're right. Let's go out to the boat and get naked."

"I forgot you have the boat with you. Let's go."

We walked out to the Bayliner and climbed aboard the rear steps. I unlocked the door to the cabin and we walked down the four steps into the cabin. I had already made up the dinette into the bed. We didn't waste any time taking our clothes off and getting under the sheets.

An hour later Patti said she was thirsty, so I got up and took two bottles of spring water out of the refrigerator. I handed one to Patti, then got back in bed.

It was already dark, so we talked for a while and then fell asleep. During the night I heard several cars drive by and heard several voices comment about the big boat in the parking lot, but no one tried to climb aboard.

The next morning I got up, got dressed, and walked on deck. Everything seemed in order and I noticed we were the only ones in the Safeway parking lot.

"I'm going for coffee, Baby."

"OK," she replied.

I walked across the street to McDonald's and bought two coffees with cream, and two croissants. I walked back to the boat, to see Patti sitting on deck on a couch. We sat there for a while watching the sun rise, enjoying our "breakfast".

Within another fifteen minutes we were on I-40 toward the California-Arizona border and Lake Havasu

By noon we had launched the boat and were racing across the lake at 30 MPH toward Copper Canyon. It was spring break and the lake was full of smaller ski boats with bikini-clad coeds and young guys in Speedos trying to get lucky.

Patti was in her own red bikini, with my "babies" stretching the fabric. She was looking hot!

As I slowed the boat, approaching the entrance to Copper Canyon, a ski boat pulled up 30 feet away and a young guy with a Nikon was motioning to Patti to take off her top for a picture. That was common during spring break, girls showing their breasts to everyone nearby. "Show them your babies, Honey."

Patti complied, posing for the guy with the camera. I turned around to drive the boat. Ten seconds later she came up beside me and said, "I showed them my bare ass, too, Honey."

"Did that excite them?"

"Yes, definitely. He took two pictures."

"Did it excite you?"

"What do you think? I'm horny already."

That's my brown-eyed girl!

We enjoyed the sun that day and liked talking with the younger set on their various ski boats that surrounded us. Ours was the largest boat in the cove by far!

That night we tied the boat up in a smaller cove that extended about 150 yards off the larger Copper Cove. All of the kids in the ski boats had returned to their respective docking facilities and we were alone. I cooked us some dinner, fried chicken, on the outdoor barbeque, and Patti added a dinner salad. We enjoyed cocktails on deck, and watched the sunset.

The next morning was hot. Patti walked on deck naked and dived into the water. She swam about 50 yards to the other side of the cove and then climbed the smooth rocks to about 20 feet above the water line.

I grabbed my Nikon and started taking pictures as she posed on the rocks. I loved taking pictures of my nude brown-eyed girl! After posing for pictures, she swam back to the boat, grabbed a beach towel, and walked to the forward deck to sunbathe.

I grabbed my Loomis six foot graphite rod and Gemco reel with six pound test line, looped a floating bass lure on the line, and casted across the cove to the opposite bank. When the ripples disappeared, I gave the lure a small pull. It took the ripples 20 seconds to abate and then I gave it another small tug.

The water exploded as the bass attacked the surface lure. I set the hook and my line started racing left and right and the rod doubled over from the tension on the line. I let the bass fight for a few minutes. Then I started to reel him in. But he had one more run left in him, so I let him run. Two minutes later I had him at the stern of the boat. I reached down and grabbed his lower lip. That's the nice thing about bass. They were indestructible. Try that with a trout, and he's a goner. Try it with a steelhead, and your thumb is sliced meat!

I let the bass go and he swam away. I tossed the lure out again.

"Is that breakfast, Baby?"

"No. I let him go. Too small. Do you want bass for breakfast, or do you want bacon and eggs?"

"I guess bass would be better for dinner. Bacon and eggs is fine. I'll go get started on them."

"Thanks, Honey."

We both got pretty red from the sun that morning. We enjoyed relaxing on the boat for another three days, but then it was time for some work.

We docked the boat at the marina just below the Lake Havasu Hotel, loaded the truck, and headed for Las Vegas late the afternoon of April 5. I had made arrangements with the sales office at the lake to dock the boat right under the hotel, and fifty yards from the London Bridge, in exchange for letting the sales manager use it to show clients around the lake when I was not in town.

We stopped at a motel that night rather than try to make it all the way to Vegas. We were both pretty tired, so we turned in early. Around midnight we both woke up to a woman's loud moans in the room next door.

Patti didn't waste any time. She started moaning out loud herself, to send a message to the couple in the adjoining room. I decided to give her some help, so I climbed on top of her. Within ten seconds, the couple next door stopped what they were doing, but Patti and I finished.

We fell asleep giggling quietly to ourselves and the couple next door remained quiet the rest of the night.

We drove into Vegas the next day, where I had a session with a film company, who was filming my new Pure Stroke 30 minute infomercial for our latest putter model at Probe Golf. After the filming was completed, Patti and I spent at least 40 hours in the editing room with the editor of the infomercial over the next four days.

Then we drove back to Palm Springs. The next day we went to Ralph's supermarket on the corner of Highway 111 and Sunrise and I helped her stock up on some food. I was leaving for Yreka the next day.

After taking the food to my truck, we walked along the shops and I saw a dark-haired wig in the window of a beauty salon. We walked in and I asked her to try on the wig. She had always been a blond, with short hair. She looked totally different in the wig.

"Do you want it?"

"You want to buy it for me?"

"If you want it."

"But it's over $200!"

"That's OK. You look great in it. It will be like sleeping with a different woman tonight."

"OK, Honey. Thanks."

April 7, 1996

I headed north to Yreka the next morning.

Probe Golf kept me busy the rest of 1996 in Yreka. Patti and I talked a lot on the phone, but I could tell she was not happy being apart.

One day in late October, we were talking on the phone, and she said, "Honey, I have something to tell you."

"What's that?"

"I'm dating someone."

'What?"

"I can't wait forever for you to move down here. I was lonely. Do you remember Mick Kaufmann, my neighbor in my apartment building?"

"I remember him."

"We've been seeing each other for a while."

"Honey, I know you're lonely. I miss you terribly. I'm trying to get the house sold and get the divorce as quickly as I can so I can be with you."

"OK. Get the house sold and complete your divorce, then come down. I'll be here when you get here."

"You'll wait for me?"

"I'll wait for you."

"Honey, I'll take care of it as fast as I can, OK?"

"OK. You take care of yourself."

"You, too, Honey."

She hung up! I was devastated.

January 3, 1997

I was tired of waiting for my realtor to get an offer on the house. He had it listed for months and the only people he showed it to were young couples that loved the house, but could not afford it! What was the point? Typical realtor!

So I decided to take my future in my own hands. I created a one-page, 8" by 11" colored brochure of the house on my computer, then ran off 50 copies.

I took a day off and went to every restaurant in the county, from Yreka south to Weed and to Mt. Shasta. I asked each owner or manager if I could put up a brochure on the wall in each waiting room.

I then went to my realtor's office and told him I would pay him 2% commission to do the paperwork if I found a buyer, instead of the 6% he'd get if he found a buyer. He agreed.

I had phone calls from potential buyers within 24 hours. Before I would show any of them the house, I qualified them financially over the phone. No sense getting them excited if they couldn't afford it, right?

I had an offer at my asking price within ten days, and we opened escrow. Katy and the boys had been living in a house in Yreka, while I was busy selling off everything in the house that Katy did not want. It took me two weeks!

February 10, 1997

Escrow closed on the house today! I met Katy at the Title Company in Yreka that afternoon. We picked up our check, went to the bank, cashed it, and split the funds 50/50.

March 29, 1997

Katy and I met at our divorce attorney's office to sign the final divorce papers. I still loved her, I just couldn't live with her. We both loved the boys. I didn't want to leave them in Yreka, but I was already three and a half years late doing what I had promised Patti I would do!

I made my plans to move down to Palm Springs. I called Patti and told her I was on my way. She did not give me the response I was hoping she would give me.

"Pete, I want you to come down here because you want to live here, not just because you want to be with me. Carol and I have made a life for us here and I am still seeing Mick."

"OK, Honey. I'll get settled down there. I just want to be close to you, so we can look into sharing a future together."

"OK, but I can't make any promises."

I hung up the cell phone. I didn't like moving so far from my sons without some definite plans with Patti, but I had to start somewhere. I felt that I had let her down, and had to take a chance on her.

As I headed south on I-5, then I called the one prson I could always count on, Gary Goldman, an attorney who had befriended me two years earlier when I played Canyon Country Club with a member there. I had met Gary in the club bar after the round, and we immediately became friends.

He answered his cell. "Hey, Gary. It's Pete."

"Hi, Pete. How are you doing?"

"I'm moving down to Palm Springs. I should be in town late tonight."

"Great. Call me when you get in."

"It will be a little late when I get into town. Why don't I call you in the morning?"

"OK. Do you have all my numbers?"

I have your office number, your Palm Springs cell, and your Washington cell number."

"Perfect. You can reach me best on the Palm Springs cell."

"OK, Gary. Talk to you in the morning."

I arrived in Palm Springs at 10:30 that night. I went to the south end of town on 111, the main street going through town and continuing toward Rancho Mirage. I stopped at the Royal Sun Inn for a room that night and to talk to the owners the next morning. The Royal Sun Inn was a member of a national barter club, ITEX, as was I. I wanted to negotiate to stay there on a monthly basis for ITEX trade dollars, since I did not know how things would go with Patti and I needed some flexibility. Renting a house would require at least a one year lease.

I met Pat and Geoff Weis, the owners of the hotel, the next morning and we hit it off. They agreed to rent me one of the two top floor suites on ITEX on a monthly basis. It was perfect. An elevator to the third floor, a fifty foot walk to the suite, queen bed, computer hookup, living room, satellite TV, kitchenette, dining room, and a large deck overlooking Palm Springs to the east, with the sunrises coming up over the distant sand dunes.

It was a short walk to the elevator, then down to the pool and hot tub, with a complimentary breakfast served from 7:00 A.M. to 9:00 A.M. every morning. Room service was included every day, unless I told the maids it was not necessary every day.

I moved in with my computer and some clothes. I called Gary and we met at his country club for breakfast. Gary was the full-time legal representative for a local gay TV station and his hours were his own. The station was his only client.

After breakfast we teed it up on his course. It felt good to beat on a golf ball for four hours and talk to the man who would become my best male friend. I thought Patti would always be my best female friend. I told Gary about the sale of my house, my divorce, my affair with Patti almost four years earlier, the fact that I was moving Probe Golf down to Palm Springs, and that I hoped for a future with Patti.

"Patti? What's her last name?"

"Thomas."

"Patti Thomas?" Is she pretty with short blond hair?"

"Here's a picture of her." I pulled out my wallet.

"Yeah. She works at Melvyn's in town here."

"Yes. Her ex used to be the chef there, and got her a job cocktailing there."

"And you know her? From where?"

"Yeah, you could say I know her. She used to work for me at Probe from 1990 to 1994; I was married to her older sister for 15 years, and had an affair with Patti four years ago. It's been on and off since then."

"So what's keeping you from seeing her again?"

"First of all, she's still mad at me for not going to her four years ago."

"Why didn't you?"

"I was still married, with two sons. I needed to end the marriage and I needed to make sure my sons were going to be OK."

"So what's keeping you now?"

"Like I said, she's still mad at me, plus she has been seeing another guy for about seven months now."

"So you just want to be close to her for when she might be ready for a relationship with you?"

"Right."

"Have you met Mel Tabor, the owner of Melvyn's? He's a member here at the club."

"No, I haven't."

"He should be in the bar when we finish playing. He usually is every afternoon."

"I'd like to meet him."

We finished the round at around 2:00 P.M. There weren't many guys in the bar yet. It was a little too early.

"I don't see Mel. Let's have a drink."

Gary ordered a scotch, and turned to me. "Jack and Water?"

I nodded. "You remembered."

Gary asked me how Probe Golf was doing. "I've cut back to making custom fit drivers, and filling bulk Probe 20/20 putter orders to pro shops and golf stores."

"I'm putting great with my Probe. Aren't you making custom fit iron sets anymore?"

"Only for personal friends."

"Great! I need two sets for myself, one to keep here at the club and one to put in the trunk of my Cadillac for traveling. And I want to buy a set for Donna."

"Donna? Your girlfriend?"

"Yep. She'll be joining us here for a drink shortly. I just called her."

It was nice seeing Gary again. My life was in a mess, and I had to get it back on track.

I had left Yreka and my sons to be close to a woman who I knew was destined to be my best friend and my soul mate. The only problem was that she hated me. Not the best situation I could imagine. So I had to be positive and move forward. Make some money and make a plan for the future. Then follow that plan. The old Dale Carnegie and Napoleon Hill training!

I played a lot of golf that spring, mostly with Gary. He had introduced me to many of the members at Canyon Country Club, and I played some rounds with quite a few of the members. My handicap was coming down again. I was a "2" handicap that spring. Gary invited me to play in several tournaments at the club, as his partner. There were many wealthy members at the club and the tournaments were expensive to compete.

Not the entry fee, but the betting! One tournament, the Gambler's Classic, had team bets on every level. As Gary's partner, I could have lost over $5,000 in three days! Not only did every team play for the winner's share of the pot, but it seemed like every team had side bets with every other team! In addition to playing for the pot, we could lose over $1,000 to each of the other 27 teams! I told Gary that was a little beyond my ability to pay off if we lost. He said not to worry, that he would cover our losses if we lost, but that he had faith in me and in my golf game.

Luckily I played well in the Gambler's Classic and we won some money.

July 15, 1997

I was in the doldrums. I hadn't heard how Patti and Carol were doing. Palm Springs is a small town, believe it or not, and everyone hears rumors about everyone else. I knew a lot of Patti's girlfriends and several guys who had dated her, but I had not heard anything in the last four months.

I got in to my suite at the hotel after midnight. As I went to bed, I started to turn off my cell phone, as I always did when turning in. But I hesitated. I had an uncanny feeling that something might happen that night and that I should leave the phone on in case someone had to reach me during the night.

I went to bed with the cell phone turned on. In the middle of the night, or I should say early morning, I awoke to the building shaking! It took me a few seconds to figure out what was happening. We were having an earthquake!

I had been through many earthquakes in southern California, so I just lay there in bed and listened to the sounds of the night. I glanced at my left wrist and noticed in the phosphorescent hands that it was 4:25 A.M.

Then my cell rang. "Hello."

"Pete, this is Patti."

"Hi! Is there anything wrong? I had a bad feeling tonight when I went to bed. There's nothing wrong with your breast implants, is there? I saw a TV documentary a few days ago about problems women are having with their implants."

"No. The men at Melvyn's are always asking me if they are real."

"What do you tell them?"

"I tell them it is none of their business! Carol and I are standing outside our apartment by the pool with bedspreads wrapped around us."

"The apartment on Riverside?"

"No. we moved from there two months ago; too many drug dealers in the building. The night before we moved, two druggies came flying through our front door to the apartment, fighting."

"Wow. Are you two OK?"

"We're fine, just standing around waiting for the manager to tell us if it's OK to go back to the apartment. Everyone in the building is out here."

"We haven't talked in a long time. I didn't think you even had my cell phone number any longer."

"I would never lose your number, Pete. You should know that."

It was good listening to Patti's voice. It was always like a tonic to my system and gave me a warm feeling inside. Besides, she was my soul mate. She just didn't know it yet.

Maybe deep down inside she did know it. That's why she thought to call me when she had to leave her apartment in the middle of an earthquake!

We talked for about half an hour, when I could hear her apartment manager announce that everyone could return to their apartments.

"We can go back to our apartments now, Pete. Sorry I woke you up."

"Patti, I always love to hear your voice. Call me any time."

"OK. Goodnight."

"Goodnight, Patti."

I was awake the rest of the night. There was no way I was going to get back to sleep after that call. I hoped Patti and Carol would be OK. And thoughts started going through my head again about Patti and getting back together with her.

March, 1998

My cell phone rang while I was having the continental breakfast at the Royal Sun. I noticed on the caller ID that it was Patti. My heart leaped.

"Hi, stranger," I answered as calmly as I could.

"Hi. Are you busy?"

"Just having breakfast at the hotel."

"I just had a big fight with Mick and need to get out of town for a while. I thought you might like to do something together."

My heart took another leap. "Why don't we drive over to Lake Havasu for a few days on my boat?"

"That would be nice. Can we take my car?

"What are you driving these days?"

"I bought a 1994 Mustang convertible, white. We could get some sun while driving."

"That sounds perfect. Give me your address and I'll come by in about an hour. Is there some place I can park my car where it will be safe?"

"The parking lot here at the apartments is safe." She gave me an address close to the Ralph's supermarket off of Highway 111.

"See you in an hour."

I went up to my suite and packed a bag. I had sold my truck and gotten a new Ford Probe about five months earlier. I drove to Patti's apartment and knocked on the door. She was ready with a small suitcase in her hand.

We got on Highway 111, driving south for four miles and then took Frank Sinatra Drive east, then Bob Hope Drive to I-10. We headed east toward the California-Arizona border. The top was down, I was driving, and it was getting over 100 degrees. I looked over at Patti and she was pulling down the top of her sun dress to give the "babies" a chance to get some sun.

I asked her loudly how she had been the last six months, trying to be heard over the wind in our faces. She had me all caught up by the time we reached the border and the Colorado River. We cut south on California Highway 95, then east on the smaller road that led to Lake Havasu. We got to the lake as it was getting dark and had dinner in the Lake Havasu Hotel restaurant before going to the boat.

Steve, the real estate broker that I let use the boat to show his clients the lake had installed a fancy stereo system in the cabin, so we enjoyed some CD's while having a cocktail on deck and watching the distant red and orange sunset over the desert. Patti went below and changed CDs. "Jungle music," she said as she came back on deck.

We had finally gotten over the tension of seeing each other for the first time in six months and were relaxing. We slept soundly; it felt good to have Patti in my arms again!

The next morning we got underway in the Bayliner, I steered out of the marina slowly, obeying the posted speed limit so as not to disturb the other boats that were docked. Patti came up from the cabin below wearing a bikini bottom and no top. She was ready to get some sun. I asked her if she could steer, so I could get my fishing rod ready. She sat in the captain's chair and smiled at me. I smiled back. We were comfortable again, together, for the first time in a long time. I had not asked about her fight with Kaufmann. I knew she would tell me when she was ready.

We cleared the channel from the marina. I walked down into the cabin for some fishing flies. When I came up Patti had removed her bottoms and was standing in front of the seat. She loved to be free from the tightness of wearing clothes.

I gave her a sighting in the distance toward the north end of the lake and she turned the boat to the right. I knew an old yacht had sunk off the northern channel to the marina and knew it would be a good place to catch some stripers (striped bass).

The depth finder indicated where we should stop, so I went forward and dropped the anchor. When I returned to the stern, I took off my bathing suit. Why not get an all-over tan while fishing?

About noon Patti said she'd go below and make us some lunch. I was fishing off the stern when I heard a high-pitched motor. I turned to my left to see a personal watercraft approaching with a guy driving and a woman holding her arms around him, sitting on the back. I sat down on the couch to hide my nakedness a little and waved. They pulled alongside and asked, "Can you tell us how to get to the London Bridge marina?"

I pointed toward the east. "See that peak in the distance? Look just below it. You can see a channel there. Just drive in that channel and follow it to the bridge and the marina on the left."

Just as they were thanking me, Patti walked up from below and noticed the couple sitting ten feet away on the watercraft. She ducked down just a bit to hide the fact that she was also naked. The couple smiled at her, said "Hi", and then gunned the motor and took off.

"What did they want?'

"Just directions to the London Bridge marina."

We had tuna sandwiches for lunch, with cokes.

I fished for another hour, catching a total of five stripers. I cleaned them on the stern and then asked Patti if she could put them in zip lock bags and put them in the refrigerator. Once she had the fish put away we headed back to the marina.

As I docked the boat, she went below and then came up wearing a bathing suit and the dark wig I had bought her many months ago. She looked like a stranger, a sexy stranger.

"Why don't we take a ride some place remote and I'll take some pictures of you in the wig?"

"OK."

We walked up to her Mustang, dropped the top, and then I drove toward the Lake Havasu golf course. The east side of the course was remote, with just sand dunes and a few Joshua trees to the east. I parked the car and got out. Patti slid over to the driver's side, put her feet on the driver's seat, and sat on the top of the seat. She took off the bikini top and posed for me.

I took over 50 shots of her in different poses, all with the wig. In the distance we heard a golfer yell. We looked over and saw him waving from about 100 yards. Patti waved back.

That evening we relaxed on deck and she finally told me about her problems with Kaufmann. "He is starting to get serious and I don't want to get serious."

"Why don't you get serious with me, Honey?"

"You know it's too soon. It would hurt Katy."

There it was again; her concern about hurting her sister.

"How long are you going to wait to get over our affair? Forever?"

"I don't know. A while longer."

The discussion turned quiet. "I think we should head back tomorrow."

"OK."

We were about three miles out of Lake Havasu the next morning when Patti said, "Let's drive back naked."

"That sounds like fun." We both took our clothes off and I drove while she leaned her seat back and lifted her breasts toward the sun.

Once we reached I-10, we passed some truckers who could see down into the car, and they honked their horns at us. I handed Patti my portable CB radio, turned to Channel 19, and she talked to a number of truckers for an hour and a half during the drive.

One trucker had his wife with him in the cab and she and Patti had an interesting conversation over the radio for over 30 miles.

As we neared the turnoff toward Palm Springs, we put our clothes back on.

"That was fun!"

I agreed with her.

As we neared her apartment building, it got a little quiet. "When can I see you again, Honey?"

She didn't answer.

"Is it going to be another six months? I miss you."

"I know. You just have to give me some time. I worry about Katy."

We parked her Mustang next to the Probe. I put my bag in my car and then turned to her. We hugged.

"Call me any time you want, Honey. You know I'll always be here for you."

"I know, Pete. I will."

I watched her walk into the apartment building.

November 1, 1998

I had been calling my sons almost every day, telling them how much I missed them. Pete asked me to come back to Yreka for a while. Pat and Geoff, the owners of the Royal Sun, had indicated to me that they might not be able to take ITEX trade dollars through the winter months due to increased cash reservations. I told them I would probably go north anyway.

I called Patti to tell her I was leaving town for a while. "OK. Drive safely."

"You're not just a little bit sad I'm leaving town?"

"Pete, Mick and I are together again."

"I understand, Honey. I just miss you terribly."

"I'll be fine. We can keep in touch by phone. Bye."

I moved out of the hotel the next day, and drove the 752 miles back to Yreka in ten and a half hours in my Probe. I did my best thinking when driving alone and I racked my brain for a plan to get back with Patti. I wondered if we would ever be happy together or would she continue to feel guilt about Katy for the rest of her life?

December 3, 1998

Katy and the boys had been living in the small house in Yreka, small compared to the huge house we had sold on the hill with 25 acres.

I looked around for an apartment I could live in through the winter, and found a nice two bedroom on Shasta Street across the street from a park, with about 40 acres of bare land behind it. I talked to Katy and we agreed to move into the apartment together, with the boys. It was time our sons had a true home, which they had not had for the previous four years.

Living together with your Ex may sound strange, but we were actually good friends. I just couldn't live with her as husband and wife. Not being married to me, I figured she would be more friendly and not the demanding wife! I was right. The boys loved our all being together. Besides, I didn't have anywhere else to go.

My plan was to try to forget about Patti for a while, and give her time to hopefully lose the guilt about our affair way back in 1993. I also wanted to spend time with my sons. Keeping in touch almost every day by phone is one thing, but there is nothing like seeing them grow up on a daily basis, helping them with schoolwork and having dinner with them every night, to hear how their day went.

Both Pete and Bob were into computers and computer games. In December, just before Christmas, Pete asked me to buy him the latest computer. We went shopping in Yreka, and I bought two identical PCs with Windows 98 so Pete could teach me how to use mine. He was fourteen years old and a genius! Katy and I talked often about the fact that Pete might never find a woman to marry who was smart enough to be his wife, to challenge him mentally.

At nine years old, he had invented a card game made up of cards with cavemen, different dinosaurs, and weapons. He ran off sets of the cards on my printer at home and he sold sets to kids all over Yreka. They played games on his game board he had created and copied one board with each set of cards.

He had entered science fairs three years in a row and took first place all three years. Needless to say, we were very proud of him. I tried to interest Pete in playing golf, but he didn't see the benefit of the game at that time. Bobby, on the other hand, loved golf, and I was giving him lessons from the time he was three years old.

December 25, 1998

I had missed a number of Christmases with the boys in the past few years. It was good to be with them this Christmas. We all went to Katy's Mom's house in Yreka. Margaret had been like a second mother to my sons and I will be eternally grateful to her for taking them in whenever Katy was out of town. We had a wonderful Christmas that year. Even Muriel's "know-it-all" attitude could not keep me from enjoying the holiday.

Pete had gotten into another discussion with Muriel about politics and, even at his young age of 14, he was more than a match for Muriel. For some reason I enjoyed watching him put her in her place, usually without her even knowing what happened! That in itself was a Christmas present to me.

Katy had been seeing a male friend in La Jolla, California, on the north end of San Diego, for over a year. Jim was a retired executive from Longs Drugs. Katy's best friend from high school had married another Longs Drugs retired executive, and they introduced Jim to Katy. The relationship was getting serious.

I never did ask Jim what he thought of Katy living with her ex-husband. I liked Jim then, in 1999, and still do today.

Katy would split her time between Yreka and La Jolla, at Jim's house. I got used to living with the boys in Yreka. I was making up for the time I had spent away from them in Palm Springs, if you can ever really make up for lost time. It's like bogeying a hole on the golf course. Birdying the next hole does not "make up" for the bogie.

I didn't talk to Patti for months. I missed her, but had to give her time to herself. I had these thoughts going through my head that by leaving her alone, we could start all over again when we got together again in the future, without her feeling the guilt about the affair anymore!

That winter I learned a lot from both Pete and Bobby about computers. I needed to get into the computer age, finally, and the boys were good instructors. I was enjoying spending time with the boys. They had grown up just the way I had hoped they would, even though I was not around all the time.

One day I came across a book in my storage unit that I had read years earlier when taking a sales training class, **HOW TO WIN FRIENDS AND INFLUENCE PEOPLE**, by Norman Vincent Peale. I showed it to the boys and suggested they read it. Bobby grabbed the book first. He read it over the next few days and told me years later that it was the best book he had ever read!

I don't think Pete ever did read it. "It's kind of corny, Dad," is all he had to say.

May 21, 1999

I was back at the Royal Sun in Palm Springs for another summer. Most residents of the Coachella Valley who had money left town by the seventh of May, due to the summer heat. The eight towns that make up the valley have a total population of about 500,000 people. During the summer, it drops to around 125,000.

That makes it easy to get a tee time on golf courses that are usually packed during the "Season", January 2 through the month of April. I didn't mind the heat; in fact, I played better during the hot season. The heat loosened up my joints, I guess.

One night I was out with Gary and Donna, having dinner, then cocktails. They went home around midnight and I decided to stop by Melvyn's for a drink. I hadn't seen or heard from Patti in a long time. I walked into the bar and I saw Patti serving drinks behind the bar instead of waiting tables. There was a stool in front of the bar, so I sat down.

"Hi."

"Hi," I replied. "How have you been?"

"Very busy tonight. Mark called in sick and we're shorthanded. Jack?"

"Perfect."

She went down to the other end of the bar and took a few orders. I sipped my Jack. After an hour, much of the crowd headed home. I looked forward to having a conversation with Patti. She came over to me, and announced in a rather high voice, to be heard over the remaining crowd, "I need a change. Why don't I go home with you tonight for some great sex, OK? No promises, just some hot sex. I need it!"

"That works for me! I'll wait until you get off at 2:00."

I watched Patti work her magic with her customers. She was the best bartender / waitress I had ever seen, because she made her customers feel special. She was like that with everyone, whether she was working or just walking around town on her day off.

She especially loved babies, and I enjoyed watching her light up when she would see a new mother walking her baby. Patti would run over to the mother and baby and exclaim, "What a beautiful baby (she would pronounce it ba-a-a-ay bee)! May I hold her?"

She would then pick up the baby and hold her until the mother begged for her child back.

I was daydreaming at the bar about Patti holding a baby when she came up to me with her purse and said, "I'm ready."

"Is your car here?"

"It's right out front. I told the valets I would pick it up in the morning. You can bring me back in the morning, right?"

"Of course."

My heart skipped a beat when she reached over from the right seat and put her hands on my arm. I knew she would always be my best friend, and I knew I would give my life for her if it ever came to that.

We made love that night like never before. She needed relief from life's stresses that night and I gave her my best. We fell asleep together around 4:00 A.M. and slept until after 10:00. Then I walked down to the continental breakfast room by the hot tub, but the food had been put away. I poured two cups of coffee, which was still perking, and took them back to my room. Patti was sitting out on the deck watching the heat rise above the town. I sat next to her and gave her a cup of coffee.

"That was fun last night, Honey. I really needed it."

"Me, too." She replied.

We talked about all she had been doing for the last six months. She and Kaufmann had been on and off during that time. That sounded familiar!

She said she and Carol were going clothes shopping that afternoon.

"Then I better get you back to your car."

"She went into the bathroom and was ready to go in two minutes. That's another thing I liked about Patti. She could get ready to go out faster than any woman I had ever known. Even if we were going out for dinner and a party, she could be ready in five minutes.

We drove to Melvyn's to pick up her car. As she got out of my car, she leaned over and gave me a kiss. "Thanks for the sex, Pete."

"No. Thank you, Honey. Are we going to have to wait another six months before we do that again?"

"You never know."

She walked to her car, glancing back with a smile on her face. I knew I would love her until the day I died. What I didn't know is whether she would ever be mine, permanently, as in man and wife. But a man can dream, can't he?

November 30, 1999

I returned once again to Yreka, to spend the winter with my sons. Palm Springs was gearing up for another season and I had to move out of the Royal Sun. I was glad once again to see my sons and wondered if I was going to spend the rest of my life in this vagabond mode, north for the winters, south for the summers. Something had to change soon.

December 24, 1999

Once again we spent Christmas at Margaret's house in Yreka. The boys were spoiled by their grandmother and we had fun playing in the snow that year. You never knew if there would be snow on the ground in town from winter to winter, and that year set a record for snowfall!

There was something about Margaret's house that was very comforting. No matter how busy we were, traveling all over California and southern Oregon, Margaret's house was home for most of us. I was still accepted as one of the family, even after my divorce from Katy. She and I were still best friends.

Sitting around Margaret's dinner table, I could learn how Carol was doing in Palm Springs, how Patti's son, Mick, was doing, and how Patti was doing. If Mick was not in some kind of trouble, everyone around the table felt relieved. He had a tendency to get into one drug or another from month to month and had been in several scrapes with the Yreka Police Department whenever he was in town.

I learned that Patti was dating a dentist down south and Carol had a new boyfriend. There was nothing like Margaret's dinner table for catching up on the family news.

January, 2000

For a few months we all got along great and I enjoyed the time with my sons. Katy and I were getting along together as well, almost as if we were a family again. But living together and not being married, made the difference. What is it about being marriage that makes a woman feel she has to control her husband? It is different when you're married. And to whom you are married makes a difference!

April 18, 2000

I had completed my income taxes with my accountant the previous week, so I returned to the Royal Sun Inn in Palm Springs under my usual monthly ITEX trade dollar agreement with Pat and Geoff. Gary had set up some interviews for me with friends of his who wanted to order custom golf clubs, and he helped me make quite a lot of money over the summer of 2000. I joined the club myself as a Junior Executive Member. At 52 years old I was the third youngest member of the club. The average age of the membership was 76!

I stayed in Palm Springs until December 20, when I returned to the apartment in Yreka with Katy and the boys. Katy was once again spending a lot of her time at Jim's house in La Jolla when I was with my sons in Yreka.

I had not talked to Patti for a long time. I had heard through Gary and Donna, his girlfriend, that Patti was dating someone else and that I was not on her good side at the time. Women! You can't live with them and you can't live without them.

At times she did not want to see me because it reminded her of hurting her sister in 1993. At other times she did not want to see me because I had not joined her in Boulder City and later in Palm Springs! I was going crazy!

December, 2000

I was back in Yreka for another winter. I hadn't seen Patti, or talked to her, in a very long time. But every morning I awakened, she was the first thing on my mind. I wondered how she was, was she healthy, who was she dating? One thing made me feel good; I knew she would keep my cell phone number and would call me if she ever needed help, with anything. That one thought gave me comfort.

April, 2001

I had decided to stay in Yreka instead of returning to Palm Springs again for the summer months. I felt the boys needed me more than ever, and Katy wanted to go to La Jolla for an extended visit at Jim's house.

Pete was spending a lot of time on his computer. He uploaded a website for Probe Golf at www.probegolf.com.

It allowed me to receive hundreds of inquiries from former Probe customers from around the world, mostly people who had purchased a Probe 20/20 putter, and wanted another one. Fortunately, I had hundreds of them stored in my Yreka storage unit, and I was able to sell them for $120 each, plus shipping.

Pete also built his own website, from which he worked to invent his own online game. The summer of 2001 was a lot of fun for my sons and for me. Katy had informed us by cell phone in June that Jim had asked her to marry him and they had scheduled the wedding for September 12, 2001.

August 1, 2001

Katy flew to San Diego to stay with Jim and plan their wedding. I would be alone with my sons, which was just fine with me!

August 14, 2001

Bobby and I drove the 26 miles to Lake Shastina to play some golf. We planned to play all day, maybe even get in 36 holes. Pete stayed home and worked on his computer.

After the first nine holes, Bob said, "Dad, I'm hungry. Can we get some lunch before playing the back nine?"

"Sure. I could go for a hamburger myself right now."

We walked into the clubhouse, sat down at the nearest table, and ordered burgers and a soft drink. The waitress was just bringing the burgers to our table when my cell phone rang.

"Pete, it's Katy. Can you drive to the Sacramento Airport and pick me up? I'll get in at 4:10 P.M."

Katy had been at Jim's house since August 1, and was supposed to be there through the month of August to plan the wedding.

"What's wrong? I thought you weren't coming back for another two weeks."

"Jim called the wedding off. Can you just please pick me up in Sacramento?"

I could tell she was trying to hold back tears.

"Where are you now?"

"The San Diego Airport. My flight leaves at 3:05."

OK. I'll get there as quickly as possible. It's a four hour drive." I looked at my watch. It was 12:35.

"OK. See you then." She hung up.

"Bob, that was your Mom. She needs me to pick her up at the Sacramento Airport in about four hours. Let's take our lunch with us in the car."

99

"OK, Dad. What's wrong with Mom?'

"I'll tell you what I know in the car."

I waved to the waitress and asked her for the check and a to-go box. I paid our bill and Bobby and I walked out to the car.

On the drive to Sacramento, I told Bobby what Katy had told me about Jim canceling the wedding for some reason. That's about all I had to tell him. Until we picked up Katy at the airport, there wasn't too much to say about Katy.

It was about 4:22 P.M. when we drove up to the terminal. Katy was sitting out front with her luggage. We stopped in front of her and she got up and grabbed her bags. I helped her with her luggage, without saying anything. She didn't talk either. She just got in the back and then laid down on the seat.

Bob turned around. "Mom, what happened?"

"Bob, I just want to sleep right now. OK? We'll talk later."

"OK, Mom."

I got behind the wheel and headed for the freeway, entering the traffic to northbound I-5, without talking. I looked in the rearview mirror and saw that Katy's eyes were closed, either sleeping or trying to sleep. I decided to drive in silence.

Two hours later we stopped in Redding to gas up. Katy woke up and was talking to Bobby as I started pumping the gas. "Hi. Get a good sleep?"

"Not really."

"Want to talk?"

"After we get back on the road."

I returned the handle of the gas pump to the tank and then got behind the wheel.

We were climbing the hill toward Shasta Lake on I-5 before she spoke. "Jim and I had a fight about his four kids. You know they are all adopted, right?"

"I didn't know that. Does he have any biological kids of his own?"

"None. All are adopted. Three sons and a daughter."

"Why were you fighting over them?"

"They all were telling him not to get married."

"Why don't they want him to get married?'

"Jim has quite a bit of money. I think they are all afraid they will lose their inheritance, because Jim will leave it all to me."

"What a bunch of greedy bastards!"

"They are!"

"So, what did Jim say to them? I can't believe he would cancel the wedding because of that. Who does he love more, you or his adopted kids?"

"His kids, I would guess. He canceled the wedding."

"Try to relax and don't think about it right now. I know things will work out for the best."

I thought of other topics to discuss. I told Katy that Bobby was having his best round of golf ever that morning, before I got her phone call.

"I'm sorry, Bob. I didn't mean to mess up your round. What did you shoot on the front nine?"

"I had three pars and six bogies for a 42 on the front. That's my lowest score ever for nine holes."

"That's great, Honey. I don't think I ever shot 42 for nine holes myself."

"I almost had my first birdie on hole number 3. I hit my tee shot six feet from the pin, and lipped out the birdie putt!"

"Wow. That would have been nice if it went in."

Katy and Bob talked about doing something together the next day, possibly shopping for some new school clothes. School was starting in two weeks.

We got in to Yreka around 8:45 P.M. "Shall I stop at Price Less Foods and get a bottle of wine?"

"That sounds perfect, but get two bottles."

"Will do."

When we got to the apartment, Katy and I sat outside, talking and drinking a Fetzer 1996 Cabernet Sauvignon. The clouds to the east over Mt. Shasta were turning orange and pink from the sunset to the west. Mt. Shasta was a beautiful mountain at any time of the day or night, summers especially. I probably took hundreds of pictures of Mt. Shasta over the years, every one of them different.

I got Katy smashed that night on wine. I figured she needed it after the day she had spent arguing with Jim and his kids.

The next morning I had just returned from taking the boys to a friend's house when the UPS truck drove up with a Red Label, overnight envelope for Katy. She signed for it and then opened it. It was from Jim.

In the envelope was a letter apologizing for his kids and a certified check made out to her for $5,000!

She started crying. "He's just buying me off!"

"I don't think so, Honey. What does the letter say?"

She started reading the letter and then calmed down. "He says he is so sorry about what his kids said to me, and for canceling the wedding. He says he loves me and that I should not worry about anything, and that we will work it out. He wants to drive up here tomorrow and take me someplace for a few days so we can be alone and talk."

"See, I told you things would be fine."

She went into the apartment and cooked breakfast for us. Jim showed up the next evening and took Katy to the nearby Amerihost Inn. The next day she called and said they were going up the Oregon coast for a few days.

"OK, Honey. You two have fun."

They were gone for six days. Jim brought Katy by the apartments the evening of August 24, and they said goodbye. He wanted to get to Redding at least that night because the forecast was for heavy rains starting the next day. He figured he would have clear sailing back to San Diego from there, and get in to San Diego that night.

That weekend we took the boys to a soccer tournament in Mt. Shasta. There was one more week to enjoy the summer before school started, so we made plans to do some things with the boys.

September 11, 2001

Katy woke me up at 7:00 A.M., shaking me hard and telling me to come watch the TV in the living room. I got up, threw on my robe, and headed to the kitchen for coffee, which was perking. As I poured a cup, I heard an announcer on the TV talking about a video of a plane hitting the North Tower of the World Trade Center. It was a day I will never forget.

Katy reminded me that the next day, September 12, was the day she was supposed to be marrying Jim and that they were supposed to be going to the Club Med in Tahiti on the 13th for their honeymoon.

November 10, 2001

Katy informed me that she and Jim were going to use their airline tickets and their Club Med reservations they had planned to use for their honeymoon and go to Club Med in Tahiti the next two weeks. I wished her well when I took her to the Medford Airport. I would have the next two weeks to enjoy being with my sons alone.

When Katy got back from Tahiti, we all went to Margaret's house for a big dinner. Katy told us about the Tahiti trip.

"The first morning we were there, Jim and I sat around a big table for breakfast, with four other couples. The conversation turned to 911 and what everyone was doing the morning of September 11, when the first plane flew into the north tower.

The guy sitting next to Katy said, "I was on the 104th floor of the north tower when the plane hit!"

She said, "The whole table went dead silent."

"Wow," I said. "That must have been weird."

"It was."

The next two hours we all talked about 911.

January 10, 2002

I figured it was time to make a move toward something more permanent for my future, so I looked around Palm Springs to rent a house full-time. I found a house in a nice, but older, part of town, just off Sunrise Way, behind Jensen's Supermarket.

I had read the rental ad in the newspaper and met the owner at the house. We liked each other and signed a one year rental agreement. The house was a three-bedroom, two bath, house about 25 years old, with an eight foot tall solid brick fence surrounding the entire back yard, with a pool. It was perfect. The house had an attached two-car garage that would be perfect for assembling putters.

March, 2002

One night I was out having a few drinks and ran into Carol. She told me she was between jobs, so I asked her if she would be interested in putting putters together for me in my garage. She asked if a friend of hers could also work and I told her to bring her friend by the next day. I gave her my address, and she said she'd be by with her friend the next morning.

Carol and her girlfriend came by the next morning and we agreed on what I would pay them. Then I took them out to the garage for some training. The arrangement worked out for all concerned.

One day the girls came into the house on a break and I asked Carol how her Mom was doing.

"She doesn't want anything to do with you!"

So what else was new? "What did I do now?"

"It's what you didn't do."

"Are you talking about way back in 1993?"

"What else would I be talking about?" She could be a real bitch at times.

I took a big breath and then let it out. I didn't need this stress again, so I changed the subject.

Two days later, Carol called me and said she had found a permanent job and that they would not be working for me any longer. That was fine with me. She asked me, since she already had a key to the house, if she could stay there once in a while if she needed a place to stay. I told her that would be fine and showed her a little idiosyncrasy in the master bathroom. The toilet had a habit of continuing to run and could overflow if she did not make sure it had stopped before leaving the house. She said she understood and would not use that toilet without checking it before leaving in the future.

I concentrated on business for the next few months, filling putter orders for golf stores that had contacted me online.

June 15, 2002

Gary and Donna were having a dinner and cocktail party at their home in Palm Springs and had invited me over the day before. I arrived at their house around 6:00 P.M. and brought a bottle of a 1995 Beaulieu Merlot to the party.

We had a fantastic dinner of grilled New York steak on the back yard barbeque, asparagus in a lemon flavored hollandaise sauce, and Caesar salad. I had had three Jacks and water when my cell phone rang around 8:30.

"Hello, this is Pete."

"Pete, it's Patti."

"Hi, stranger. What are you up to?"

"I was wondering if I could ask you for a favor."

"Sure. You know me. Always willing to help you out. What's up?"

"I was hoping to drive down to San Diego to visit Katy and Jim. I've had some problems and need to see family for a little while. I don't have any money for gas."

"OK. Where are you now?"

"I've been helping Jody Klein with her house here in Norco. I can drive over to Palm Springs, but I'm worried about having enough gas to make it."

"Why don't I meet you halfway? Do you think you can make it to the Morongo Casino on I-10?"

"That shouldn't be a problem. I can be there in thirty minutes."

"OK, I'll meet you at the gas station by the casino in thirty minutes."

"OK. Thanks. I appreciate it."

"No problem, Honey. See you then."

I told Gary about the phone call and asked if he'd mind if I left and then came back.

"No problem, Pete. We both know you're still in love with Patti."

"It shows that much does it?"

"I know how it is. See you in a bit."

I thanked Gary for the hospitality and for understanding. I walked outside and got in my Probe, then headed for I-10 heading toward Los Angeles.

Twenty-five minutes later I turned off I-10 at the Morongo Casino off ramp. I didn't know what Patti was driving in those days, but I spotted her short blond hair beside a purple convertible at the gas pumps right away. As I go closer, the car looked like a Chrysler Sebring convertible.

I drove up on the other side of the gas pump where she was parked and got out.

"Hi, Patti. When did you get the Sebring?"

"About three months ago. How are you?" We hugged for a few seconds. She was cold. The high desert gets cold at night.

"I'm OK. Just a little lonely and want to visit my sister."

I took out a credit card and started gassing her car. While the gas was flowing, I handed her a hundred dollar bill. "Will this be enough after I fill the tank?"

"That's more than enough. I really appreciate it."

"No problem, Honey. Say "Hi," to Katy and Jim for me."

I returned the gas nozzle to the pump when it stopped pumping, put the cap back on the tank, and turned to her. She gave me another hug, a peck on the cheek, and then got in her car.

"Drive safely, Honey. I worry about you."

"I will."

I watched her drive out of the station, then turn onto I-10 heading west. I guessed she was taking I-215 down to I-15 toward San Diego.

I drove back to Palm Springs, to Gary's party, wondering when I'd see Patti again. It was tough being in love with someone when you couldn't be with her and not being sure as to why!"

Gary's party was still going strong when I got back to his house.

July 25, 2002

I turned in early that night because I was feeling kind of low and didn't want to go out. My phone rang around 9:00 P.M.

"Pete, it's Johnny."

Johnny Drummond was the youngest member of our club, at 36, with a beautiful wife.

"What's up, Johnny?"

"I'm down at Las Casuelas. Come on down and I'll buy you a drink."

"I'm kind of tired, Johnny, and not in the mood for a drink."

"Hey. I know you've been down in the dumps, lately. But you have got to come down here now. There's a hottie dancing out on the dance floor by herself and she looks just like Patti! Short blond hair, great body, and a smoking personality."

"I don't know, Johnny. I'm not feeling much up to meeting someone new right now."

"Oh, come on. One drink. If you see her and you're not interested, you can go home immediately."

"OK. One drink. I'll be there in ten minutes."

When I arrived, Johnny was sitting at the bar, with a drink in his hand and a big smile on his face. I sat down beside him and the bartender placed a Jack and water in front of me. Johnny had told him what I drink.

"OK, where is this goddess?"

"Right there on the dance floor, dancing by herself."

Johnny was right. Dancing by herself was a five foot, six inch beauty, great ass, short blond hair, and the best legs I had seen in a long time. She was dancing in a blue and yellow flowered sun dress. When the song ended, she sat down at a small counter on a stool by herself. I walked over to her and asked if I could buy her a drink.

"Sure. A white wine."

Her name was Katie Phillipsen. She lived in Riverside, but came to Palm Springs all the time to play tennis at the Palm Springs Tennis Club, where she had a membership.

Johnny and I sat with her and enjoyed our conversation. Johnny said he was going to call another female friend of his and suggested we meet them at his house for a swim. Katie was up for it and said she needed to take her car to Johnny's so she could leave at a reasonable hour. I told her to follow me in my car as we both walked to the parking lot.

Thirty minutes later we were naked in Johnny's heated pool on the fourth fairway at Canyon Country Club, with Johnny and his friend, Teresa.

Katie and I went to one of the bedrooms while Johnny entertained Teresa in the shallow end of the pool.

The night ended with Katie and me exchanging phone numbers just before she drove home. That night started an 18-month romance with Katie. It was exactly what I needed to get Patti out of my head.

I learned that Katie was a former singer in a band and had traveled all over the world with the group. She was also famous for raising world champion Alaskan Malamutes, as I was to learn the first time I went to her house on over an acre, and had six Malamutes jump all over me! She also had a teaching degree, and was currently teaching music to ninth graders at a Riverside County high school.

August 8, 2002

I had taken Katie out on three dates over the next week. She was smart, pretty, and a lot of fun. I met several of her female friends at the Palm Springs Tennis Club and even got my own tennis racquet out of storage to play a little tennis with her.

I had been on the phone almost daily with the boys and they asked me if I would come up and visit them for a while. I decided to go north for a few weeks.

I called Johnny Drummond and asked him is he would keep an eye on my house while I was away for about six weeks.

"Sure. Just hide a key for me and I'll check on it every few days."

We agreed on a hiding place for the key and I said Goodbye. I also reminded him that Carol Thomas had a key to the house and that she was authorized to stay there if she needed. I loaded my Blazer and headed north for the all-day drive to Yreka.

I enjoyed being back with the boys, helping them with their projects, and playing golf with Bob.

About a week later, Johnny called me.

"Pete, we have a problem with the house. I just came by to check it and found the living room flooded with water. It looks like the main toilet overflowed."

"You've got to be kidding me. Carol is the only person who is authorized to stay there. I'll give her a call. In the meantime, can you do me a favor and call someone to clean it up?"

"I've already done that. I can have a cleaning crew come in, roll up the carpet, dry everything out, then replace the carpets. $500 total."

"OK. Do it. Give me your bank account number and I'll transfer the $500 to you."

We concluded the banking arrangements and then hung up.

I tried calling Carol's number, but got her voicemail. I left her a message to call me. She never did. Boy, was I getting tired of doing Patti's kids favors. It always came back to bite me on the ass. But I was in love with her and knew I always would be. The things we do for love.

I kept in touch with Katie by phone during the six weeks I was away. I was anxious to see her again.

September 20, 2002

A said goodbye to my sons and drove back to Palm Springs. Before I left, Pete asked me if he could come down and visit in January for a few months.

"What about school?"

"I have a bunch of projects going on right now. I can take the winter semester off and catch up next summer."

"OK. Give me a call when you are ready to come down."

I drove all the way south that day, 752 miles to the house. When I got to my house that night around 9:00 P.M., the garage door was open, as was the door from the garage to the house. My largest TV was missing from the living room, my fax machine was missing from my office, and my large Probe professional golf bag with my golf clubs was missing from the den! I called Johnny.

"Pete, I was at the house yesterday and everything was fine."

"Well, today the garage door was wide open and the house was wide open, and a lot of things have been taken from the house."

Johnny came over in his cream-colored Jaguar convertible and we took inventory of what was missing. I had pretty well gotten it right the first time. He drove home. I wasn't having much luck trusting friends and "family" with my valuables.

I walked across the street. I figured it was about time I met the neighbors. I knew there were two older men living there; probably gay since Palm Springs was famous for homosexuality. One of them answered the door. Yep! Gay.

"Hi, I'm Pete, and I moved in across the street a while back."

"Hi. I'm James."

"I've been gone for about six weeks and noticed when I got in last night that the garage door was open. I was wondering if you saw anyone around the house yesterday."

"We saw one guy go in the house two nights ago."

"Did he drive up in a car?"

"Yes. It was a very nice convertible, light brown, or tan in color."

"Could it have been cream colored?"

"Yes, I would say that."

"Could it have been a jaguar?"

"Now that you mention it, yes, it could have been a Jaguar."

"And he went in the house two nights ago? When did he leave?"

"He left that same night, about half an hour later."

"Did he close the garage door before he left?"

"No, I'm sure it was still open when he left."

"So the garage door was left open all night?"

"All night, all day yesterday, and all last night."

"Thanks, James. That clears up the mystery."

I walked back to my house. I was furious with Johnny. I later asked him about when he was at the house, but his story made no sense. I was convinced that Johnny, or someone he knew, had been in the house and had taken the items that were missing. I never did get to the bottom of the mystery.

January 17, 2003

I played golf that morning with Bill and Tom, two of the older members of the club, and then walked into our pro shop. Our pro, Jeff, was behind the counter taking inventory.

"Hi, Jeff."

"Hi, Pete."

"Jeff, I have to be in Tulsa, Oklahoma next week on business. Can you call the head pro at Tulsa Country Club and set up a reciprocal round there for me next Wednesday?"

"Pete, do I look like I have time to make a phone call?"

"Sorry to bother you." I walked out. So much for private country club privileges.

Pete called me from Yreka and said he could drive down with Evgeni Kostitsyn, his college composition piano instructor, if Evgeni could stay at the house for a while.

"What's a while?"

"A month or two."

"Yeah, sure. Come on down."

They arrived the next evening. Two days later I had some friends over from the country club for a barbeque in the back yard. During the barbeque, I mentioned the story about our pro, Jeff, not having time to call Tulsa Country Club and get me on the course.

Pete overheard the story and said, "Dad, that sounds like a service we should start." I thought about the idea, but dismissed it at first. The private country club business was very private and it was not a service we could publicly advertise easily.

A week later, I went to Pete and said, "Pete, if you build the website, I'll operate the business and we'll split the profits."

I explained what would have to be included in our website and he got to work on it. It became Reciprocal Golf, www.reciprocalgolf.com, and we have been operating that business since February of 2003.

March, 2003

Evgeni was driving me crazy at the house. Being Russian, he was from an entirely different culture. For one thing, he ran around the house with only a tiny pair of European briefs. With our living room window open most of the time, the neighbors could see him, and I didn't want them thinking we were all gay!

I had asked Pete if he had talked to Evgeni about paying any sort of money toward the rent, since it was obvious he was not in any hurry to move.

"No, Dad. He is giving me free composition lessons on the piano, so I didn't want to mention any rent."

The next thing I knew, Pete was spending many hours on his computer, building a website for Evgeni, at www.cdkmusic.com. When I asked Pete how much Evgeni was paying him to build the website, he said, "I'm not charging him since he is giving me free lessons."

We discussed the fact that in my opinion, Evgeni was taking advantage of Pete, but Pete didn't care, so we dropped the subject.

The next time I asked Katie out on a date, she asked if she could bring one of her Malamutes over.

"Sure. My son is visiting and he'd love to see one of your dogs."

Katie brought Velvet, a two-year-old female by the house, and Pete was in love with the dog. That night, a Thursday, Pete, Evgeni, Katie, Velvet and I drove down to the weekly Palm Springs Street Fair that occurs every Thursday night from 6:00 P.M. to 10:00 P.M. I suggested to Pete that he walk ahead of the rest of us with Velvet, while we hung back and looked at the booths.

Pete went ahead of us and we watched all the girls come over to him and ask if they could pet Velvet. Talk about a chick magnet! Pete was in heaven. At one time, over 15 pretty girls were surrounding Pete and Velvet.

The Fair ended and we returned home. Katie and I went into the master bedroom, and Velvet slept in Pete's room.

A week later I made a deal with Katie to buy Velvet for $500, including a giant travel cage that barely fit in the back door of my Blazer. While Evgeni was visiting, he had borrowed some money from me, about $1,200. One night I heard my new fax ring. It was from Spain, and it was Evgeni's first distribution contract for his CD company. The contract mentioned US$7,500 that would be wired to Evgeni's bank account the next morning.

By noon the next day he had gone to his bank and paid me back the $1,200. He was now also ready to move back to Weed, CA to once again teach piano.

At the same time, Pete and I decided to drive north to visit family and friends and he wanted to bring Velvet to meet the family.

July 14, 2003

Pete and I loaded the Blazer, with Velvet in her travel cage in the very back, and headed north. Evgeni had left two days earlier in his car. We arrived in Yreka around 8:00 P.M. I was used to making the drive in less than eleven hours, but had never had a dog with me before. Walking a dog at a rest area every two to three hours can add a couple of hours to a 752 mile drive.

Katy and her Mom loved Velvet and took many walks around Yreka with Velvet, attracting a crowd wherever they went. We visited for ten days and then drove back to Palm Springs. We were beginning to learn that Malamutes were not easy dogs to care for. Velvet thought she was a member of the family and wanted to go everywhere with Pete and me.

And if we didn't take her with us when we went out, she would demonstrate her dissatisfaction by tearing up the carpet, or chewing up a piece of furniture. It was getting costly.

After a while, we learned we could trick her into thinking we were in the back yard instead of leaving entirely. We would lock her in her cage in the dining room, with a carrot and water, and tell her we were just stepping out to the back yard. She could see us through the sliding glass door.

Then we would walk around the side of the house and go out through the locked gate. We would then push the Blazer about fifty yards, so we could start the engine without her hearing us leave. If we weren't gone more than two hours, we usually got away with it. Any longer than that and she would start howling loudly. One day we came home to find the police out front, in answer to a phone call saying that someone was harming a dog!

September 1, 2003

Pete had to go north and register for school, but asked me if I would ask Katie to take Velvet for ten days until he could have her shipped somehow to Yreka. I asked Katie if that would work and she said, "Sure, no problem."

But after Pete registered for classes, he came to me and said, "Dad, I don't think buying Velvet was such a good decision. She's too hard to care for and I'm going to be too busy with school to have her up here. Do you think Katie would take him back?"

I had seen this coming, so I said, "Sure, I'll give her a call."

Katie was not happy with Pete's decision and we drifted apart. She kept Velvet, but she kept to herself and never returned my phone calls after that! Wow, what I went through trying to keep others happy. I began to wonder if I'd ever have a life of my own that I could control.

October 2, 2003

Pete informed me that his living arrangements at college had not worked out with his roommate. He said he could take his classes that semester from home, via the internet, and asked if he could continue living with me.

I told him that I was thinking of moving to Oregon, at a bed and breakfast fishing resort on the upper Umpqua River and use ITEX trade credits to stay there through the winter steelhead run. He said that sounded like fun, and that he could use the alone time to work on his projects on his computer.

We loaded the Blazer and headed for the Bed and Breakfast east of Roseburg.

I ran Reciprocal Golf from my cell phone and computer and fished for steelhead almost every day. Pete was working on his projects, which were many, and often confusing when he explained them to me. It was fun having a genius for a son. When he wasn't working on his computer, he would ask me to go on daily trips to nearby waterfalls or to Crater Lake during the day. It was winter and many of the places he wanted to visit were snowed in, including every time we tried to drive south to Crater Lake from the north. I might someday see Crater Lake, but not that year.

March, 2004

Pete had been talking to his Mom on his cell phone, and he learned she had moved to Grants Pass, OR to be near her best friend from high school, Mickie. Katy was also pursuing a certificate in hairstyling from a Grants Pass styling school.

We had spent three and a half months at the Bed and Breakfast using ITEX trade dollars to pay for it, and it was time to move on. Katy agreed we would upgrade to a three bedroom apartment in Grants Pass just two blocks from the styling school she was attending. Pete registered for classes at Rogue Community College in Grants Pass.

June 14, 2004

I had learned by spending some time around Margaret's dinner table with Katy and my sons that Patti was living with her best friend, Jody Klein, at Jody's house in Norco, California. I also learned that Jody had breast cancer and was driving to Tijuana, Mexico several times per week for a special cancer treatment.

I had read online about a new juice called Noni juice that was made from a plant in Tahiti. The juice was supposed to help fight cancer.

I decided that knowing about the Noni juice was going to be my way to see Patti again. I packed up my Blazer with some clothes and my golf bag and drove all day to Palm Springs. I spent the night at the Royal Sun Inn and then called the last phone number I had for

Patti. A voicemail answered the phone and I did not recognize the woman who had recorded the message.

"Hi, this is Pete Baumann. I was trying to find Patti Thomas's phone number. My number is 760-xxx-xxxx. If you know Patti, can you please ask her to call me? Thanks."

That was all I could think to do at that point, so I called Gary in his office. He answered on the first ring, and we agreed to meet at his golf club for lunch.

June 16, 2004

My cell phone rang as I was having the continental breakfast at the Royal Sun Inn. I had made a deal with Pat and Geoff to stay there for a few days until I could make some plans.

"Hello."

"Pete, it's Patti. I got a message to call you."

"Hi. Thanks for calling back. I heard you were living with Jody Klein in Norco, California."

"Yes. I've been living there for a few months.

"Honey, I heard Jody has breast cancer."

"Yes, she does."

"I was reading about a new juice that is made from a fruit in Tahiti that is supposed to fight cancer. I ordered some to take myself, just as prevention, and was wondering if you'd like to introduce Jody to it. It couldn't hurt."

"No, it couldn't hurt. Do you have some now?"

"No, but it will be delivered to me in Oregon in a few days. Why don't I call you when I have a few cases, and I'll bring it over to you girls?"

"That would be great, Pete. Call me when you have it. Here's my new cell phone number."

I wrote down her phone number on a breakfast napkin. "OK, Patti, on another subject, I just had a physical and learned there may be a problem with my heart. I'd like your permission to add you to my life insurance policy as a beneficiary along with Pete and Bob. Would that be OK with you?"

"Why would you want to do that?"

"You were my best friend for a long time, Patti. If anything should happen to me, I've made sure the boys would get some money, $100,000 each. I'd feel a lot better if I knew you'd get the same amount if anything happens. Would you do that for me? It would make me feel better."

"If that's what you want, it's OK with me."

"Thanks Honey. I appreciate it. Can I get your social security number so I can give it to my insurance agent?

"Sure, it is xxx-xx-xxxx."

"Thanks Honey. I'll call you in a few days."

"OK. Thanks. Bye."

I stayed in Palm Springs for one more day to play 18 holes with Gary and then drove back to Oregon. The shipment of a dozen cases of the Noni juice arrived two days after I returned to Grants Pass.

June 26, 2004

I loaded my Blazer with the cases of Noni juice and then headed south toward Palm Springs. This time I was hoping to make contact with Patti on a more permanent basis. I called her from the road and told her I had a quantity of Noni juice in my car and would be in her area by that evening.

"That's great, Pete. Just bring it here to Jody's house in Norco."

"What's the address?"

"Call me when you turn west on I-10 and I'll give you directions from there."

"OK, Honey. It will be around 8:00 P.M."

"I'll be here."

I relaxed while driving and enjoyed the nice weather and light traffic. As I drove down I-5 into Newhall, north of Los Angeles, I decided to touch base with Patti. She answered her cell on the first ring.

"Hi, Patti. I should be in your area in one hour. I just hit some traffic near Newhall."

"OK, call me in an hour. I'm just watering the plants in the front yard."

It was starting to get dark as I neared the turnoff toward Norco. I dialed Patti's number. She answered, learned exactly where I was and gave me directions to Jody's house. She stayed on the phone as I drove.

"Norco is horse country. There are 2.5 horses for every person in the town. Jody has two horses here in her back yard right now and a couple of bulls that she ropes from one of her horses. Where are you now?"

I gave her the cross streets.

"You're only five minutes away. You'll pass a bunch of houses with corrals out front. We're at 1246 Via Dorsalis Way."

A few minutes later, she said, "I think I see your lights. I'm ready to open the gate when you get here, so the dogs don't get out."

I drove another 200 yards and then I saw Patti standing by an open gate to the driveway. She was wearing an orange colored bikini, and looked thin, almost emaciated! I hung up my cell and waved. She smiled and waved back.

The driveway was crowded with the largest pickup truck I had ever seen. It had a huge cab and double wheels on each side of the bed. The bed was piled high with hay, and painting supplies.

I tried to pull to the left side of the pickup, away from the house, but my Blazer was pushing a small tree. I backed up in the semi-light and heard a thud. I put it into park, and then walked to the rear of the Chevy. I had hit the lower part of the fence with my bumper. No visible damage, just some discoloration.

"Just pull forward two feet and then park it."

"OK."

I parked the Blazer, and then got out. Patti walked up to me in the bikini. My babies were stretching the fabric of the top, and were looking magnificent. We hugged, and her breasts against my chest felt great.

"Hi, Patti. You look good."

"No I don't. I'm too thin."

"You look good enough to eat."

She smiled and gave me a peck on the cheek. I wanted to devour her right then and there, in the front yard.

She helped me carry my bags into the house and started to show me around.

"It's getting late. You can put your things in the guest bedroom for tonight. What are your plans for tomorrow?"

"I'll unload the Noni juice and go over the instructions on how Jody should take it with water or mix it with fruit juice. I also have some printouts from the website on how it helps cancer to disappear from the body. I'll go over that with both of you. Then I'll drive to Palm Springs and start looking for a place to live. I'm moving back down from Oregon."

"I'll cook us some dinner. Jody is at Lowe's getting some materials to repaint her back porch."

"Sounds perfect."

Patti was cooking as I unpacked in the guest room. The aromas from the kitchen were making me hungry.

We enjoyed dinner in the dining room while watching a DVD movie on Jody's large screen TV.

It was getting late. I told her I was tired from the drive and was ready to turn in.

"Want to join me?"

She laughed. "Jody will be home any time now and we are going to start working on her back porch."

"At night?"

"With the breast cancer, Jody works all hours of the day and night. She wants this place looking good because she wants to sell it."

"OK, Honey. Don't work too late. Goodnight."

"Goodnight."

I awakened to the sound of power tools in the middle of the night. I looked at my watch. It was 3:05 A.M. I got out of bed and followed the noise. It was coming from the garage. I opened the door from the kitchen to the garage about one inch, and glanced through the opening. Jody and Patti were drilling a piece of wood on a workbench!

I figured it wasn't my business, so I closed the door and went back to bed. It took me over an hour to fall asleep.

June 27, 2004

I awakened around 7:30 A.M., and looked around. I was still tired from the long drive the day before, and had to remind myself where I was. I threw on my robe and walked out into the kitchen. I didn't see anyone, but smelled freshly brewed coffee. I found a coffee mug and poured myself a cup. I wondered if the girls were asleep, since they had been up late. I walked outside to enjoy the morning on the back porch.

"Good morning!"

I looked around and saw both Patti and Jody feeding a horse and a bull in the fenced back yard.

"Good morning. You two are up early."

"We haven't been to bed yet," replied Patti.

"You're kidding. That's not healthy."

"There's a lot of work to be done around here."

I sat down in one of the four chairs surrounding the back yard glass table and took a sip of coffee. The girls came over and sat down.

"Hi, Jody. It's been a long time."

"Yes, it has. How are you, Pete?"

"I'm OK, now. It feels good to get back to some southern California weather."

"The weather has been nice. It's not 105 degrees like in Palm Springs, but it's been around 85 to 90 over here."

"Well, we're going to relax a little bit before Patti and I get back to work. Would you like some breakfast, Pete?"

"Coffee is fine right now, but thanks."

The girls went into the kitchen to make something for breakfast. I was enjoying the quiet in the back yard. It looked like Jody had over an acre in the back, with horse corrals, heavy metal fencing, and an outbuilding for tools.

Ten minutes later the girls came out with scrambled eggs, toast, and juice, placed the food on the table, and went back inside. A minute later they came back out with a coffee pot and two coffee mugs and sat down. It was nice just sitting and talking with two beautiful women while enjoying a delicious cup of coffee.

When I learned the girls were going to sleep for a few hours, I told them I was going to run over to Palm Springs an hour to the east to take care of some business with Gary, my attorney.

"Is it OK if I come back tonight and stay another night? I want to go over the use of the Noni juice with you and Patti."

"No problem. Stay as long as you like."

"Thanks. I'll see you two tonight."

When I said I had to go to Palm Springs for the day to see Gary about business, I neglected to mention that we would be playing 18 holes of golf while talking about business!

I was in good spirits and felt better than I had in many months. I was close to Patti again, in proximity if not in her heart. But I was following my plan to get back together with her, one day at a time.

After golf, I had one drink with Gary before heading back to Norco. I was anxious to see Patti again. I got back to Jody's house around 6:00 P.M. and smelled something delicious as I walked in the front door.

"What is that exotic aroma?"

"Shrimp on the barbie," replied Patti.

She and Jody were in shorts and halter tops, and barefoot, making a salad while dinner cooked. Patti handed me a glass of red wine. She was drinking something that looked like chocolate milk. "Is that a White Russian?"

"Yep. Some things never change."

I had tried for years to get Patti to drink something healthier, but I never made a big deal out of it. All I would do is occasionally make the suggestion, just like her smoking. A White Russian had a ton of sugar in it, from the cream, the vodka, and the Kahlua. With her family having a disposition toward diabetes, she would be better off drinking something with less sugar in it.

"This wine is perfect."

"Wait until you try my barbecued shrimp!"

"I can't wait."

After dinner, the girls went out to the back porch to continue working. The porch was about 60 feet long and fifteen feet wide. Jody wanted to sand all of the wooden trim, then stain it a dark walnut color. I decided to join them.

"May I do something to help?"

"We're OK. If you want to do something, how about doing the dishes?"

"I can do that. In fact, I'm an expert at doing dishes and cleaning up kitchens after eating."

"Perfect. Thanks."

Around 10:00 P.M. I was ready to turn in. I went out back and saw that the girls were sanding away on the wooden trim.

"The kitchen is like new. Now may I help with the porch?"

"That's OK, Pete. We have weeks of work to do around here. You relax."

"OK, if it's all right with you, I'm going to turn in."

"Goodnight. Sleep tight."

It took me a while to get to sleep. I felt guilty about sleeping when the girls were working so hard. What Patti had said to me about Jody made sense; she had breast cancer and didn't want to waste time sleeping when she wanted to make her house look good to sell it. But Patti needed sleep. I lay awake for hours before I could fall asleep.

June 28, 2004

The next morning I was glad to see that both girls were sleeping, Jody in her master bedroom and Patti in her room. Jody had three dogs in bed with her. I believe Patti had told me that Jody had five dogs, a Jack Russell, two yellow labs, and two Border Collies.

I made some coffee and then got on my laptop to check on business. I had three Reciprocal Golf members who had called our 800# to request play at private country clubs. It took me twenty-five minutes to make the phone calls and set up the three rounds of golf for my members and their guests. That was enough work for the day.

I walked out the back door and looked around. I noticed where the girls had left off sanding the trim on the porch. I picked up a hand sanding block, put a new piece of sandpaper in it, and started sanding. I was able to complete about twenty feet of trim before I heard a noise inside from the kitchen. I dropped the sanding block and went inside. Patti was pouring a cup of coffee, with creamer.

"Good morning."

"Hi. Were you sanding outside?"

"Just getting a little exercise. It's a pretty day outside."

Just then Jody came in. "Good morning."

"Morning," we both chimed in together.

As Patti poured Jody a cup of coffee, they discussed what they had to pick up at Lowe's Building Supply for the work ahead that day. They were dressed and out the front door within ten minutes, saying they'd be back in a couple of hours.

An hour after they drove off to Lowe's, the front doorbell rang. I answered the bell. A blond young lady was outside.

"Hi. I'm Pete, a friend of Jody's and Patti's. The girls are shopping at Lowe's."

"I'm Sandy."

"Hi, Sandy. Would you like a cup of coffee?"

"Sure."

Sandy sat down at the kitchen table and we started talking. I learned that Jody was like a demon possessed when it came to fixing up her house to sell it. I also learned that Sandy's nickname for Patti was Cinderella.

"Why Cinderella?"

"Because Patti tries to work hard helping Jody finish this house and gets very little rest. Jody works Patti all night long sometimes and she will work for 24 hours without any sleep! Patti feels she owes it to Jody because Jody doesn't charge her any rent."

"I noticed that the first night I got here."

"Pete, don't let Patti get sick from overworking."

"As if there was anything I could do about it."

"All I'm saying is try to help her if she needs help."

"Sandy, I have been doing my best to do just that for over ten years."

"Good. Don't stop."

The girls returned from Lowe's around noon with a truck bed full of lumber and cans of stain. I helped them unload everything next to the garage. Within five minutes they were back sanding the trim on the back porch.

That evening, Patti asked me if I could give her a ride over to Palm Springs to see Carol the next day. She informed me her Sebring convertible was not running very well.

"Of course, Honey. Anything you want. Do you want me to see what can be done about fixing your car?"

"No. Not right now."

I was glad to see that Patti got some sleep that night, although I could still hear power tools going strong out in the garage until the early hours of the morning.

The next morning I drove Patti to Palm Springs. She asked if I would drop her off at Carol's apartment for a few hours. That worked for me. It gave me time to meet with Gary about a business project we were working on. I picked up Patti later that afternoon. As we drove back to Jody's house Patti talked about Carol quite a bit. I caught up on the latest news that night.

The next day the girls were back at it on the back porch. I told Patti I was going to look for a place to live in Palm Springs that day and might not be back for a few days.

"OK. You be safe."

"I always am, Honey."

August, 2004

I spent the next three days looking in the classifieds for rentals, staying at my old reliable Royal Sun Inn during each night. It was nice seeing Geoff and Pat again. I had found a few possible places to rent after three days, but nothing confirmed.

When I returned to Norco, Patti was looking glum. "What's wrong, Patti?"

"Carol just called me. She told me the other day that she is pregnant. I didn't want to mention it to you at the time, but now she needs help. She wants to move up to Sonora to live with Mick until she has the baby. My car wouldn't make it."

"Who's the father?

"She's not sure. She said it had to be one of two guys she's been with."

"And she doesn't know which one is the father?"

"No."

"So what can I do to help?"

"Is there any chance you can take her to Mick's? Do you know where Sonora is?"

"Somewhere up in the mountains in central California I think. Isn't it close to Yosemite?"

"Someplace up there."

"Sure, Honey. I can do that. When does she want to go?"

"I'll call her cell and find out."

Patti and Carol made their plans over the phone. I waited to hear the outcome, so I could do whatever was needed to help them both. Finally, Patti let me know their decision.

"Carol can get a ride from Palm Springs this afternoon. She can be here by 7:00 P.M. Do you mind if she brings her cat? She has a travel cage."

"No problem. We can start north this evening and miss all the traffic."

"That's great, Honey. I don't know what I'd do without you."

"I keep telling you that. When are you going to finally believe it?"

Carol was dropped off at Jody's by 6:30 P.M. We all had a quick bite of dinner and then got on the road. The drive north out of Los Angeles was a little slow due to the evening rush hour traffic, but once we reached Newhall, the freeway opened up. Traffic was moving at 70 MPH, the legal speed limit.

When we were opposite Bakersfield, my cell rang. It was Patti, checking on our progress.

"We're moving along just fine, Honey. The cat is meowing quite a bit, but we're just fine."

I handed the phone to Carol so they could chat for a few minutes. Then she hung up.

I had estimated that we'd make it to Sonora around 2:00 A.M. Driving at night never bothered me; I enjoyed the silence and did my best thinking when driving. Carol slept a couple of hours and I put my right arm behind her seat to calm the cat down when it started meowing again. Carol slept and I calmed the cat with my hand strokes and my voice as we moved north at 70 MPH in the darkness.

Around midnight Carol awakened and asked where we were. "Just turning east off of Interstate 5, heading up the mountains toward Sonora. We're pretty much on schedule."

She helped me stay awake by talking and working the radio, finding music that we both liked. We arrived at Mick's house at 2:15 A.M. Carol had called her Dad on her cell and written down directions to his house. After Carol unloaded her things and her cat from the Blazer, I sat and talked for about thirty minutes before hitting the road back down the mountain.

At 4:00 A.M. my cell rang. It was Patti.

"Hi, Honey. What are you doing up at this hour?"

"I'm just worried about you. Aren't you tired?"

"I could use a little sleep. I see a motel up ahead. I'll stop and sleep for a while, then call you and let you know where I am and how I'm doing. OK, Honey?"

"Ok. I'll try to get some sleep myself. Goodnight, Pete."

"Goodnight, Patti. You know I love you."

Peter Edward Baumann

"I know, Pete. I know. Bye."

I pulled into the parking lot of a small motel, checked in, and then hit the sheets. I slept until 8:00 A.M. I checked out after filling up my travel coffee mug with a nice local brew, then got on the road. I didn't want to call Patti because I was afraid I'd wake her up. I waited for her to call me.

She phoned me at 9:45.

"Good morning. Did you get some sleep?'

She said she slept like she hadn't slept in a long time.

"That's good, Honey. You needed it."

"So where are you?"

I just got onto I-5 heading south. It will be clear sailing from here. I'll call you in a couple of hours and let you know my progress."

"OK. Drive safely. Bye"

"Bye, Honey."

It always amazed me how Patti and her mother said, "Bye" the same exact way. "Bah-eeee". They sounded so much alike when on the phone.

By 3:30 P.M. I was driving down the hill into the Newhall Valley. I saw Magic Mountain in the distance off to the right. I decided to call Patti and report my progress. She seemed excited to hear from me when she answered.

"Hi. Where are you?"

"I'm entering Newhall, Honey, next to Magic Mountain. I should be there in less than two hours."

"Great! Is there any chance we could go out to dinner when you get in?"

"I'd like that. Any place special you'd like to go?"

"How about TGIF's?"

"Thank God It's Friday?"

"Yes."

"Perfect. I could go for a steak."

"OK, Honey. I'll see you in two hours. Drive safely. Bye."

There it was again. "See you in two hours, Honey." I hit END on my cell.

It was exactly 5:30 P.M. when I drove up to Jody's gate. All five dogs were waiting for me inside the gate. I was just wondering how

I was going to open the gate to drive in without the dogs running off when Patti came out the front door. She called the dogs and they responded immediately to her voice. The dogs entered the side door to the garage. Patti closed the door, so I opened the gate and drove inside.

"Hi, Honey."

She ran up to me and gave me a hug. "Hi. Carol just called and said to thank you with a kiss when you got back. She is so happy to be at Mick's, so she can have her baby away from her friends in Palm Springs."

"So where is my kiss?"

"Right here." She kissed me hard and I kissed her back.

We went in the house. "Would you like to take a bath with me before we go to dinner?"

"Let me think. Would I like to get naked with you in the bath tub, is that what you're asking me?"

She smiled. "That's what I'm asking."

"Well, since you put it so nicely, yes, I would love to take a bath with you."

"I'll go run the water. Have a glass of wine in the meantime."

"Sounds great, Honey."

I walked into the bathroom and saw that she was already naked and climbing into the tub. I was right behind her. She scooted forward, so I could sit close behind her. My erection was already poking her in the back. She reached behind her, grabbed me, and said, "What's that?"

"Have you forgotten already? It's only been, what, about two years? You need to get out more, Honey."

"I haven't forgotten. It's just been too hectic around here for a long time."

I scrubbed Patti's back, and then moved to my babies in front. Her nipples were hard as rocks. She washed my feet, while massaging them. They were sore and her massage felt great. I massaged her neck and could feel her stress slowly fade away.

Neither one of us wanted to get out of the tub, but the water was getting cold. We got out and dried each other off.

"Let's get dressed and go to dinner."

"OK. Pete, I want to thank you again for all your help with moving Carol up north. I hope you know how much it means to me. If I can ever do anything for you, anything at all, just let me know."

"Oh, I can probably think of something."

She smiled her deadly smile that always melted my heart.

We were both dressed and ready to go within fifteen minutes. I drove her Sebring with the top down as she gave me directions to TGIF's. She said her car could go short distances, but that it overheated after an hour or so. It was a bit nippy with the top down, as well as a little noisy. We made small talk during the short drive. I asked her how she came to be living with Jody.

"I was working at a restaurant, but couldn't make enough to pay the rent. Jody invited me to live with her if I agreed to help her fix up her house so she could sell it. Before she invited me to live with her, I was actually considering stripping or prostitution to get by."

"You're kidding, Honey."

"You don't think I could make a living that way?"

"Sure you could. You'd be the sexiest stripper or hooker on the planet, but you're better than that, Honey. You could do anything you wanted if you put your heart in it."

"You've always told me that, Pete. I wish I had believed that twenty years ago when I was younger."

"No time like the first day of the rest of your life, Honey."

We got to TGIF's and sat near the fireplace. It was cozy and warm. We both ordered the top sirloin steak, medium, and baked potatoes with the works. Patti immediately hit it off with our waitress. Patti was the best waitress I had ever known, always going out of her way to please her customers. This young lady was very similar and Patti complimented her on the great job she was doing.

I had to laugh when a table of four young guys across the aisle from us gave the waitress a bad time, trying to come on to her. Patti called her over and gave her some experienced advice on how to handle such childish behavior. Patti insisted I leave a 30% tip for her when we left!

We got back to Jody's house and then relaxed in front of the large TV with a drink, my red wine and Patti's White Russian. At midnight we got up to go to bed.

"Want to join me tonight for some great sex? It's been a long time."

"I want to, Pete, but I'm worried about what Jody will think. She's still working in the garage."

"Does that girl ever sleep?"

"Sometimes she works all night long."

"I noticed. I guess we're lucky she isn't insisting that you work all night with her."

"I told her that after what you did to help Carol, she owes me a night off so I could spend time with you."

I pulled her close and whispered in her ear, as I nibbled on it, "OK. But join me in my room later if you can."

"I will."

"Promise?"

"I promise."

I kissed her on the neck and then went to my room. I had a hard time getting to sleep.

I woke to a movement beside me. It felt like naked flesh. Since I usually slept naked, I wondered if I was touching myself at first. But as I got the sleep out of my system, I knew it was Patti. Her firm breasts were on my chest, and I felt her warm stomach against mine. She kissed me firmly on the mouth and I responded fully.

The sex that night was incredible. At first it was quick, then over. We were both too anxious. It had been a long time. Then we slowed down and enjoyed every move. After what seemed like a lifetime, we were both spent, and she fell asleep in my arms.

As the light to the east was coming through the window, she woke up.

"I don't want to be here when Jody gets up, Baby. I'll see you in a little bit."

She kissed me and then got out of bed and went next door to her room. The last thing I saw was her fantastic ass going through the door as it closed.

Our relationship was getting back to what it had been years before. Patti was helping Jody finish the back porch, while I spent time in Palm Springs looking for an apartment for us.

One night Patti said something about having to go to Palm Springs to see someone. She didn't say who she had to see and I was getting concerned.

"Are you having second thoughts about getting back together with me, Honey?"

"No, I just need to do something and I need you to trust me."

"Ok. I'll be here when you get back."

She drove off in her car at around 9:00 P.M. I turned in around 11:00. When I woke up around 2:00 A.M., she was not back and I was getting more and more worried.

I tried to call her on her cell, but only got her voicemail. I think I left at least five messages on her phone that night.

Around daybreak, she came in the front door.

"Where have you been, Honey? I've been worried. Are you OK?"

"I'm fine. I was on my way back from Palm Springs, but my car overheated and it took me forever to get a tow truck. It was right in the middle of "no-man's-land", the winding stretch of road between here and the desert."

"Why didn't you call me, Honey? I left my cell on in case you needed to reach me."

"I didn't want to wake you up."

"Did you accomplish your mission last night?"

"Yes. It's all over now."

"Was it Kaufmann you had to see, Honey?"

"It doesn't matter. It's over."

I dropped the subject. To this day, five years later, I still don't know what that night was all about. What was important is that she was safe and with me. I would try to make sure that never changed.

The next few days were spent trying to figure out what to do about her car. She had had it towed that night to a garage in Norco and its engine was shot according to the garage owner. I also learned that Patti was behind on her car payments to the bank and that they were looking for the car. I told her not to worry, that we had my car, and that we'd be fine.

Two days later, she asked me for a favor. "Pete, the neighbors have an old Dodge in their back yard. They say it runs; it just needs a windshield. They'll take $400 for it. Could you loan me the $400? I'll pay you back."

"Let's go over and look at it."

We checked out the small Dodge four-door coupe. It needed a paint job, and a new windshield, and two tires. Patti wanted it, so I said, "Sure." I gave her the $400 and told her I'd give her the money for the windshield and two tires.

I wasn't really into her getting some clunker, but I knew Patti needed the self-esteem of having her own transportation, and not being dependent upon me, or anyone else for that matter.

I had decided to take an apartment on Sunrise Way in Palm Springs in a small complex of about 34 units. It had a pool and a hot tub just below our apartment. We arranged to move in. One day I followed Patti from Norco to the apartment in her Dodge, to make sure she made it.

September 1, 2004

Within a week we were moved in. We had even picked up some furniture she had in a storage unit in Palm Springs. What did not fit in the apartment we put in my storage unit. I still had a storage unit I used for a work area when I put together golf clubs for customers.

It had been eleven years since our affair in 1993. I was hoping and praying that we could finally be happy together.

Katy had been living with Jim in La Jolla for two years and was happy. The rest of Patti's family was still in Yreka; small town people, which is just fine if that is all you want out of life. Patti was the only person in her family to leave the small town of Yreka with the guts and inclination to go out into the world by herself.

I felt that enough time had passed for her family and her sister to forget about the affair and let her live in peace, and let her be happy.

I was so wrong!

PART THREE – *Together At Last*

September, 2004

We were finally settled in at our own place. Our first night in the apartment, we were watching a movie from the couch and Patti started hiccupping. She could not stop. I wondered at the time if she was stressed from the move, because stress can cause hiccups.

I reached over and pulled her head toward me. Then I kissed her hard on the lips. Her hiccups stopped. We continued kissing for another thirty minutes, with no hiccups. The kiss had stopped the hiccups. From that day forward, for years, we knew how to stop her hiccups.

Now that we were settled down in one place, I decided I needed to get new cell phones for my sons and me and for Patti. Patti and I went to the local Verizon store the next day and I bought four new phones on one two-year plan. I suggested that Patti give her new phone number to the members of her family.

"Carol isn't allowed to make long distance phone calls from their house in Washington, so she can't run up their phone bill!"

"That's not a problem. I'll call my 800 number providers, and have them set up an 800 number on your cell phone number so Carol can call you free of Carolge whenever she wants."

"You can do that?"

"Of course. I'll also have an 800 number go to your Mom's house in Yreka, so you can both call your Mom free of charge whenever you want."

"Wow, Baby. That would be great!"

"No problem, Honey."

We were finally getting settled in our new home. One of the things that always amazed me was how quickly Patti could get ready to go out on the town whenever we decided to do so. She could get in the bathroom and "put her face on" and do her hair in five minutes!

One night I asked her if she wanted to go out to dinner.

"Sure."

Love Was Not Enough

She disappeared in the bathroom, but did not come out for a very long time. I went in to see what was taking so long. She was busy with something in her mouth. When I looked closer, I noticed she was gluing several false fingernails to her gums with Super Glue! She was evidently missing several of her front teeth and was gluing false fingernails in their place.

"Honey, I didn't know you were missing some teeth. When did that happen?"

"When it happened doesn't matter. What does matter is that I lost three of my teeth."

"OK, Honey. So what do you want to do about it? Should I find a dentist down here?"

"I'd like to have all of my teeth pulled and get dentures."

"You're too young for that, Honey. Let's set up an appointment with a dentist."

"No, that would be too expensive. It will cost less to have them all pulled and get dentures."

One thing that I always loved about Patti is that she was not extravagant. She was the thriftiest woman I knew.

"OK, Honey. I'll see what I can set up to have your teeth pulled and replaced with dentures, if that's what you want."

"That's what I want. Thanks, Baby."

I knew dentists were expensive, so I went to my "plan A" I had used for years; I called ITEX, one of the barter clubs to which I belonged. I learned there was a dentist in Morongo Valley, a forty minute drive to the west, who could pull Patti's teeth. It would be about 5,000 trade dollars on my ITEX account. I had that. We set up an appointment.

Then I found the nearest denture lab on ITEX. I found one in Redwood City, CA, just south of San Francisco. I called Rob, the owner, and told him that I sold custom fit golf equipment on ITEX. He asked me if I could make his twelve-year-old son a custom set of golf clubs.

"Of course. How much would it cost my girlfriend to get custom dentures?"

"I would think it would be about what a set of golf clubs would cost. Why don't we trade straight across?"

"That works for me." We agreed on the exchange.

I told Patti about what I had set up and she was excited.

"That's great, Honey. When can we do it?"

I told her about the appointment to have her teeth pulled, then asked her, "What can you do after having your teeth pulled, in the time period before you get your new dentures?"

"I have Mom's old set of dentures. They will work until I can get my new ones."

"Great, Honey. Then it's all set."

Two weeks later we drove to Moreno Valley to see the dentist for the first part of the procedure. He knocked Patti out and then pulled all of her teeth in one session. That had to hurt! When he was finished, he asked me to join Patti in his recovery room. I went into the room and could tell she was in serious pain.

I held her hand and tried to console her, but I wasn't much help. I could just try to imagine the pain she was in.

When she indicated to me she was ready to leave, I walked her out to the Blazer. I had already picked up a frozen slush drink for her to sip on during the drive home, to try to freeze her gums and relieve the pain.

When we got home, she took some aspirin and went to bed. It was one of the roughest nights we have ever spent together!

The next morning she was feeling a little better, and each day that passed was an improvement.

October 12, 2004

The process of having her fit for dentures was time consuming, because it would require three trips to Rob's lab in Redwood City. We arranged to drive north to Redwood City for the first fitting and then continue north to Yreka to visit her mother.

October 27, 2004

We left for Redwood City at 8:00 A.M. It took us much of the day to reach Redwood City. We stayed in a Colony Inn for the night so we could be at Rob's lab first thing the next morning.

We walked in to his lab at 9:00 A.M. Rob walked up to me and introduced himself.

"Hi, Rob. This is Patti. I'm Pete." We shook hands.

"Patti, come on over here and have a seat. I'll bring out the sample trays."

Patti and I took a seat at a long table. Rob's assistant brought out seven different trays of "sample" teeth. Patti's eyes got wide and she exclaimed, "Wow. Look at all those teeth! And look at the different levels of whiteness in each tray."

Patti was like a little girl in a candy store. Rob explained the differences in the size, shape, and whiteness levels to her in each of the trays. I told them I was going to the car to check my business emails on my laptop while they looked over the samples.

"Take your time, Baby. We'll be just fine."

I was glad to see her smiling and having fun for a change.

I got back about an hour later and Patti was more excited than I had seen her in a long time. "Look, Honey. I picked out my new teeth."

She showed me two sets of teeth, uppers and lowers, lined up in a mounting fixture. I had to admit they were beautiful.

Rob told us it would take him about two weeks to set the teeth into a denture set. We thanked him and said we'd be back through, heading south the next time, in two weeks.

We got in my Blazer and headed north on Highway 101 for the Bay Bridge.

While I drove, Patti called her Mom's 800 number. Margaret answered on the first ring.

"Hi, Mom. It's Patti. Pete and I were just at the denture lab and they let me see the most beautiful collection of artificial teeth I could ever imagine! I spent over an hour picking out each tooth that they will use to build my dentures. I am so excited!"

I could only hear Patti's end of the discussion, but I could tell Margaret was also excited about Patti's new dentures. They talked for about half an hour before Patti said, "Bye." She had told Margaret we were on our way to Yreka for a visit and that we should be there at around dinner time.

We arrived at Margaret's house in time for dinner. It was nice being there around the dinner table with Patti, instead of just being there with my sons to try to learn how Patti was doing down south.

Patti was excited about her new teeth and was ready to discuss her new teeth for a long time with anyone who would listen.

As I expected, Muriel immediately started asking Patti questions about why Rob was doing this, and why wasn't he doing that! She always irritated me, but it was nice to see Patti getting irritated with her little sister for a change, if you can call a 400 pound woman little!

Finally I was glad to hear Patti say, "Muriel, you're full of s**t."

That was my cue to change the subject.

"Has anyone heard what Pete is doing at SOU? He's taking a film making class so he can learn more about how he can produce movies in the future."

Muriel then had to inform all of us how much she knew about raising children.

"Peter, when are you going to stop spoiling your son and teach him about the real world? Teach him how to get a real job, like digging ditches."

"Muriel, I encourage my sons to follow their dreams, to be what they want to be. If I can help them achieve their dreams, I do so."

"Pete will never be a movie director or producer. Teach him to stop wasting his time."

"Muriel, I'll make you a deal. I will raise my sons the way I think they should be raised, and you raise your sons exactly the way you think you should raise them."

"I don't have any children."

"Exactly!"

I got up from the table and poured myself another cup of coffee. What I really needed was a Jack.

Patti loved her family. No question about it. But she had the common sense to tell a family member when they didn't know what they were talking about. That was usually the situation when Muriel opened her mouth. For years she seldom went out in public because she did not know how to get along with people. She had talked Margaret into converting her garage into a pet grooming station so she could work on dogs at home and not go out.

In short, Muriel could get along with dogs much better than she could with people.

I have a younger sister who is very intelligent. She graduated from USC with honors. But whenever the family sits around and discusses politics, she pipes up and says the United States stole Texas, Arizona, New Mexico and California from Mexico, and that we should return those four states to Mexico. She also believes we stole the rest of the country from the American Indian tribes!

We love her, but we know when to tell her she's terribly confused.

Patti and I stayed at Margaret's house for about ten days. I would have loved to get a motel room for that visit, but Patti would still have stayed at her Mom's, so what would be the point of a motel?

I was keeping in touch with Rob in Redwood City regarding the progress he was making with Patti's dentures. It would be another few days at best.

Pete and Bob were also visiting and the house was pretty crowded. I always traveled with one of my inflatable queen-sized beds for just such an occasion. We set it up in the living room, where

Pete was sleeping on Margaret's rollout couch. Bob was sleeping in Margaret's room, Julie in her room, Muriel in her room.

The last night we were in Yreka, Patti and I were sleeping on the inflatable bed, and around 2:00 A.M. I decided to mess around a little bit. Patti was sleeping on her right side, facing away from me, so I inched up behind her. She moved back against me to indicate she was in the mood also. It was pitch black in the house, so we started making out.

Just as we were reaching a climax, a shadow walked by. I could tell it was Julie, Patti's cousin, walking into the kitchen. Julie lived in the house full-time. She must have realized what was going on, because she started walking faster. I didn't want to stop, because that would have let Patti know we were not alone, so I continued, and finished just as Julie was walking back to her bedroom.

To this day I don't think Patti knows we were not alone that night. But you never know with Patti. She loved to take chances, especially when it came to sex, as did I.

The next day we stopped by my storage unit in Yreka where I had been working on the junior, custom fit set of golf clubs I had been making to trade for Patti's dentures. We drove out of Yreka heading west. We decided to take the circuitous route back through Redwood City to Palm Springs to pick up her new dentures. We drove west through Scott Valley, just to see the beautiful scenery. We drove by Trinity Lake, close to where I used to fish for steelhead, often with Patti coming along for the ride.

We stopped for the night at a beautiful log-cabin-type resort after a nice dinner in their dining room. We were somewhere west of Redding, CA, near the original mining town of Shasta, CA.

The next day was beautiful. We drove down 299 to Redding, then south on I-5 to 505, then west to I-80 into San Francisco. South seven miles to Redwood City and we were in Rob's lab. Patti couldn't contain her excitement at picking up her new dentures.

When we met with Rob, he had Patti try on her dentures and asked her to tell him if they hurt her mouth anywhere. She indicated several spots that did not feel just right. Rob marked those spots with a marker.

"You two go out and have a nice lunch and come back in an hour and a half. I'll have these finished by then."

"Will do."

We found a nice Chinese restaurant nearby and shared a dish of chicken and broccoli. By the time we returned to Rob's lab, Patti's dentures were ready for another fit. They were perfect! Rob was quite pleased with his son's new golf clubs. I explained to him that once his son grew another four inches, he should call me and I'd extend the shafts again and regrip each club free of charge.

We said goodbye and then headed south on Highway 101 to the cutoff over to Interstate-5. From there it was clear sailing toward Palm Springs. We spent the night at a Santa Nella motel and drove into Palm Springs the next day. We were home and Patti had her new teeth. I was current with all of my Reciprocal Golf's member play requests. Patti was happy, so I was happy. I had my soul mate, best friend, and lover with me, and all was well with the world!

December 25, 2004

We spent Christmas for the first time together, in our apartment in Palm Springs. Patti had had a nice artificial Christmas tree in her storage unit and it was perfect in the apartment.

The New Year looked promising.

February 14, 2005

We went out to a nice restaurant for dinner on the main street in Palm Springs for Valentine's Day. The evening was beautiful, but not as beautiful as Patti. When she smiled, she lit up the night. We ate outside so we could enjoy the 80-degree weather.

I had signed up the owner of a nearby tanning salon on Reciprocal Golf a few days earlier and he loved the idea of trading tanning sessions for golf. Two days before Valentine's Day, Patti had gone by for a tanning session and when she smiled with her new teeth, her tanned complexion made her radiant.

At dinner that night, she mentioned that she had talked to Carol earlier in the afternoon. Carol was eight months pregnant, and Patti wanted to go to Sonora, CA, to be with her daughter during the birth of her first grandchild.

"Whatever you want, Honey. We can drive up there whenever you are ready. I'll visit for a day and then drive back. Stay as long as you want and just call me when you are ready to come home.

"You are so good to me, Pete. I don't deserve it."

"Of course you do, Honey. I would do anything for you, you know that. You are my best friend and soul mate! You make me happy."

"And you make me happy, Baby. I love you."

"I love you, too, Honey."

February 22, 2005

We left Palm Springs that morning at 8:00 A.M., heading west on I-10 to I-210 through Pasadena, and then connecting with I-5 North. The morning was clear, with no smog at all. Patti was reading a paperback while I drove. She had packed a nice lunch for us and I had a tuna sandwich around 11:00 A.M. We stopped for gas opposite the Bakersfield Exit.

When I was driving, Patti usually chose the radio stations in the car. But when she was reading a book, I'd take over that responsibility. I never had to ask her if she liked a station when I was turning the tuning knob; I would just watch her feet. If I changed to a station and one or both of her feet bounced to the music, I'd leave that station on. If her feet did not bounce to the music, I'd move on to the next station. Simple as that!

We continued north on I-5 until we reached the south end of Stockton, then turned east toward the Sierra Nevada Mountains. We were taking the very same route Carol and I had taken when I took her to Mick's house. Sonora was in the mountains about 60 miles from Yosemite National Park.

We arrived at Mick's house around 4:00 P.M. Patti rushed inside too see Carol while I unloaded her bags from the Blazer. Mick was evidently not around at the time, which was fine with Patti and me. We visited for an hour and then I left the girls to drive into town to find a motel for the night. I drove back to the house and smelled spaghetti and fresh garlic bread as I walked through the door. Dinner was relaxing and the girls caught up on the latest news.

Around 9:00 P.M. Patti and I drove to the motel for the night. The town of Sonora was founded during the California Gold Rush of 1849 and had many interesting buildings. We agreed we'd take some time in the morning to explore the town.

A winter storm had the temperature down to freezing that night, and it was good lying naked next to Patti under the covers that night. There's a lot to be said for shared bodily warmth!

The next morning Patti called Carol and told her we were going to walk around the town and explore and find a nice place to have breakfast. We found a nice quaint little restaurant on the main street that had hundreds of old artifacts from the gold rush days hanging on the walls. I love history, especially American History, and couldn't sit down long enough to eat.

Around 9:00 A.M. we drove back to Mick's house. I hugged and kissed Patti goodbye and then got on the road back down the mountains. I didn't know when I'd see her again, but knew we'd stay in touch by phone every day until Carol's baby was born. I drove straight through to Palm Springs that night and arrived at the apartment around 11:00 P.M.

March 10, 2005

Gage Wilson was born today to Carol Thomas in Sonora, California. Patti called me that morning to tell me all about the delivery. She was a first-time grandmother and couldn't be happier!

"Does that mean you're ready to come home, Honey?"

"I want to stay for another week or so to spend time with my grandson. Is that OK, Baby?"

"Honey, you can stay as long as you want. I just miss you."

"I miss you, too, Baby. Just one week more, OK?"

"That's fine, Honey. I can drive up to pick you up whenever you are ready to come home."

March 19, 2005

I left Palm Springs that morning to drive north to Sonora to pick up Patti and bring her home. She had called the night before and told me how well Carol and Gage were doing and said she was ready to come back.

About four hours into the drive, my cell phone rang. It was Patti, and she was crying uncontrollably.

"Pete, Jody died."

"When?"

"Yesterday. Amy has been trying to reach me, but I didn't get her messages up here. I should have been there with her."

"I am so sorry to hear about Jody, Honey, but you can't be everywhere at one time, Honey. Carol and the baby had to take priority."

"I know, I just wish I had seen her recently. It's been months!"

I paused while I heard her give out a big sob and then blow her nose. She came back to the phone.

"Where are you now?"

"I'm on I-5 just north of the Grapevine. I'll call you when I get closer, Honey."

"OK. Please drive carefully. There is a big winter storm heading this way and it's supposed to drop and lot of snow this afternoon. There are already stories on the radio and TV about roads closing."

"You know me, Honey. I'm always careful when driving."

"I know. I'm just worried about you in this weather."

"I'll be fine. I'll call you when I have an estimated time of arrival."

"OK. I love you."

"I love you, too, Baby. I'll talk to you later."

She hung up the phone. I could tell she was still crying.

When I reached Kettleman City, I decided to take a shortcut rather than continue to Stockton on I-5. I turned on Route 41 toward Fresno, then into the Sierra Nevadas toward Yosemite. Driving through Yosemite National Park is impossible due to the height of the mountain peaks, so I turned west and followed Route 49 north.

The weather was getting bad, with high winds and rain. I was dodging fallen trees everywhere and listening to the radio to try to learn if any nearby roads had been closed. I glanced at my cell phone to see if I had a signal and noticed I had one missed call. It had to be Patti trying to reach me. I was driving less than 20 MPH to avoid fallen trees and watching my cell phone to see if and when I could get a signal.

Ten minutes later I had a signal, so I pulled over on the shoulder after checking if any traffic was following me. No one else was around, so I stopped and called Patti's cell. She answered immediately.

"Hello." I could barely hear her.

"Hi, Honey."

"Where are you?"

"I'm on Route 49 about thirty miles south of Sonora. I decided to take a shortcut."

"Is the road open? The news says they are closing roads all over the place because of the storm."

"So far it appears to be open. There are some wet areas where I have had to drive through about six inches of water, but no snow yet."

"Pete, I'm worried. They say this is the worst storm in years."

"Honey, I'll be fine. If it gets bad, I'll stop somewhere and call you. We're not on any kind of timetable, so I'll get there when I get there. Don't worry."

"I can't help it."

"Sure you can, Honey. Take a deep breath and then let it out. I'll call you when I know for sure if this road goes through, OK?"

"OK. Call me soon."

"I will."

I continued on Route 49, sometimes barely moving due to the water on the road. The rain started to turn to slush, then to snow. After another hour I saw a sign to Sonora pointing to the right, on Route 120. 19 miles still to go. I drove through a small town called Moccasin and then Chinese Camp. Both looked almost completely abandoned except for a few houses. I passed a sign showing I was at 7,662 feet elevation. Another six miles and I turned right on 108. Six miles to Sonora.

I entered Sonora and the town looked like it had just been hit by a tornado. Debris was everywhere. I pulled over in front of a bar and went inside.

"Jack and water," I said to an old lady behind the bar.

"Coming right up."

I sat on a bar stool and dialed my cell.

"Hello!"

"Hi, Honey. I'm in Sonora, at a bar on the main street, having a Jack. I didn't even want to try to find Mick's house in this rain. I'm one hundred feet from the Best Western we stayed in last time I was here."

"Hold on a second."

I could hear her call to Carol, and bring Carol up to speed. Then she came back on the line.

"Honey, stay right where you are. Carol will drive me down there. Can we get a room at the Best Western again for tonight?"

"I'm sure we can. I only see two cars in the motel parking lot."

"Give us fifteen minutes, Honey."

"I'll be here."

I told the bartender I was going across the street to get a room and would be right back.

I registered for a room, #1, the same room we had the last time, and then returned to the bar. Patti and Carol drove up ten minutes later. We hugged, and then Carol drove back to Mick's house, her truck disappearing within one hundred feet in the rain.

"Let's go to the room, Honey."

She smiled and nodded. We were barely inside the room when I had her clothes off, and she had mine off, and we jumped into the bed.

"Slow down, Baby. I'm not going anywhere!"

We had been apart for too long.

The next morning we went to the same little restaurant on the main street for breakfast. I spent ten minutes looking at the artifacts on the wall again until our food was served.

After breakfast, we checked out of the motel and drove to Mick's house. It took Patti an hour to say goodbye while I loaded her bags into the Blazer. By 10:00 A.M. we were on the road. This time I wasn't taking any chances; we would drive straight downhill toward Stockton to I-5, then south to Los Angeles and Palm Springs.

Patti was reading a different paperback on the return trip. We got home at 7:30 P.M. We were both spent. Patti was still stressed about Jody's passing. The next morning, she took one of our antique nightstands from the bedroom out to the front deck and started sanding it. I asked her what her plan was and she said, "These nightstands need sanding and staining."

I figured she needed something to do for therapy to deal with Jody's death. I was impressed over the next week with her craftsmanship! I guess she had learned a lot about working with wood when she lived with Jody.

The next few weeks were relaxing for both of us. I worked about an hour each morning taking care of Reciprocal Golf Members' play requests and then usually played 18 holes with Gary. Patti occasionally came along to ride in the golf cart, but she usually stayed at the apartment and worked on the nightstands, or watched game shows. She loved to increase her knowledge by watching Jeopardy, or Who Wants to Be A Millionaire?

In the afternoon, we'd take a walk together around the neighborhood.

One afternoon in June we were taking our usual walk, when I stopped and pulled a ring out of my pocket.

"Patti, will you marry me?"

She looked at me, and then said, "We're doing fine. I don't want to hurt Katy."

"Honey, how long are you going to feel guilty about us? Forever?"

"I don't want to hurt my sister. Someday, Honey. I promise."

May 14, 2005

Bobby and Pete drove down to Palm Springs from Yreka to visit for a few days, and to deliver Bob's white Chrysler, Sebring convertible to me. The Chrysler needed some repair work and Bob wanted to take my older Chevy Tahoe four-wheel-drive SUV up north for a while, so he could go out in the wilderness with his buddies, four-wheeling.

I took the Sebring to several garages in Palm Springs for their opinions about what needed fixing. The air conditioning unit no longer worked and it was difficult just getting to the condenser with all the other parts in the way.

I left the Sebring in the garage for a week and then received a phone call that it was fixed and to drive over and pick it up. The bill came to over $880.

We didn't need two cars, so I decided to try to sell it on eBay and in the local Desert Sun Newspaper. I was asking $5,700 for the convertible.

The third day of my auction on eBay, I received a message from an eBayer in Rancho Bernardo. I talked with him on the phone, and it sounded like he was a serious buyer. He told me he'd probably pay $4,800 for the car as-is.

Patti and I drove over to Rancho Bernardo that afternoon, a Friday, she in my Blazer and I drove the Sebring. We found his house and were surprised to see all of the different vehicles in his driveway and parked on the street in front of the house.

We parked both vehicles and I walked up to the front door and knocked. Mark came to the door and introduced himself.

"Hi, Mark. I'm Pete. We talked on the phone about my Sebring convertible."

"Yeah, Pete. Let's take a look at it."

He grabbed a notepad and walked down the walkway to the car. He started asking how this worked on the car, and how that worked. He asked questions about the car as if he were a used car dealer deciding what he'd pay for the car, which is exactly what he turned out to be!

Patti and I were becoming furious that Mark would waste our time without telling me on the phone that he had a used car dealership license and that he would be buying the Sebring for resale.

Finally, he said he'd pay $4,100 for the Sebring. I didn't respond to his offer, but simply told him he was a jerk for not telling me ahead of time that he was buying for resale. "Mark, we wouldn't have wasted our time and an hour drive in each direction if you had been honest on the phone. Get lost."

Patti got in the Blazer and I got in the Sebring and we backed out of the driveway. On the drive back to Palm Springs we spoke on our cell phones about what an ass Mark was, to waste our time like that.

When we got back to the apartment around 7:30 P.M. Friday night, I noticed I had another message from an eBayer on my computer. This eBayer was a soldier at Fort Irwin Military Reserve Base northeast of Barstow, California. We exchanged messages on the eBay website. I learned that he was expected to be at his friend's wedding in Las Vegas that Sunday afternoon. He said that he'd give me my asking price of $5,700 if I would deliver the Sebring to him at Fort Irwin Sunday morning by 10:00 A.M.

When I asked him if he would be able to get $5,700 cash at 10:00 A.M. Sunday, he said the base bank opened at that time on Sundays and he would have the cash.

Patti and I made plans to get up early Sunday and drive the Sebring and Blazer to Ft. Irwin. That morning was a clear, brisk, high desert morning, with a temperature around 57 degrees when we left Palm Springs. It was projected to reach a high of 97 degrees by noon.

I led the way in the Sebring, with the top up, west on I-10 toward San Bernardino, with Patti following in the Blazer. It warmed up quickly as we drove. When I pulled into a gas station to gas up, Patti pulled in behind me at the next pump.

"Pete, after we gas up, is it OK if we switch cars, so I can drive the Sebring with the top down the last part of the trip?"

"Sure, Honey. If that's what you want."

Patti jumped into the Sebring and operated the controls to the convertible top. Within a minute the top was down and covered.

I drove out of the gas station in the Blazer, and Patti followed in the Sebring. I should have known what Patti had in mind when we switched cars, but didn't think of it until we reached the entrance of Fort Irwin. I noticed in my rear view mirror that she was adjusting her blouse as we slowed down at the military gate and the guard in uniform was eyeing Patti in the convertible behind me.

The guard instructed me to park in the parking lot to the right and for Patti to follow me. We parked side by side and then got out of the cars. Patti had a big smile on her face.

"It was so nice and warm after we gassed up, I decided to pull down the front of my dress and get some sun on my titties while I drove the last 45 minutes."

"I figured you were doing something like that, Baby. Any time you want to get some sun on my babies is fine with me."

I called her breasts my babies because I had paid for them back in 1993. Based on the attention the gate guard showed to Patti as we walked over to him, I think he had an idea what she had been doing as well when she drove up to the gate.

"Sir, you will have to phone your contact on base and have him bring a day-pass here, so you can drive on base."

"No problem. Here's his name and his phone number."

The guard handed me the phone, and I called Steve, the soldier we were meeting to sell the car. He drove up from inside the base about five minutes later. He parked his truck, we three jumped into the Sebring, and with Steve driving, we drove through the gate onto the base. As he drove, I explained the different features of the car to him.

He drove into a parking lot in front of the Base Exchange building and parked.

"The car is just as I had hoped. Do we have a deal at $5,700?"

"Deal. I brought the paperwork, so all we need is the cash."

Steve looked at his watch. "The base bank just opened. Let's go."

We followed Steve into the building and Patti and I sat at a table and had coffee while Steve went to the teller's window. Within thirty minutes we had completed the sales papers and the Sebring belonged to Steve. Patti and I asked if we could shop for a few souvenirs at the Base Exchange.

"Sure. I'll wait while you pick out what you want and I'll use my card to pay for it."

Patti picked out two desk carvings made of clear glass, with a lighted table mount for each, and I picked out a NAVY baseball cap. We handed them to Steve and he paid for the items at the checkout.

We said goodbye to Steve and wished him luck at his friend's wedding that afternoon in Las Vegas. Patti and I jumped into the Blazer and headed back toward Barstow. We took it slow and easy that afternoon driving back to Palm Springs. We stopped for a nice lunch along the way and got in that afternoon around 4:00 P.M.

June 21, 2005

Carol and Nolan Wilson, Gage's father and a former chef at a Palm Springs restaurant, were scheduled to get married that summer, and Patti wanted to attend the wedding, obviously. They were going to be married in Winthrop, WA, where Nolan's family lived. My son, Pete, was asked if he would video the wedding, not with the usual Sony home video camera but with the Canon XL2 camera I had bought for him to film a movie he had written for a psychology class in college.

I arranged for Patti to fly into Medford, Oregon, from the Palm Springs Airport so she could join her family for the drive to Washington. She would be gone for at least two weeks, so I caught up on some business on my computer, and played a lot of golf, mostly with Gary.

Patti called me from her cell phone at least once a day for the week she was gone. I always loved hearing her voice over the phone and could tell her mood from the tone of her voice. I could tell she was having fun. She always did when she was with her family.

When she returned two weeks later, she had a pile of pictures to show me and we spent many hours going through them.

Patti was happy, and when Patti was happy, I was happy.

October 30, 2005

The summer heat was finally gone, to be replaced by cooler days and even cooler nights. We enjoyed the evenings especially and went out to the Street Fair in downtown Palm Springs every Thursday.

Patti loved visiting each booth at the Fair, buying little things for our apartment.

On Thanksgiving, we went to a local restaurant and ate dinner while watching an NFL game on the big screen. It was fun to relax and laugh together when we could, without some family member having some kind of crisis wherein we'd have to stop our lives and help them out. The break did us both as lot of good.

December 20, 2005

Patti wanted to go to Carol's house in Winthrop, WA, for Christmas, so we went. We left Palm Springs four days before Christmas and drove the entire 750 miles that day. I drove the entire way and Patti read a paperback part of the way, looked for good radio stations part of the time, and opened the cooler for food when we were hungry.

She was always fun to have in the car when traveling. Some couples argue about little things, such as which route to take, or they fight. She never did; we never did. It was almost as if we were too comfortable together, if it can be possible to be too comfortable! We just "were" when we were together. No stress, nothing but peace and quiet.

We arrived just after dark, which was around 5:00 P.M. in northern Washington that time of year, and there was quite a bit of snow on the ground. Carol and Nolan were renting a single-wide trailer that year. Dinner was ready and we were starved.

I inflated the two-foot-tall inflatable bed I always carried in the Blazer when we traveled. We set it up in the living room, in a corner. We turned in early that night because we were tired from the long drive that day.

The next morning we all drove half a mile to Nolan's parents' house to visit. The house was full of family visiting from out of town. We spent that day playing with the kids, talking about politics and the weather, eating great food, and just relaxing.

Patti and I left earlier than Carol, Nolan, and Gage. We wanted some time alone. We got back to the trailer and jumped onto the inflatable for some intimate time. Twenty minutes later there was a knock at the front door. Patti jumped up and put on a robe, and then answered the door. It was her cousin, Tom.

"If you had gotten here five minutes earlier, you would have caught us f**k**g!"

"Just my luck. A day late and a dollar short."

Tom came in and Patti gave him a hug. I had met Tom earlier in the day, so introductions were not necessary. Tom visited for about an hour when Carol, Nolan and Gage came in. Patti asked Tom if he wanted to stay for dinner, but he had some things he had to do before heading home.

On Christmas Eve, Gage was taken to bed early so we adults could stay up and wrap presents. Most of the gifts under the tree were for Gage, and we had fun showing each other what we had bought for him.

The next morning we all got up the usual time and had fun watching Gage grab at the wrapping paper. He was only nine months old, so we adults were acting like little kids, showing him everything so we could get a smile out of him.

Patti and I left Winthrop two days later. One problem with running a golf service online is that you work seven days per week. I had to be available every day to check my emails, so I could take care of any Reciprocal Golf members who might want to play over the holidays. Cell phone and wireless laptop signals were few and far between around Winthrop, so it was not easy picking up my emails. I needed to get back to civilization.

We drove back to Palm Springs in one day, and relaxed around the pool the next day. There may have been snow on the ground in Winthrop, but it was 82 degrees in Palm Springs.

New Year's Eve was a warm 77 degrees at 10:00 P.M. We went to a beautiful house in La Quinta where one of Patti's friends lived. The house was on one of the fairways on the Arnold Palmer Course at the PGA West Resort.

We danced until midnight and ate some fabulous food. At one point, one of the men suggested that all of the women get together for a group picture in the living room. I took about five pictures myself with my digital camera and was amazed the next day when I transferred them to my computer. Every single woman, all 15 of them, in the group picture was blond!

January was beautiful. The snowbirds, people from Canada and the northern states that come to Palm Springs for January through

May, were driving into town in droves. The valley's population jumps from 200,000 to over 800,000 during January.

On Valentine's Day, I took Patti out to a special dinner once again. We went to L.G.'s Steakhouse on Palm Canyon Drive and ate outside on the veranda, next to one of the outdoor fires. It was a great evening.

February 27, 2006

Carol was having another baby, and Patti wanted to go to Washington for the birth. I drove her to the Palm Springs Airport to fly to Spokane, WA, where Carol and Nolan would pick her up.

The baby wasn't due until the tenth of March, so Patti was visiting for a few weeks before Silas Wilson was born. Patti was in seventh heaven once again with her two grandsons to care for. She called me every day to tell me how much fun she was having with the boys and with Carol.

It wasn't until early April before she was ready to come home.

April 29, 2006

It was my parents' 60th wedding anniversary and we were invited to a brunch at Air Force Village West, the retirement facility where they lived in Riverside, CA. We left Palm Springs at 10:00 A.M. and arrived at 11:00 A.M. They had vacated the house they had there the previous month and were staying in the SNF, the Secured Nursing Facility.

I didn't get the memo, because I showed up in a coat and tie, where everyone else was in Hawaiian clothes. Patti's new flowered red and white dress was perfect. My older brother, Scott, was down from Seattle, with his new fiancée, Claudia, brother Brian was there with his wife, Debbie, and my younger sister, Debra, was there. The rest of the people there were older residents of SNF.

Mom and Dad looked well, in Dad's Hawaiian black and white flowered shirt, and Mom's white and grey Hawaiian dress. Mom was having trouble staying awake. Patti was her usual charming self, helping out with the serving of the food and Champagne. One old fellow walked up to her and asked her if she was an actress. Patti smiled and said, "No."

"You should be, young lady. You are beautiful, and have a lot of class."

"Thank you." She smiled her great smile and blushed."

After brunch, Patti asked Mom if she'd like to be taken outside in her wheelchair for a while, since it was such a pretty day.

"That would be nice."

Patti pushed Mom's wheelchair toward the exit.

Dad walked up to me with his walker and asked, "Pete, can we talk for a minute?"

"Sure, Dad."

We sat down in the corner of the banquet room.

"Peter, when are you and Patti getting married?"

"I wish I knew, Dad. I have asked her to marry me, but she is worried about hurting Katy."

"How would it hurt Katy? You and Katy have been divorced for eight years now, and she is living with someone else, right?"

"Correct. For about five years."

"How long do you think Patti will want to wait?"

"Who knows, Dad? Who knows?"

"Well, I want you to know how your mother and I feel. We loved Katy, but knew you two had problems. She is now with another man. Your mother and I love Patti, and we think you two are perfect together. We'd like to see you get married, preferably sooner than later. We're not young anymore, you know?"

"Dad, I'll do my best to make it happen."

"Please do, Peter. We both want to live to see you two get married."

June 1, 2006

Today was my birthday; fifty-eight years young. Patti and I went out to dinner to celebrate.

It was exceptionally hot that summer. Patti loved to lie on the blowup swimming pool mattress and float in the pool in the hot sun. She tanned much better than I did. One week we drove over to my Bayliner on Lake Havasu and enjoyed running around naked on the boat for five days.

One evening Patti was sitting in my lap as I steered the boat and I was making figure-eights on the lake, jumping our wake on each turn. We hit a big wave and Patti fell out of my lap and onto the deck. The engine stopped and we were dead in the water, about one hundred yards off of one of the casinos on the shoreline.

I tried and tried to start the engine, but it would not start! It was getting dark and cool, as the high desert nights tend to be. Finally I waved down a ski boat and they towed us in to the nearby marina using a ski rope. We thanked them for the tow and then looked around the marina. No one was visible, so I told Patti we may as well tie up to the dock for the night. I didn't see any other option, and she said, "Great. We'll have an adventure!"

Most other women might have complained about being stranded at a strange marina for the night, but not Patti. She was game for anything.

We changed from our bathing suits into some warm clothes, then walked up the ramp to the shoreline and looked around. The casino building was closest, so we walked toward it, Patti placing her hands in the crook of my arm. We were pleased to learn that the casino had a nice restaurant, so we sat down for dinner. We had a nice, peaceful dinner while watching couples trying their best to win some money at the tables a hundred feet away.

At midnight we walked back to the boat, entered and locked the cabin door, and turned in for the night.

The next morning I went outside and noticed that the marina personnel had not come to work yet. I took out my fishing rod, put on a purple rubber worm and cast from the stern of the boat. On the second cast I had a hit on the worm and my line pulled tight.

I didn't know what kind of fish I had on the line, but it was big and strong. I had been fighting it for a full seven or eight minutes when Patti came out of the cabin in a hot red bikini.

"Morning, Honey. I may have breakfast on the line."

"Cool. Can I try to reel it in?"

"Sure. Come on over."

I showed her how to hold the rod and how to operate the spinning reel. First I showed her how the drag was set, so she could pull on the fish without breaking the line, if the fish decided to run. Once she had the knack, I sat back and watched as she had fun playing the fish. She was taking her time pulling in the fish, but I didn't care. I was having fun watching my baby yell and scream, jumping up and down in her bikini.

I don't know who was tired first, the fish or Patti, but after about fifteen minutes she sat down next to me and said, "Here, you take it."

I reeled in the fish within thirty seconds.

"Oh, sure, I tire out the fish and then you pull him in after he's exhausted."

"You did tire him out, Honey. It's a carp. They get big and heavy in lakes like this, but they're not good to eat. Too many bones and not very tasty. But as long as you had fun fighting him, that makes it perfect!"

"It was fun. I've never done that before."

The marina personnel showed up for work, and I asked one of them, Don, if he could look at the engine. He got his toolbox and started checking everything he could find on the engine. After two hours, he mentioned, "This reminds me of the time I tried to find out why a personal wave runner stopped running. After an hour, I learned that the guy riding it had pulled out the safety cord and stopped the motor."

I almost laughed out loud. I ran over to the throttle and looked for the safety cord. It was not connected. I plugged it in and then told Don I was going to try to start the engine. It fired right up!

"Don, I feel like an idiot. The safety cord was pulled out of its socket!"

I gave Don a hundred dollar bill and thanked him for his time. We pulled out of the marina and headed back across Lake Havasu toward our dock by the London Bridge.

We drove home the next day, this time with our clothes on! It was a boring drive.

July 4, 2006

We drove the one mile to South Palm Canyon Drive around 9:00 P.M. to have dinner and watch the 4th of July fireworks. South Palm Canyon Drive is in the heart of Palm Springs. Highway 111 coming into town from the north opens to four lanes, all going south one way, with restaurants on either side of it. The main stretch is seven blocks long.

We ate outside as usual. After the sun goes down during the summer days, it cooled off from the daytime temperature of 115 to a nice 80 to 85.

After dinner, we took a walk along the sidewalk and looked at all of the art displayed in the galleries. At one point, I turned to Patti and asked, "Honey, when are you going to let me make an honest woman out of you? Marry me. I love you."

"I know you do, Pete. I love you, too. We're doing just fine right now. I don't want to mess things up with my sister."

July 6, 2006

It was my son, Pete's, birthday, so I called him on his cell phone in Yreka to wish him a happy birthday. I hung up the phone.

Patti was talking to her Mom on her cell inside the apartment. I had my coffee on the front deck, reading one of my Clive Cussler books. I owned all of his hardbacks and was reading this particular one for the third time in twenty years.

Patti came outside with her coffee cup and sat down.

"Baby, what would you think of moving back to Yreka?"

"I don't know, Honey. I moved away from there because of the cold winters. And I know how much you hate that white shit that falls from the sky!"

She laughed. "I know, but I'm worried about my Mom's health. I want to live closer to her in case something happens."

"If you want to move, Honey, we'll move. Would it be OK if we moved to Lake Shastina?"

"That would be fine, Honey. It's only a half hour drive to Yreka."

I walked to the manager's apartment and gave her notice that we would be moving.

Two days later we drove to Lake Shastina and looked around for a house to rent. We found a cute three-bedroom, two-bath house right on the fourth fairway of the Scottish Nine, with a view right across the fairway at Mt. Shasta seven miles away. We met with the owner and signed a one-year lease and gave her a check for $2,700. Then we drove back to Palm Springs to prepare to move.

August 1, 2006

The two previous days we had loaded our things from the apartment and my storage unit into a large U-Haul Truck. I went to my doctor's office at 8:00 A.M. that morning so they could inject my back with a painkiller. They told me to take it easy for at least three days to give the shot a chance to work.

I did not tell them I was going to be driving a U-Haul truck 750 miles north that day. Patti's son, Mick, was helping us move. I started out driving the truck, with Patti riding with me and Mick following in my Blazer.

After a few hours, I stopped for gas and Mick pulled in behind us at the pumps. Mick and I switched places, with him driving the truck and Patti riding with him. I followed in the Blazer. We drove all day long and got in at around 9:00 P.M. at the Lake Shastina house. It was still light out due to Lake Shastina being farther west than Palm Springs.

We took a few sleeping bags and pillows into the house to sleep on that night and started unloading the truck the next morning.

Mick was a big help unloading the U-Haul. He was a hard worker. I often wonder if he would have developed into a more responsible young man if his dad had encouraged him in whatever it was that he wanted to do in life. But his dad had constantly criticized him when he was younger, and Mick was like a lost soul, with no goals in his life for him to strive toward.

Thinking about how Mick was raised made me think quite often about my own sons and what might have changed if I had gone to Boulder City in 1994 with Patti, or if I had immediately followed her to Palm Springs two years later. I knew that my staying in Yreka helped my sons grow into mature, responsible young adults. At the same time I knew it had hurt my chances of being happy in the future with Patti.

But that was all in the past and there was nothing I could do to change the past. I knew I had to concentrate on our future together.

Once we had unloaded the U-Haul and carried everything into the house, we moved the furniture around to where we wanted it. Over the next few weeks I obtained a hot tub for the outside deck, facing Mt. Shasta. I also had an internet antennae installed on the roof so my laptop could receive a signal and I could better take care of Reciprocal Golf business.

October 2, 2006

Patti asked me if I'd take her into Mt. Shasta to see Dr. Parker. We had moved back to Siskiyou County because Patti was worried about her mother's health and wanted to live closer to Margaret. At the same time, she and I both missed living in Palm Springs. She was evidently depressed about the move, because she asked Dr. Parker if he could give her something to lift her spirits.

He gave her a prescription for Lexapro, an anti-depressant. She would end up taking that drug for six months before she came to me and said she no longer needed the anti-depressant. She was very proud of herself when she stopped taking the Lexapro. I was not satisfied living in a small town either, but had moved to keep Patti happy. Both of us enjoyed the more active lifestyle we could live in a place like Palm Springs. Siskiyou County, California, could be quite boring at times.

As things turned out 22 months later, I wish we had never left Palm Springs!

November 6, 2006

Patti often took the Blazer into Yreka to visit her Mom. Today I decided to drive into town with her, to take care of some errands while she visited. I called Margaret's house after I bought some supplies at Wal-Mart and asked if anyone wanted some Taco Bell for lunch. They did, and I took their orders over the phone.

After driving through Taco Bell and picking up the food, I drove to Margaret's house on South Fairchild Street.

During lunch, I told everyone about Pete asking me to produce his independent film, SPIN OF FABRICATIONS, which he had written for a philosophy class at Rogue Community College in Grant Pass in 2004.

"How much money does he want from you," asked Muriel.

"Pete thinks he needs about $8,000 for the camera equipment and lighting equipment. He plans to do all the work himself, so he won't have to pay anyone else."

"What about actors?"

"He has talked with several friends and a couple of actors at the Shakespeare Theatre and they have agreed to act in the film for a small royalty. Most of them just want to be able to add their work on the film to their respective resumes."

"What a waste of money, Pete. Tell him to get a real job and stop wasting his time on dreams!"

"Muriel, we've been over this before. I encourage my sons to go after their dreams and help them financially whenever I can."

"So you're going to give him the money?"

"As I can come up with it."

"And did he say how long it would take to finish the movie?"

"He thinks it will take about three months to finish it."

"I'll bet you he doesn't finish it in time."

"In time for what, Muriel? If it takes longer, it takes longer. Period."

Patti jumped into the conversation and I was happy to see she was on my side. "Muriel, you are the most negative person in the world at times. Why can't you help lift people up instead of trying to let them down all the time? Besides, it is none of your business what Pete wants to do to help his son."

I couldn't have been more proud of Patti than I was at that moment.

December, 2006

We were going to celebrate our first Christmas in Siskiyou County in a long time. Patti's artificial tree we had used in the apartment in Palm Springs was once again perfect for our house at Lake Shastina.

Christmas Eve we drove into Yreka, where we had a great Christmas dinner at Margaret's house. Muriel reminded everyone that she would wake them up at 4:30 in the morning. And I reminded myself of the reason I was against staying at Margaret's that night!

I knew I would have lost that discussion with Patti, so I was in Yreka for the night. Muriel had to be tolerated every now and then to keep the peace!

March, 2007

It was that time of year when Patti started missing her grandsons. I arranged time to drive her to Washington this time, taking my portable office with me. It was nice owning a service business that I could take care of from anywhere with a cell phone and wireless laptop signal.

We had fun visiting Carol, Nolan, and the grandsons. Nolan was the chef at a snow skiing and golf course resort in Winthrop, and he did a fantastic job preparing the dinner we had after driving out to the resort with Carol and the boys. The history of the area amazed me as I listened to Carol tell us about it at dinner.

I have always enjoyed American History, clear back to the 1700's. I had read the entire collection of James Fennimore Cooper's series **The Last of the Mohicans** about the mountain men that opened up our country when I was eleven and twelve years old.

The next day I talked Patti into leaving the boys for a few hours so we could drive around the valley and explore. We enjoyed driving through the various small towns in the valley and stopped to investigate some of the older buildings.

We had lunch at a great old building that used to be a hotel, but was converted to a sports bar. We ate hamburgers while watching a golf tournament on the large screen TV in the restaurant end of the building. We struck up a conversation with the couple sitting next to us and learned they were from San Diego, where I had gone to high school and college while working at Sea World.

Patti told them about living in El Cajon for several years, before moving to Siskiyou County, CA.

After another hour of exploring the valley, Patti mentioned that she had better get back to her grandsons. We drove back to Carol's trailer for the rest of the day. I had some business phone calls I needed to make, providing I could get a good cell phone signal from their location.

We spent a full week visiting in Winthrop before we decided to head south to Lake Shastina.

June, 2007

Summer was on its way and Patti and I got into the routine we used to follow in Palm Springs; we started taking walks around the house every afternoon. We were on another afternoon walk when I decided to pop the question for the fourth time; or was it the fifth time?

"Patti. Will you please marry me, and make me the happiest man in the world?"

She took my left arm into her arms and squeezed. "Pete, I do love you. I really do. We're doing just fine right now. Why do you want to change that?"

"I don't want to change anything, Honey. I just want the whole world to know that you're mine."

"I am yours, Pete. Nothing will change that."

Patti was right; nothing would change the fact that we loved each other, that we were best friends. But neither of us realized at that time that things would change if one of us became ill, as I was to learn the hard way fourteen months later!

August 2, 2007

I went to my doctor's office for my annual checkup that morning. Dr. James Parker had been our family doctor in Mt. Shasta for over 20 years. He had also been Patti's family doctor for the previous fifteen years. Patti adored Jim, and he thought the world of her.

The next morning, my cell rang; it was Dr.Parker.

"Pete, Jim. Can you come into my office this afternoon for the results of your tests yesterday?"

"Sure. What time?"

"I have an opening at three."

"I'll be there."

I told Patti about the call. "Say 'Hi' to Dr. Parker for me."

"I will, Honey."

I arrived at Dr. Parker's office at 3:00 P.M. sharp. In the waiting room a nurse came in and took my blood pressure. Dr. Parker came in a few minutes later.

"Pete, how are your boys doing?"

"Well, Pete's still at S.O.U., and working on his independent film when he has time. Bobby is still at P.U.C. in St. Helena. He should graduate next year, in June."

"Are you going to get me a DVD of Pete's movie when it's finished?"

"You'll be the first person to get one."

"Thanks. I'm looking forward to seeing it. The reason I wanted you to come in, Pete, is because your PSA test came back high, at 5.05."

"PSA test, that's the prostate test, right?"

"Correct. We need to make an appointment with a Urologist."

"Dr. Carter is the only Urologist in the county, isn't he?"

"I believe he is."

"OK. I'll give his office a call."

"Let me know what he advises you do, OK?"

"I will."

When I got home, I told Patti that I probably had prostate cancer and that I would know for sure after seeing Dr. Carter. She took it in stride."

"So Dr. Parker thinks he found it early?"

"He says it's probably early, but we'll know for sure after I see Dr. Carter in Yreka."

I made the appointment the next morning. They could see me in two days.

"I want to go with you to the appointment, Baby."

"That's fine, Honey."

We drove to Yreka two days later for my appointment. Dr. Carter did his own blood test while we waited. He came into the waiting room and sat down.

"Pete, Dr. Parker caught it early, but you do have prostate cancer. We have plenty of time to decide which course of action you want to take. We can remove your prostate, we can give you radiation treatments from outside the body, or we can schedule a new technique that has been used for about ten years. We don't do it in Siskiyou County, but I'll give you a phone number to call to find out the nearest place you can have it done. It is called Brachy Therapy. The Urologist places radioactive seeds, like tiny pieces of metal, inside your prostate. The radioactive seeds kill the cancer from inside the prostate."

"How successful has the Brachy Therapy been?"

"As far as I know, it has been very successful. I have a book here that you can take home with you to read. It covers all three treatments. Read it over and then let me know which way you want to go."

"Sounds good, Doc. Thanks."

Patti and I drove back to Lake Shastina after the appointment with Dr. Carter. Once home, I started reading the book the doctor had given me while Patti cooked dinner. Within thirty minutes I knew I was going to opt for the Brachy Therapy, the radioactive seeding. Now all I needed was some advice as to where to have it done.

I went to my laptop and searched for "Brachy Therapy" and "prostate cancer".

The first website to come up was about prostate cancer treatment in California. I learned that California had a program for resident men over the age of 18 that was offered free-of-charge. I wrote down the phone number to call for more information. It was after 5:00 P.M., so I made a note to call them the first thing in the morning.

The next morning I called the phone number I had taken off the website the night before.

"California Impact Program, may I help you?"

I gave the young lady that answered the phone the details of my situation, and she asked me if I had a fax number. I gave her my 800 fax number, and she said I would be receiving a form to fill out and then fax back to her office. The fax came through within an hour, I filled it out immediately and then faxed it back. Within thirty minutes someone called me on my cell. These people didn't waste time!

I learned that the closest place I could go to have my prostate checked on their state program was the University of California, San Francisco. The young lady told me their office would fax the Urology Department in UCSF by the end of the day, and for me to call the UCSF Urology office the next day. I wrote down the phone number she gave me and thanked her for her help.

I called UCSF the next morning and made an appointment to visit them the following week.

"Honey," I called out. "Do you want to go to San Francisco next week with me to see a Urologist about my prostate?"

"I love San Francisco. Let's go."

I called my ITEX barter office in Medford, OR and asked my broker what hotels they had in San Francisco. "Queen Anne's Hotel is a nice place to stay. Look it up on the internet and let me know if you want to stay there next Wednesday night. You can see your doctor the next morning."

I called Patti and asked her to come into my office to check out the Queen Anne's Hotel. It looked beautiful, so I made the reservation with the ITEX office.

August 8, 2007

The following Wednesday we drove to San Francisco and checked into the Queen Anne. I learned it was over one hundred years old and was originally a boarding and finishing school for young women. The decorations were late 18th Century.

The hotel didn't have its own restaurant, so we asked at the bellman's desk where we could get some dinner. He told us to drive down the hill one block and then hang a right on Fremont St. and we'd find a number of good restaurants.

We did so and stopped at a nice dinner house on the second corner. We enjoyed a nice dinner and then returned to the hotel for a good night's sleep. We were both tired from the six hour drive from Lake Shastina. My doctor's office appointment was for 10:00 A.M. the next morning.

We drove the 1.5 miles to 1600 Desiderada Drive the next morning to the UCSF Medical Center. We had to circle the block twice before we found parking in the high rise parking structure across the street from the Medical Center.

My appointment was with Dr. Shinohara, one of the Urologists who had originally developed the new Brachy Therapy treatment procedures used today. Patti waited in the waiting room while I saw Dr. Shinohara for several tests. We were free to return home.

By noon we had crossed the Bay Bridge and out of the city and the heavy traffic.

I had to come back in about two months, so we decided we would stay for two days next time so we could take some time to see the city.

We arrived home around 6:00 P.M., had a nice dinner, and then turned in for the night. It had been a long two days.

Labor Day Weekend we stayed home and relaxed. I played some golf while Patti drove into her Mom's house in Yreka and visited for a while. We seldom liked to travel on three day or four day weekends, due to the increased traffic on the highways, and air travel is such a pain these days!

Fall at Lake Shastina is beautiful. The temperature during the day is around a high of 75 to 80 degrees.

October 16, 2007

I was due to return to San Francisco for my next prostate tests the next day. Patti was looking forward to seeing some sights in the city this trip, so I made reservations for the evening of the 16th of October at Tarantino's Restaurant on the Wharf on ITEX. Of course we would be staying at the Queen Anne again on ITEX for both the night of the 17th and the 18th of October.

My appointment with Dr. Shinohara involved a few more tests on my prostate, and some tests just to make sure I would not encounter any problems during the actual surgery. In other words, I was otherwise healthy enough to go through the radiation seeding process.

That night we walked around the San Francisco Wharf, and Patti bought a few souvenirs. She bought me a computer disk filled with pictorial scenes of San Francisco Bay and we bought some shot glasses with various scenes of San Francisco.

Dinner at Tarantino's was delicious. We both had fillet and lobster tail with baked potato and asparagus. The view of the fishing boats moored along the wharf gave us an aura of past trips out to sea, with a safe return.

December 25, 2007

Christmas that year was in Yreka, at Margaret's house. Katy and Jim had driven up from La Jolla, and Patti's son Mick drove up from Palm Springs. My sons drove in from their colleges. Pete brought some footage from his independent film, **SPIN OF FABRICATIONS**, and the living room filled up with family to watch the footage on the big screen TV.

Muriel was the only family member to stay in her room while everyone else watched the movie footage. What a bitch! If my son's film makes his career in the movie industry, I can just hear her now, "Pete was lucky."

February 2, 2008

Patti was dejected because Carol had not been able to bring the boys down from Washington for Christmas.

"Why don't you fly up there for a few weeks, Honey, and visit?"

"It's too expensive to fly, Pete."

"No, it's not. I'll look into the flight schedule. When would you like to leave?"

"In two days would be perfect, Baby. Thanks so much."

Patti flew out of Medford the morning of February 4, 2008. She had a stopover in Portland and then on the Spokane where Carol and Nolan picked her up for the three hour drive to Winthrop.

She called me at 10:00 P.M. after arriving at their house. She said it was cold, with about three feet of snow on the ground. I could tell she was happy and excited to be with her grandsons again. I could hear Gage and Silas laughing in the background.

I felt warm inside. I missed Patti already, but hearing her on the phone, laughing and talking to the boys, made it all worthwhile.

She stayed in Winthrop for two and a half weeks and then flew back to Medford through Portland. I picked her up at 8:15 P.M. and on the ride home I told her I had to go to San Francisco one more time for checkups before the actual prostate seeding the end of April.

March 16, 2008

We drove south on I-5 for my last appointment with Dr. Shinohara before my prostate radiation seeding on April 30, 2008. The doctor explained to me exactly what I should expect during the surgery. If all went well, I would be in and out of surgery in an hour and a half. We'd be able to drive home within two hours after the operation.

At Patti's urging, I booked the Queen Anne Hotel for two nights, just as we had done previously. This trip we visited many tourist attractions on the San Francisco Wharf the first night we got into town. Then we turned in fairly early because I had to be at the medical center at 7:30 the next morning.

Everything went perfectly that trip for my pre-surgery meeting. We then did some sightseeing around town. I never wanted to live in a big city, but visiting all of the tourist attractions in San Francisco had its charm. It was a nice place to visit.

We drove home the next day. It was a beautiful day to drive.

April 29, 2008

We drove south from Lake Shastina the six hours to San Francisco and unloaded our bags at the Queen Anne for the fourth time in six months. This time was the real thing.

We checked in at the UCSF Medical Center at 7:15 A.M. the next morning and I was called to the waiting room within twenty minutes. Patti seemed a little anxious that morning, but when Dr. Shinohara came in and explained the procedure, she calmed down.

Two male nurses came in and wheeled me about fifty yards into the operating room, while Patti walked alongside, holding my hand. She kissed me as the nurses told her that was as far as she could go. One nurse had already given me a shot, and I was dozing off just as the nurses pushed my gurney through the double doors to the operating room.

The next thing I remembered, I was waking up in the recovery room, and Patti was standing beside my gurney.

"Hi, Baby. How do you feel?"

"A little groggy, but OK. Am I out of surgery already?"

"You are, Honey. Don't you remember anything?"

"Nope. The last thing I remember was going through the double doors to the operating room. How long was I in surgery?"

"Less than two hours. Dr. Shinohara said everything went perfectly."

"That's good. How long before we can leave?"

"Whoa. Wait a little while to make sure you are fully awake. The doctor said he would come in and check on you before he can release you."

"OK, Honey. I'm sure glad that's over with."

Dr. Shinohara came in less than thirty minutes later and asked how I felt.

"I'm ready to go home."

"Good. Let me tell you what to expect in the next few weeks."

He handed me a small plastic case shaped like a 35 mm film case, but it weighed about half a pound. He also handed me three folded filters that looked like coffee filters. He explained that I had to urinate through a filter for the next week, and if any tiny metal cylinders about 3/16 of an inch long came out and were caught in the filter, to put the cylinder in the lead-lined plastic case. I was to bring the case back with any cylinders I had in the case on my follow-up visit in one month.

"How many radioactive cylinders did you plant in my prostate?"

"Sixty-two, total."

"OK, Doc. Nice job!"

"Any time. Now I need you to go to the men's bathroom and urinate, so I know everything is functioning properly."

I did as he instructed and then came back and told him everything was working just fine.

He gave me his card and told me to call his office if I had any problems, or if I had any questions. I thanked him and then got dressed. Patti helped balance me as we walked out of the building and to the Blazer on the fifth level of the parking garage.

"Do you feel good enough to drive, Baby?"

"I feel great, Honey. Let's go out to dinner at Tarantino's, then back to the Queen Anne for some fun."

"Should you be messing around after having sixty-two radioactive seeds put in your prostate?"

"Probably not. I guess we should have asked the doctor that question!"

June 2, 2008

That morning my cell phone rang; it was Muriel.

"Peter, this is Muriel."

"What can I do for you, Muriel?"

"You can tell me why you're having your Verizon cell phone bill mailed here at the house to Patti!"

"What are you talking about? My cell phone bill comes here at our house."

"Then why is Patti's bill for her phone being mailed here?"

"What makes you think it is her cell phone on my plan that you are looking at?"

"It's right here in front of me!"

"Muriel, what you are looking at is probably an old bill for Patti's cell phone from before we got together four years ago. It is not the bill for her cell phone that is included on my plan."

"Are you sure?"

"Yes, Muriel, I am sure. Goodbye."

God help save me, save us, from that woman, and I use the term loosely!

June 3, 2008

That spring and summer we upgraded a number of things in the house. Patti had asked me if we could get a bigger bed. We had had the queen-sized bed ever since we had moved into the apartment in Palm Springs in 2004.

We went shopping in Yreka for a new bed and bought a king-size bed at Black's Furniture. Their personnel delivered the bed the next day at our house at Lake Shastina. We moved our old bed into the guest room and moved that older queen-sized bed into Julie's bedroom in Yreka.

Patti had also mentioned to me how slow the water pressure had gotten in both showers. I drove into Yreka and bought two new shower heads with adjustable controls. We could now run five different types of spray, from a massage setting to a hard spray.

Anything I could do to make her happier in the house was worth the cost. A new window air conditioning unit kept the master bedroom cooler, so that room became her favorite room in the house.

July 4, 2008

That year, the city of Yreka was celebrating our Independence Day with fireworks at the County Fairgrounds at 9:00 P.M. Patti and I drove into Yreka at 7:00 that evening for dinner at her Mom's house. Then we all jumped into two vehicles and drove one mile to the fairgrounds to park where we could see the fireworks easily without getting out of the cars.

Patti and I drove back to Lake Shastina at 10:30 that night and turned in early. The next few weeks we spent some time repairing the few bare spots that had not filled in in our back yard and generally fixing up the outside of the house.

When we had moved into the house in August of 2006, there was nothing but bare dirt and sage brush surrounding the house. We had purchased the fertilizer and the grass seed during the fall of 2006 and after a year and a half, the yard was looking pretty good.

Patti and I had shared the chore of mowing the lawn during the eighteen months. The yard had become so full that the deer kept lying down on the grass to rest and turned the grass brown in some spots as a result.

July 28, 2008

The next item Patti asked me if we could buy for the house was a big-screen TV. The TV in the master bedroom was a 20-inch RCA flat screen that weighed a ton.

We drove to Wal-Mart together and picked out a forty-two inch Vizio TV. We decided to put it in the master bedroom, because Patti could now relax in her new king-sized bed, enjoy the cool temperature from the new air conditioner, and watch her game shows on the new, larger TV!

She was in seventh heaven. And I was happy because she was happy.

August 3, 2008

The first week in August, Muriel talked Patti into asking me to drive them to Crater Lake, Oregon. I had never seen Crater Lake and had heard how amazingly blue the water looked from the rim of the crater. We took my Blazer out of Yreka and drove north into Oregon, then northeast on Route 62 toward Crater Lake.

We arrived at the Ranger Station and tourist center at noon, picked up some brochures and a map and drove to the rim. The tourist center was quite interesting and had a display showing how the crater had been formed during the last 7,500 years.

By the time we returned to Yreka, it was getting dark. We had dinner at Margaret's house and then Patti and I drove home to our house at Lake Shastina.

August 14, 2008

Muriel invited everyone in the family to go to Grants Pass, Oregon that day to ride the Hell's Excursion Jet Boats on the Rogue River. That does not mean she intended to pay for everyone. I paid the $35 per person for myself, Patti, and my son, Pete.

Muriel, Julie, Margaret, Katy, Patti, my son, Pete, Julie's son, Gerald and his one-year-old daughter were included in the group.

The jet boat ride was entertaining, exciting, and informative. For example, we rode the jet boat through the very same canyon where John Wayne and Katherine Hepburn rode the raft with all of the dynamite in True Grit.

Bald eagles were to be seen everywhere! The country was beautiful. Patti had the biggest smile on her face than I had seen in months. The noise of the engines drowned out anything Muriel tried to say, so it was one of the best days of the year!

Unfortunately, the happiness was not to last. Nine days later the roof would fall in on our happy home.

PART FOUR – Heart Attack

August 23, 2008

It was Patti's fifty-fifth birthday today. I wished her Happy Birthday when she awakened and asked her if she wanted to go out to dinner that night to celebrate.

"That would be nice."

But as the day progressed, Patti said she did not feel very well. She spent most of the day in bed, watching her favorite game shows. At around 5:00 P.M., I asked her if I could cook her something for dinner. She said she was not hungry and would eat something later if she felt hungry.

She went to bed early that night.

August 24, 2008

The next morning, I asked her if she wanted to go out to Sunday brunch to celebrate her birthday, but she said she was still feeling poorly. Around noon I heard her vomiting in the bathroom. I knocked on the bathroom door and asked if I could get her anything.

"Thanks, Honey, but I just want to sleep."

"OK, Baby. I'll watch some football in the living room so you can sleep. Let me know if I can get you anything, OK?"

"I will."

Two hours later I heard her vomiting again and I went to the bathroom door once again. "Honey, can I do anything for you?"

"My chest hurts and it's not getting any better."

"Do you want to go see the doctor?"

"It's Sunday, Honey."

"I know, but we can go to the Emergency Room at the hospital."

"I just want to sleep."

The rest of the day Patti tried to sleep, but was in too much pain. At 8:00 P.M. she came into the living room and asked if I had any kind of sleeping pill. I found some Tylenol P.M. and gave her two of them. She went into the bedroom and tried to sleep.

I was just dozing off on the couch around midnight when Patti came into the living room and said, "Honey, I think we should go to the hospital."

"OK. Put something warm on and let's go."

I helped her out to my Blazer and then started the engine. I drove out of the driveway and Patti leaned over and put her left arm around my right arm, and her right hand on my right hand.

As I drove the thirty minutes to Yreka, Patti said, "I love you, Pete."

"I love you, too, Honey. I won't let anything bad happen to you."

"I know you won't. You always take care of me. You're my best friend."

She became very quiet, so I squeezed her hand for assurance while I drove.

I parked in front of the Emergency Room entrance at Fairchild Medical Center in Yreka at 12:30 that night. No one was visible. We went into the Emergency Room, and I told the first female nurse I saw that Patti had been vomiting all day Saturday and then again all day Sunday. I then told her that Patti had been complaining of chest pain starting Sunday afternoon.

She helped Patti into a gurney in the center of one of the rooms. A male nurse came into the room. "If she has been vomiting all day long, her esophagus is probably irritated. That would cause the chest pain."

I told him not to make light of her chest pain complaint, because she very seldom ever complained enough to go to a hospital. I suggested that he take her complaint about chest pain seriously.

The male nurse left the room and the one female nurse was standing with her back to Patti, setting up a drip bag from the ceiling. I was standing beside Patti while she sat up in the gurney.

The nurse, without looking back from hanging her drip bag, asked me to leave the room because I was in the way, and to go sit in the waiting room around the corner.

I did not trust the way the nurse was acting, with her attention elsewhere. I only trusted myself to watch Patti, so I told the nurse I would sit down on the chair in the room, ten feet from Patti and the gurney.

That decision on my part saved her life, because about 30 seconds later Patti's body seized while the nurse was still trying to get the drip bag to work properly. She was still standing with her back to Patti. I watched as Patti's body became rigid, and then fell head first to her right, toward the floor, and away from the nurse on the other side.

I jumped up from the chair and barely got my left hand under her head and my right arm under her torso before she could hit the floor! I was able to stop her fall, but could not lift her dead weight back up to the gurney. I called for help and within a few seconds there were five nurses at my side, lifting Patti back onto the gurney.

One female nurse had a breathing bottle over her mouth, squeezing it every few seconds. A male nurse started giving her CPR, depressing her chest at a regular rate, while watching the clock and counting the seconds. At two minutes, he yelled "clear", and shocked her with the paddles.

He continued administering CPR, and at another one and a half minutes he notified the others on the team that he was going to shock her again. He was counting down, "five, four, three...." when Patti's body reacted and she took a big breath inward.

She was alive!

The team of nurses wheeled Patti into another room and hooked her up to life support. I was told they would scan her to see exactly what had happened and try to determine how long her brain had been without oxygen. I told them I would call her family and notify them of the events of that night.

I reached Patti's Mom's house at about 1:30 A.M. and told them we were at the hospital. They arrived about thirty minutes later.

We were informed by one of the doctors that they planned to have Patti transported to Rogue Valley Hospital in Medford, Oregon by medic chopper within a few hours. After I waited at the Yreka hospital with Margaret, Muriel, and Julie, Patti's cousin, for three hours, the Medic chopper crew arrived. I drove Margaret to her house for a few minutes to pick up some additional clothes and then we drove to Medford.

When Margaret and I arrived at Rogue Valley Hospital, we were instructed to wait outside Surgery while the doctors operated on Patti and inserted a stint to open a collapsed artery to her heart.

After that surgery, they wheeled Patti into ICU and hooked her up to the life support unit. We were told she would not wake up for at least two days. I drove Margaret back to Yreka.

The next morning I drove from Lake Shastina to Medford. Margaret, Muriel, and Julie were at the hospital. They told me that Mick, Patti's son, was flying in from Palm Springs and that Carol was driving down from Washington. Katy was also flying in from San Diego.

We tried to see Patti, but were told she was still on life support, and that they would not try to bring her out of it for at least another 24 hours.

The third day Patti was awake and the nurses told us that only two of us could go in and see her at a time. She looked drugged and completely out of it so we did not stay very long.

August 27, 2008

After the third day, I realized that I needed to have Patti signed up for the Siskiyou County CMSP (County Medical Service Provider) to help with her medical expenses due to the heart attack. I knew I had to obtain approval for her on the program before the end of August, for her to qualify. I was able to accomplish that by August 28th. As a result, CMSP was able to cover about $180,000 of her medical bills and the $19,000 cost for the medic chopper from Yreka to Medford.

I was scheduled to have full knee replacement surgery on my left knee at the Mt. Shasta Mercy Medical Center on September 2. I considered delaying my surgery, due to Patti still being on life support by the 2nd, but was told by her doctors she was doing fine.

September 2, 2008

I went ahead with my knee surgery on September 2. I woke up from the surgery that afternoon. An hour later my cell phone rang. It was my older brother, Scott. He informed me that our father had just passed away the night before! Dad had been in a nursing home with our Mom for over six months, and had not been doing very well. His passing was not a shock.

What did upset me was the fact that I had failed my Dad; I had not married Patti before his death. I remembered how much he was hoping that he and Mom could attend our wedding.

Scott discussed the funeral arrangements and told me not to worry about making it to the services, which were to be in Riverside, California in a few days. I would be laid up after the surgery for about three weeks.

My oldest son, Pete, came down to Lake Shastina to help me during my recovery period. I had told him I had lost my appetite after the knee surgery and not to cook much for lunch or dinner. We both mostly ate chocolate shakes, diet drinks blended in the blender for three weeks. I dropped from 217 pounds to 188 pounds in that three week period.

I was miserable being laid up in bed for those three weeks, not so much due to the pain, but because I could not drive yet, and Patti was still in the hospital in Medford, and then released to her family in Yreka. I could not visit her and was going crazy not knowing how she was. I had been told that she had suffered memory loss from her brain being without oxygen for almost four minutes.

I didn't know if she even remembered me, and if she did, how much! I did know that Carol planned to take Patti up to her house in Washington as soon as she was well enough to travel, and that thought was driving me crazy. I had to know if Patti remembered me, remembered us.

Even though I could barely move with my knee, I limped around our house at Lake Shastina looking for something I could use to make Patti a special gift. I wanted it to be a compact booklet with pictures of us, of our house, with information she could use to be independent in Washington, and not completely dependent upon her daughter.

I found a small photo album in one of my desk drawers that would suit my purposes. I spent a full day producing small photos from my laptop computer and placing them in the photo album. Then I typed information in the booklet about her bank account I had opened for her months before, so she could call the bank's toll-free number from her cell phone and check her balance. I had typed my number in the booklet for her to call when she needed money transferred into her account and she had her debit card in the booklet to use to buy her grandsons, Gage and Silas, gifts from her.

Then, to get her independence started, I placed five $20 bills into the slot on one page.

As soon as I could get around on my new knee and bend my leg enough to get into my Blazer, I took the booklet and drove to Yreka to see Patti at her Mom's house.

As I parked in front of the house and got out, I heard Patti's voice. "You look all stove up."

She was sitting on the front porch on her Mom's rocker.

"Hi, Honey."

She looked at me with a confused look on her face, as if she didn't recognize me. My knee still had the sticky tape on the surgical incision showing because it hurt too much to pull it off. As I limped up to the porch, I smiled at her, and she smiled back. I was glad to see there was recognition in her eyes.

She got up from the rocker and walked through the front door with me. I was in a lot of pain, but tried not to let it show. My head was also disoriented from my pain medication, two Norco tablets every four hours.

I sat down at the dinner table with Margaret and watched Patti walk around in the kitchen. I was still studying her, to see if I could detect differences from before the heart attack. Just as I was feeling all alone, like she did not know me, she came over, sat down next to me in a chair, and reached out with one hand and held my right hand and squeezed it. I looked at her and she smiled again while looking in my eyes.

I took out the small paper bag I had brought with me, and handed Patti six DVDs of her favorite movies. I told her I had heard she was going to go north to Carol's house for a while and I wanted her to take the six movies with her. Her favorite, Romeo and Juliet was on the top and she noticed it. "Romeo and Juliet, my favorite!"

Then I handed her the photo booklet, opened it, and then went through each page with her explaining that I didn't want her to forget about our relationship while she was in Washington. Her hand squeezed mine once again and she smiled. I then went through the pages that showed her bank account information, her cell phone information so she could call me whenever she needed money deposited into her account, and the slot with the $100 cash in it.

She thanked me for being so thoughtful.

I promised myself that I would not bring up the fact that I knew it was a bad idea for Carol to take her Mom away from Yreka, and from me. I had had that conversation on the phone already with Katy, and she had asked me not to bring it up.

But I knew the trip was a mistake. First of all, Carol's Dad, Patti's ex, Mick, was already living in her home in Washington. And I knew Patti would go crazy having to be around Mick all the time. Mick was the one person Muriel would not allow in their house as well. But I didn't place much stock in what Muriel wanted. She was one messed up piece of work, a "know-it-all" with whom you could not discuss any topic without her telling you how much of an expert she was on the subject. And the sad thing was that she rarely knew anything about anything!

Another reason I did not want Patti to go to Carol's was because Carol smoked and Mick smoked. Patti's doctor had told her that if she did not stop smoking she would die! But Carol told me she had quit smoking, and so had Nolan. I didn't believe a word of it.

I still tried to convince the family that she should not leave Yreka. But what did I know? Trying to explain anything to Muriel and to Julie, the cousin, was like beating your head against the wall! I don't know how many times I heard Muriel, the all-time Old Maid of the family, tell me that I spoiled my oldest son, Pete, by encouraging him to dream about becoming a famous movie director. "Tell him to get a real job like digging ditches or waiting tables."

Muriel, who was too afraid to even answer the door when she was supposed to go on her very first and only date with a man, was always giving advice to others who had children, on how to raise them!

So, no one in the family considered that I might know what I was talking about when discussing Patti going to live with Carol and her ex! But before I returned to our house at Lake Shastina, I went over the information in the photo booklet one more time with Patti and reminded her how to use her cell phone to call me, especially if she needed money transferred into her account. I did not want her to be totally dependent upon Carol while she was in Washington.

I said goodbye to Patti and gave her a hug. Then I went out to my Blazer before I fell apart. I could feel the tears starting to appear and wanted to leave before that happened.

September 15, 2008

Carol left Yreka with Patti, heading for her home in Washington. I learned many weeks later from Patti that Carol had immediately lit a cigarette in the car as soon as they were out of sight from Margaret's house, even though Patti's doctor had told her she must quit smoking or she would die.

It was two days before I tried calling Patti on her cell phone. All I got was her voicemail. She had completely forgotten about having her cell phone with her or how to turn it on. So I called Carol's house phone.

"Hello."

"Hi, Carol. It's Pete. Did you guys get home OK?"

"Yeah, of course."

"May I talk to your Mom?"

"Mom, telephone!"

Then a pause. "Hello."

"Hi, Patti. It's Pete."

189

"Hi."

"I tried to call you on your cell phone, but I don't think it is turned on."

"Oh. I forget where I put it. I'm so stupid."

"Don't say that, Honey. Your brain was just damaged a little from the heart attack, but it will get better and soon you'll be back to normal."

"You think?"

"I'm sure of it."

"OK, if you say so."

"I say so. I'll just call you when I can on Carol's phone, OK?"

"OK. Take care."

She hung up. I guess I couldn't hope for more that first call.

I got in the habit of calling her at least once per day, sometimes twice if I had something to discuss with her. I reminded her to use her debit card if she needed to buy anything, especially something for Gage and Silas. She loved those boys and anything I could do to help her relationship with the boys was a good thing.

I missed Patti terribly, but just hearing her voice on the phone was like a shot of adrenalin to me.

My knee was mending nicely and it was good to be able to walk without flinching with every step.

October 27, 2008

I called Patti at Carol's house around 10:00 A.M. This time Patti answered herself on the first ring. She was home alone with the boys.

"Hi, Honey. It's Pete."

"Hi. Pete."

We talked for about fifteen minutes about how she was doing. She said she was pretty confused about everything. I was surprised Carol had left her alone with the boys. After fifteen minutes, she shocked me with what she said next.

"Pete, can you come up and bring me home?" This was totally unexpected.

"Drive up there and get you?"

"Yes."

"How does Carol feel about that?"

"She doesn't want me to leave, but I can't stay here with Mick any longer. He drives me crazy, walking around in nothing but his briefs all the time, as if he had a body that anyone would want to look at."

"How does Nolan feel about you leaving?"

"He doesn't want me to leave any more than Carol wants me to leave, but I have to get out of here."

"OK, Honey. I need to do a few things for business, which I'll do tomorrow. Then I'll call you and if you still want me to drive up and bring you back, I'll drive up on Wednesday, the day after tomorrow, OK?" I didn't want to drive 750 miles all day and find out I had to fight Carol, Mick, and Nolan to get Patti out of there!

"OK. And Pete, is it OK if I stay with you?" That was another shock to me.

"Of course, Honey. After living together for the last four years, I don't think there would be a problem with you staying here."

She laughed.

"OK, Honey. We'll plan on it. I'll be up in two days. But we'll still talk tomorrow."

"OK. Bye."

My heart jumped! My brown-eyed girl wanted to come home and for the exact reasons I had told her family she would. I got caught up on my business bookkeeping that day and the next.

October 29, 2008

Wednesday morning I got on the road by 7:00 A.M.

I turned north on Highway 99 six miles from Lake Shastina and then called Bob from my cell.

"Hello."

"Hi, Bob. Guess what I'm doing."

"What?"

"I'm on Highway 97 driving north to Washington to bring Patti home."

"What?"

"Yeah. She asked me two days ago to bring her back to Lake Shastina. For the same reason I predicted she would; she could not stand living in the same house with Mick any longer."

"That's great, Dad. Good for you."

"I'll pick her up tonight. It will be dark by the time I get there. We'll just drive a little ways back, to civilization, and then get a room for the night. That will be interesting staying together in one motel room after all this time."

"Yes, that should prove interesting."

"Talk to you later, Bob."

"OK, Dad. Good luck."

As I got closer to Winthrop, Washington, I called Patti wherever I had a cell phone signal.

"Where are you? I thought you'd be here by now."

"I know, Honey. It's dark, and the traffic is moving very slowly. I'll be there in about half an hour."

"OK. Hurry."

I drove up to the house around 7:00 P.M. Patti was actually out in front of the house with a heavy winter coat on, waiting for me, which I thought was odd. She ran behind the Blazer as I drove up the driveway. Carol was standing outside as well, yelling something at Patti. It was obvious they were still arguing about Patti's leaving.

"Hi," I said as I got out of the Blazer. No one answered me.

Patti opened the back door of the Blazer and was putting two large plastic tubs with her clothes in them into the Blazer. Then she walked over to Carol and hugged her daughter. Carol was crying and screaming that she had failed her mother. Patti got in the right hand seat, closed the door, and said, "Let's get out of here."

I backed down the driveway and headed south back to town. I placed my right hand on her left knee and said, "Hi, Baby."

"Hi."

"I thought we'd drive about an hour back to a larger town, then get a room for the night."

"That sounds good to me."

"I have missed you so much, Honey," I said.

"I missed you, too."

We drove in silence for the next 45 minutes, watching for deer. When we reached the main highway, I saw lights 200 yards to the left and drove toward them. I saw a sign to a motel and turned toward it. I pulled up in front of a dimly lit motel, got out, and walked to a door marked "Office".

"Hi,"

"Hi. What can I do for you?"

"We need one room, non-smoking." I had forgotten to ask Patti if she still smoked.

We entered the room and Patti noticed the NO SMOKING sign. "A non-smoking room?"

"I forgot to ask you if you were still smoking."

"No problem. I don't smoke much anymore and if I do I can go outside."

Patti started getting undressed and into her pajamas. I was glad to see she still undressed in front of me. As she put her pajama top on, my babies stood out as perky as ever. I couldn't help it. I walked up to her, stooped down, and kissed the left nipple, and sucked it into my mouth just for a second. She smiled and then buttoned her top.

As she climbed into the queen bed and under the covers, I said, "Honey, I can't believe you stayed in the same house with Mick for as long as you did."

"How long was I there?"

"Five and a half weeks."

"Five and a half weeks? It felt like six months!"

I got into bed and turned toward her. "It feels good to lay beside you again, Honey."

"Yes it does," she replied. She put her right hand on my chest, pulled up close to me, and was asleep within ten seconds. I thought about everything that had transpired that day. I had so many thoughts going through my head; it took me over an hour to fall asleep.

The next morning we drove south through the state of Washington without speaking, until we stopped for gas. I hate to admit it, but we were so comfortable together that we were like an old couple, not having to speak to know what the other is thinking. For the rest of the day, we just relaxed and enjoyed the silence for the ten hours it took to return to Lake Shastina.

October 30, 2008

We had been home for one day and were back to our relaxed, comfortable mode. Patti was cooking dinner when her cell phone rang.

"Hello."

I could tell it was Carol on the other end. I could tell Patti was not pleased with the conversation. In fact, she could not get a word in herself, so she handed the phone to me and said, "Here, you talk to her."

I took the phone and said, "Hello."

"Pete. We're supposed to get my Mom's disability check delivered up here, not down there."

"Carol, what are you talking about?"

"I applied for Mom to get her disability check in town here and we should have it mailed here to my house. Not to your house down there."

"Carol, I don't know anything about any disability check for your Mom and why are you arguing about it on the phone? Your Mom doesn't need the stress."

She started rambling on about Patti's disability check and wouldn't let me say anything, so I hung up. Twenty seconds later, Patti's cell phone rang again. I answered it.

"Pete, this is Mick. Let me tell you why we should get Patti's disability check mailed here."

I hung up the phone and put it down on the counter. It rang again, and I let it ring.

"That was weird. Why are they bugging you about a disability check?"

"I don't know."

We dropped the subject. I had learned long ago not to try to figure out Mick's or Carol's way of thinking. Patti and her mother, in my opinion, were the only two people in that family with any common sense at all, and Patti had always had more common sense than I did myself. More often than not, I would ask her opinion about things, including my own family's decisions and her advice usually made sense to me. Most people follow their own family members' advice without giving it any thought, just because they are family.

Prior to her heart attack, Patti always knew when to follow her family's opinion or advice and when to tell them they didn't know what they are talking about. She especially did that with Muriel, which made me proud of her. Muriel never hesitated to state her uninformed opinion about men, even though she had never had any relationship at all with any man. When she gave such advice to Patti, Patti had the common sense to tell Muriel that she was full of s**t.

November 3, 2008

I contacted an attorney in Redding, California, about looking into having Patti approved for disability, so she could start receiving funds from the state because of her mental confusion and memory loss after the heart attack.

I paid the attorney a $1,200 retainer, for which he guaranteed success in his efforts to have her approved for disability. As far as I was concerned, it was a done deal.

After all, the attorney said he had never failed to obtain disability status for his clients in the previous 18 years and he would return the $1,200 retainer if he failed to accomplish that goal in Patti's case.

November 16, 2008

I took Patti to Dr. Parker's office in Mt. Shasta to get his opinion of whether or not she qualified for disability. Patti adored Dr. Parker. He had prepared a mental test for her to take, by writing down her answer to each written question.

She took about five minutes to answer the questions. Dr. Parker came in and looked over her answers. At the first answer, he laughed!

"What's so funny?" I asked.

"The first question I asked her to write one complete sentence, with a subject, a verb, and an object. She wrote, "My doctor is the best doctor in the world."

Patti smiled at me as he read her answer.

She did fairly well on the test, the only wrong answer being the name of the medical center next door. Dr. Parker said she was doing very well under the circumstances.

Patti thanked the doctor by giving him a hug. She was one of his favorite patients. We then drove back to Lake Shastina.

When we returned home, I called my attorney in Redding. He had set up a doctor's appointment for Patti in Redding for January 28, 2009, 8:00 A.M. The attorney said that this particular doctor was a specialist in mental damage after a heart attack and that his diagnosis would guarantee approval of Patti's disability application.

I told Patti that I had marked it on my calendar.

December 17, 2008

I drove Patti to her heart doctor's office in Medford, Oregon for her follow-up appointment. Her doctor told her she was doing great, but that she had to give up smoking. His exact words to her were, "Patti, if you don't quit smoking, there is a 50 percent chance you will not live for another year!" She promised him she would give up cigarettes.

As we drove south on Interstate 5, Patti called her Mom on her cell and told her, "Mom, the doctor says that I am doing so well, I don't have to see him again for a whole year."

OK, so her brain had a little problem understanding things. It had only been three and a half months since the heart attack. She had the rest of her life to get better.

On the drive back to Yreka, I asked her if she'd like to stop and have lunch with Pete on our way through Ashland. "Sure. That sounds nice."

I called Pete and we agreed to meet for lunch at the China Panda restaurant right across the street from his house in Ashland in thirty minutes.

He was standing right outside the restaurant when we drove up and parked. The three of us were eating pork ribs when Patti's cell phone rang. She answered it; it was Carol.

As she talked to Carol during lunch, I was only a foot away and could hear both ends of the conversation. "Mom, Pete doesn't know what he is doing! He doesn't know how to get you your disability benefits at all. He'll just screw it up!"

"Honey, can you tell Carol you will call her back, and hang up your phone, so we can enjoy lunch with Pete?"

She did as I asked, and we continued enjoying listening to Pete talk about finishing his independent movie. Patti's phone rang again. This time it was Muriel.

"Patti, Pete doesn't know what he is doing with regard to getting you approved for disability! Let me take care of it for you."

"Muriel, Pete has more experience than you do in business and I have complete confidence in him."

"But I'm your sister and I should be the one who takes care of you! I can get your disability for you, not him."

I once again asked Patti to hang up the phone so we could enjoy lunch with Pete. She did as I asked.

Talk about the ultimate irony! There was Carol calling Patti on the cell phone that I got her, and calling the 800 number I had arranged to ring on Patti's cell phone, so Carol didn't have to pay for the call, telling Patti I didn't know what I was doing! And right after Carol called, Muriel did the same thing.

After paying the check and saying goodbye to Pete, we headed back to Yreka in the Blazer. My patience with her "family" was about to end. What I did next has haunted me for over a year, because I believe something snapped in Patti's brain as a result of my decision.

"Honey, I have been patient with your family, but I can't continue to do so. Before your heart attack, you had the common sense to tell your daughter and Muriel when they didn't know what they were talking about. I couldn't help but hear them both telling you on your cell phone at lunch that I didn't know what I was doing with regard to getting your disability benefits approved. I am fed up with their stupidity! You have to decide if you want me to take care of you or not."

I could tell she was taken aback with my attitude at that moment, so I tried to calm down. It was the first time I can recall ever raising my voice to her, but I was so fed up with Muriel's stupidity, and Carol's lack of faith in me to take care of her Mom, that I had to say what was on my mind. Maybe they were both too stupid to even recognize, or admit, that I had saved Patti's life that night, by trusting my own instincts, and not the nurse's!

I honestly think something snapped in Patti's head that day, caused by my verbal attack on her family.

When we got to Yreka, I suggested that I drop her off at the local Wal-Mart so she could finish her Christmas shopping she had mentioned that morning. I had a few errands to run myself.

"Just take me to my Mom's. I want to stay there for a few days and visit her."

I couldn't talk her into coming home with me, so I stopped in front of her Mom's house. She got out and walked to the front door. I drove home to Lake Shastina alone.

The next morning I called Patti on her cell and asked her if I could take her out to lunch.

"That would be nice."

"I'll pick you up at 11:30, Honey."

"OK. I'll be ready."

She was standing on the front porch as I drove up. She got in the front seat and leaned over to kiss me. We drove to the China Dragon, the only restaurant you could usually depend on being open in Yreka those days.

We sat down and ordered General Chicken and fried rice. As the waitress brought our food, I apologized to Patti for my comments to her about her family the previous day. "Just don't attack my family. I love my family and don't want to hear you say anything bad about them!"

For the next thirty minutes I tried to tactfully explain to Patti that I had a guarantee from my attorney that he would get her approved for her disability application, but every time I started a sentence, she would say, "Don't attack my family. I love my family."

I finally gave up trying to explain my feelings to her. I paid for lunch and we left. I asked her if she would come home to our house at Lake Shastina with me, but she said she was staying with her Mom through Christmas. I gave in and dropped her off at her Mom's house, kissing her goodbye before she got out of the Blazer.

We talked on the phone the next few days, but I could tell something had changed in her head.

December 21, 2008

My cell phone rang the first thing in the morning. It was Bob. "Dad, something is going on. I don't know what it is, but Aunt Muriel just asked me if I could bring her and Aunt Patti out to your house. She didn't say why. Do you know anything about it?"

"That's news to me. I guess we'll find out why when you get here. I'll see you then."

"OK, Dad. See you soon."

I was watching a golf tournament on TV when Muriel walked through the front door about forty-five minutes later. She didn't say a thing. She had two large plastic containers in her hands and walked right past me toward the master bedroom.

"Muriel, may I help you?"

No reply. She kept on walking.

Bob and Patti came through the front door next. "Hi, Honey. What's going on?"

Patti was crying. I looked at Bob for some indication of what was happening, but he just shrugged his shoulders. I asked Patti again what was wrong.

"You want me to move out of the house!"

"No I don't, Honey. Where did you get that idea?"

"That's what you said."

"Honey, I never said that. I told you that I have missed you not being here. I want to spend the rest of my life with you. I want to grow old with you."

I pulled her close to me and hugged her tight. She wouldn't stop crying.

Meanwhile, I could hear dresser drawers opening and closing in the master bedroom.

"Bob, come with me. I may need a witness." I walked down the hall to the master bedroom. Bob and Patti followed.

"Muriel, what's going on?"

"I'm just doing what Patti asked me to do. She says you want her to move out of the house."

"I wonder who put that thought in her head!"

"Not me. I'm just following Patti's wishes."

I turned to Patti. "Honey, do you want to move out?"

"No, but you said that's what you wanted."

"I never said that, Honey. I want you to stay with me, forever if that's what you want."

"I'm so confused," she said as she sobbed. "I don't know what to think."

Muriel continued to empty Patti's drawers in one of our dressers, putting her clothes into one of the plastic containers.

"Muriel, stop it, now!"

"I'll just get some underwear and socks that she needs at Mom's."

"Muriel, get out of my house." I was close to putting my fist in her face.

She took the two plastic containers with Patti's clothes and headed for the front door. Bob was consoling Patti. I put my arm around her shoulders and walked to the living room with her.

"Honey, believe me. I don't know why you would think that I wanted you to move out, but that is not true. I love you and I want to be with you for the rest of our lives. Will you believe that?"

"I don't know what to believe. I'm all messed up. Muriel said you wanted me to move away, so she said we would come out here and get my things."

"Listen; let's just forget about it right now. Your things will be safe here. You just get better and when you're not so confused, we'll talk. OK, Honey?"

"OK."

Bob walked Patti out to his Saturn Vue, where Muriel was sitting in the front, right seat by herself. What a bitch!

If I had done at that moment what I was thinking of doing to her, they'd lock me up and throw away the key! Maybe not.

Patti got in the back seat. Bob came over to me and we talked while standing outside his Saturn.

"Dad, let me take them back to Yreka and calm done. I'll try to find out why Patti is so confused."

"Bob, you and I know why she is confused. Muriel has been telling her what to think and do."

"I know, Dad. Everybody just needs to calm down."

"OK, Bob. You take them back to Yreka."

"OK, Dad. You take care."

I knocked on the Saturn window and waved to Patti. She looked up.

"I love you, Honey. I'll see you later."

She was still crying, but waved to me as they drove off.

December 25, 2008

Katy had called me the night before and asked me if I'd like to come by her Mom's house for Christmas Day. I said, "Sure."

I had put together five pictures of her and the boys in a picture frame to give to Katy for Christmas. I had gifts for Pete and Bob as well.

Two days earlier I had gone by the local travel agency and picked up something special for Patti and was anxious to give them to her.

I arrived at Margaret's house around 11:00 A.M. I noticed that most of the presents that had been under their Christmas tree were gone. It was obvious they had already opened most of their presents

Margaret, Patti, Katy and Bob went into the living room, so I joined them. Katy grabbed a gift from under the tree and gave it to me. "Merry Christmas, Pete."

"Thanks Honey." I opened the gift. It was a pair of warm, tan, winter slippers.

"Thanks, Patti. These will come in handy this winter."

Patti smiled when she saw I liked the present.

I handed a wrapped gift to Bob. He opened it and saw it was a set of Stetson men's cologne. "Thanks, Dad."

Katy opened her gift from me and noticed it was a picture frame with five pictures of her and her sons. "Thanks, Pete. But I didn't get you anything."

"Not a problem. I just thought you'd like those pictures.

I handed Patti's present to her. She opened it and saw it was a calendar from me showing that we were going to Hawaii in February for a Christmas present to both of us.

Patti had never been to Hawaii. I had lived there for three years from 1959 to 1963, when my dad was stationed there with the Navy. I had been back about six additional times on vacation or business with the Senior PGA Tour.

Patti smiled at the idea of finally going to Hawaii. She understood she needed to go through the four travel magazines I had put in her present, so she could let me know which island, or islands, she wanted to visit on her first trip there; the magazines covered the big island of Hawaii, Oahu, where most of the population was located, Maui, and Kauai.

The rest of the day we all visited and ate dinner. I was reluctant to leave that evening, because I missed Patti terribly, but I had to drive home alone. She was not ready to come back yet.

December 27, 2008

I called Margaret's house and asked Margaret if I could take her out to lunch.

"Sure! Where do you want to eat?"

"How about the China Dragon?"

"Perfect."

"I'll be there at 11:30 A.M."

"I'll be ready."

I drove to Yreka and arrived at Margaret's house at exactly 11:30 A.M. As soon as I opened the front door, Margaret was standing there with a sweater over a dress. I walked her to the Blazer, looking around to see if I could see anyone else in the house. No one was visible.

We sat in the first booth to our left in the dining room. We each ordered General Chicken and fried rice, and the hot tea.

"Margaret, I'm having a tough time dealing with everything right now. It is tough...."

"Losing your best friend. I know." She had finished my sentence for me.

"Yes. I don't know what to do."

"Pete, you need to let Patti decide for herself what she wants out of the future."

"I know, Margaret. But I'm afraid she will get the wrong advice if she stays in town with Muriel and Julie. Excuse me for saying so, but I know Patti better than anyone else in your family. You only know her when she is in Yreka. You don't know how she has loved living out in the world outside this small town."

"That may be, but right now my advice to you is to let her heal on her own and decide what she wants to do."

"OK, I'll try to do that."

We ate our lunch and made small talk while finishing our meal. I took Margaret back to her house and walked her to her door.

"Thanks, Margaret, for the advice. I'll try to follow it."

"I think it's best, Pete."

January 10, 2009

Three days earlier I had informed everyone in the family that I wanted to call for a family meeting at Margaret's house for January 10. Margaret was in La Jolla with Katy and Jim. The purpose of the meeting was to agree on the best way to care for Patti, and help her regain her memory.

I had prepared a list of items to discuss at the meeting and had given each family member a copy ahead of time. Muriel, Julie, Patti's son Mick, and Patti would be there.

I arrived at the house at 5:00 P.M. I could feel a cold chill in the air as I walked in. No one would look me in the eye. I had the feeling I was wasting my time, but what the heck. I was already there.

I called the meeting to order and everyone sat down at the dining table. I covered the past four months, from the night of the heart attack to the present. I informed everyone that I was working on Patti's disability application through an attorney in Redding. I explained that I would be taking Patti to Redding the night of the 21st of January, so we could make her 8:00 A.M. doctor's appointment the next morning. This was the doctor's appointment that had been set up by the State of California and not the doctor's appointment that my attorney in Redding had set up.

I watched Patti closely during the meeting. She seemed uneasy and was not paying attention. Julie was acting strangely as well, as was Muriel. I had the feeling they were all going through the motions of a family meeting, but that they had rehearsed ahead of time their own agenda. When I mentioned my taking Patti to Redding the night before the January 22 doctor's appointment to get Patti's disability approved, Julie spoke up.

"We'll take care of Patti's disability. It's time she got on with her life and got over her guilt."

There it was. If Patti still felt any guilt over our affair of 1993, it was because her family kept reminding her of it!

I started to say that I had arranged for the doctor's appointment, but Muriel jumped in with, "I have been in touch with the State of California and have all the information for following through with Patti's disability application."

There it was, again. They had gone around me, to take over Patti's welfare.

"Patti, do you want me to take care of your disability application, or do you want Muriel and Julie to follow through?"

"They're my family. They will take care of me."

"OK, you two take care of seeing that Patti makes the January 22 doctor's appointment. But I have made additional arrangements for her to see another doctor, a doctor who is guaranteed to get her approved by the State."

"We'll take care of it, Pete."

That was a laugh, Muriel and Julie taking care of anything successfully.

January 15, 2009

I called the house in Yreka and told Muriel that there might be some things she could use in her dog grooming shop still left in my carport, such as the window air conditioning unit I had bought the previous summer for Patti to cool the temperature in our house.

She said she'd drive out that afternoon to look around. She showed up at 1:00 P.M. and had Patti in her truck. Patti walked right up to me and handed me the cell phone I had given her more than four years earlier.

"Pete, take this phone back. I don't want to be dependent upon you anymore."

"Hang on to it, Honey, in case you need to get a hold of me sometime."

"No, I can't be dependent upon you anymore."

She handed the phone to me and then walked out to the truck.

Talk about a rehearsed skit! I wonder which one of the old maids had Patti practice that skit before driving out to Lake Shastina.

I learned later that my son, Pete, had stopped in at the Yreka house the day before and told everyone that if they wanted Patti to move on, without me, she had to tell me herself that we were finished. In her diminished mental state, that made sense to her, and that's what she did.

I confronted Pete about what he had said the next day. "Dad, I thought I was doing you a favor. You can do so much better than Aunt Patti. Find a pretty, smart woman with whom to spend the future."

"Pete, if you knew the history Patti and I have shared, for 15 years, you might understand the meaning of a soul mate. You did not do me a favor."

That day Pete wrote a letter to Patti in Yreka, stating he was wrong in giving her the advice to leave me. But we have no way of knowing if Patti received that letter. We never did hear from her about it.

January 22, 2009

I woke up that morning remembering that Julie was taking Patti to see the doctor that the State of California mandated that she see in Redding, to determine if she deserved disability.

No one called me to let me know how it went, so I could only guess. Four days later I called Katy in La Jolla and asked if she knew anything.

"Patti was turned down by the State of California for disability."

"I knew that if I left the responsibility for getting Patti's disability approved in Muriel's and Julie's hands, they would screw things up." I hung up the phone.

I went to my laptop and emailed to Muriel's email address everything I had done to get Patti her disability approved through the Redding attorney. I figured that if the family would not allow me to get her approved, then I may as well tell them how to get her approved instead! I gave Muriel in my email the attorney's contact information and the details on Patti's doctor's appointment in Redding for the 28th of January. After all, the attorney had guaranteed me that the doctor she was going to see on the 28th would guarantee her approval by the state, or the attorney would refund my $1,200 retainer! All she had to do was to show up for the doctor's tests.

All I could do after that was hope that Muriel didn't screw things up.

January 31, 2009

I had been selling off, or should I say giving away, everything in the Lake Shastina house during the last two weeks. I was anxious to get out of there. Without Patti living with me, I didn't want to stay in the house anymore. I had advertised my "Moving Sale" in the local newspaper, with "everything goes; make offer" in the ads.

I hired a cleaning crew from Yreka to clean everything in the house and offered everything that was unsold in the house to them as a bonus. "Just take everything that is remaining in the house. You can have it."

I was anxious to get on the road to Palm Springs, play some golf and forget the past four months. I called Katy from my cell phone as I drove through Redding on I-5.

"Hi. Have you heard if Patti's been approved for disability yet?"

"I don't think she has. I told you before that she was not approved after the doctor's visit in Redding about ten days ago."

"But what about the doctor I had arranged for her to see on the 28th?"

"Did you tell Muriel about that appointment?"

"I emailed everything to her about that appointment and that it was a "done deal" if she kept the appointment."

"Pete, Muriel does not handle confrontation very well. She told me some time ago that she had blocked your email address from her computer, because she did not want to read anything from you any longer!"

"That's just great. She can't handle confrontation, so she hides with her head in the sand?" What a moron!" She has not only kept Patti from getting approved for disability, but also cost me another $1,200 retainer due to her stupidity!"

"That's Muriel for you. She just can't handle things, so she hides from them."

"That's the story of her life for the last 40 years."

February 1, 2009

I loaded some clothes and my golf clubs into the back of my Blazer and headed south on I-5 toward Palm Springs. I arrived at 8:00 P.M., after dark. I checked in at the Royal Sun Inn.

The next day I relaxed by the pool and worked on my laptop. I met quite a few snowbirds from Canada by the pool that day and enjoyed listening to strangers talk about their homes in Canada. It let me get my mind off of Patti.

I called my attorney and best friend, Gary, that evening. We met at his golf club for a drink and he explained to me that Canyon Country Club was no longer private.

"The economy has changed and the club could no longer turn down requests by the public to play here."

Gary and I agreed to meet at the club the next morning for a round of golf. We teed off at 9:00 A.M. and were able to play in less than four hours.

After a couple of drinks, I went back to the motel to take care of a little business. Gary could not play the rest of the week, because he was flying to Las Vegas on business. I called the pro shop and arranged to play at the club again the next morning.

When I showed up in the pro shop the next morning, I was paired with a Dr. Jon Andersen, a psychiatrist from Sweden with an office in New York. He told me that he knew Gary when I mentioned Gary's name.

After riding together for the first nine holes, Dr. Andersen had learned my whole story about my on and off relationship with Patti for the last 15 years. I also brought him current about Patti's heart attack and memory loss. When I told him that her family had taken Patti to live with them, he said, "Pete, that is not good."

"I have helped counsel couples for over twenty years in similar situations. It is imperative that Patti continue living where she lived before the heart attack! That is with you."

"Jon, we were never married. So I have no rights when it comes to caring for her."

"It makes no difference. What is important is that she continues life as she was living before the memory loss. That is critical to her recovery. You were not married, but Patti chose to live with you for the last four years, correct?"

"Correct."

"From what you have told me, Patti's personality was quite different from the rest of her family members. She was not satisfied with living in a small town, and liked the exciting life that larger cities could provide. She was outgoing, an extrovert, and liked meeting new people and interacting with new people. Is that about it?"

"That's about it."

"Did you try to talk the family into having both you and Patti see a counselor together, to put your lives back together as a couple?"

"I tried, Jon, but I was not dealing with rocket scientists here."

"Pete, you've heard the saying, "you can choose your friends, you can choose your lovers, but you can't choose your family. Right or wrong, you are stuck with your family."

"Of course. I have a younger sister who thinks we stole Texas, New Mexico, Arizona, and California from Mexico, and thinks we should give them back."

"You're kidding!"

"No, I'm not kidding. She also thinks we stole the rest of the continent from the American Indians. She thinks we should give it back to them."

"And just where does she suggest that 350,000,000 Americans go to live?"

"Who knows? She's kind of the outcast from the family."

"It sounds to me that Muriel is the outcast from Patti's family."

"She should be. But Patti's childlike personality since the heart attack and her memory loss has influenced her to protect everyone in her family. Two years ago she would tell Muriel to get lost when she didn't know what she was talking about."

"That's all the more reason that a professional psychiatrist needs to talk to her and to you together, as a couple. She chose you to live with for four years. You two have a history together for 16 years. If Patti is to recover fully and return to the outgoing personality she used to be, it is imperative that you get her away from her family and get counseling together."

"That's not going to happen at this point in time."

"Then mark my words, Pete, someday Patti will resent what her family is doing to her right now. She will eventually hate her family if and when she gets her memories and her personality back."

The more I talked with Jon about Patti's condition, the more excited I became about things working out for the better. I learned a lot from Dr. Andersen that day, during the round of golf and over dinner that evening. I made careful notes of his suggestions, so I could write everything down on my laptop later on.

I came away from that first meeting with a long list of things that had to be done to make sure Patti recovered fully, and properly, from her heart attack and her memory loss.

When I returned to the Royal Sun, I got busy typing a general letter of my findings, so I could personalize the information and send it to the family members who mattered. I first emailed my son, Bob, telling him how excited I was to finally have some professional advice, some direction.

Bob replied back, "Dad, that is fantastic. Now all you have to do is educate Patti's family about the importance of doing what Dr. Andersen says to do."

"Yeah! That will be Mission Impossible."

"First you have to convince Nona (Margaret) that it is important."

"I agree, but Margaret doesn't have the strength any more to take on Muriel."

"Yeah, Dad, but you have to try, for Aunt Patti's benefit."

Then I sent the same email to Katy at Jim's house. The next day I drove to Jim's house, and had a chance for a one-on-one meeting with Margaret when Jim and Katy went shopping. Once again Margaret advised me to give Patti a chance to decide for herself what she wanted in the future.

I mentioned to her my concerns that Patti would not get the chance to decide for herself what she wanted, because she was under the influence of Muriel and Julie in Yreka.

Margaret then made me feel good when she winked at me and told me she knew Muriel and Julie were not following her instructions, and were filling Patti's head with what they wanted her to think, and decide.

"Pete, mark my words, they will be sorry for not allowing Patti to think for herself."

"I hope you're right, Margaret, because Dr. Andersen warned me that Patti would not heal properly if she is taken from the same surroundings she knew before the heart attack."

Unfortunately, I learned months later that Margaret no longer had the willpower or physical strength to stand up to Muriel, and was unable to follow through with her comment about Muriel's actions to turn Patti's head away from her past relationship with me.

I remembered the day Bob had brought Muriel and Patti out to our house at Lake Shastina, clear back on December 21, 2008. Someone had convinced Patti that I wanted her to move out of our house back in December of 2008. That's why she had come into our house crying, and saying, "Pete, you want me to move out!"

I also learned in early 2009 that Muriel also put thoughts in Patti's head such as, "Patti, your relationship with Pete was based upon alcohol!" To put that thought in Patti's head is ludicrous, because Patti drank much more from 1997 through 2004, before we started living together.

After meeting and talking with Dr. Andersen, I tried to get Patti to communicate with Dr. Andersen via email, but Muriel interfered, and asked Dr. Andersen in an email, "How do you know Pete isn't stalking Patti?"

It became obvious to me in late February of 2009 that Patti would have no opportunity to heal properly as long as she was under Muriel's spell. I was not dealing with intelligent people.

As a result of that conclusion, I became more and more depressed. As Dr. Andersen had explained to me, by Patti remaining under Muriel's and Julie's influence, she would not get the opportunity for her mind to heal the way modern medical science required her to heal.

Dr. Andersen explained that, as a result, Patti would be as happy as a pig in the mud living with her family, but would never recover fully and be the person she had been previously. Another way he explained it to me was, "Ignorance is Bliss."

"Pete. Have you ever seen a Hollywood movie wherein a family member goes through a trauma, and instead of getting proper medical help, the family has that family member committed to an institution, wherein the family member lives the rest of his or her life on medication? They are drugged, so they can't think for themselves, and spend the rest of their life in blissful ignorance."

"Yes, Jon, and whenever I see that happen, I am enraged that modern medicine would allow that to happen."

"Unfortunately, Pete, it happens more often than you would believe. The medical community in European countries has recognized that realization much more than in the United States."

"In Europe, if Patti's family kept her away from the man she had chosen to live with for four years, the government would step in and make sure she could receive counseling together with you, the man she chose to live with."

Normally, every family member has the common sense to tell other family members when they are wrong. From what you told me, Patti had that common sense before the heart attack and the memory loss."

"Yes, Jon, Patti had more common sense than the next five people put together, before her heart attack."

"It is obvious to me, Pete, that Muriel and Julie are dead wrong in their actions. Making Patti continue to feel guilty about an affair you two had fifteen years ago is dead wrong. Keeping Patti from you, the man she chose to live with, whether you were married or not, is not going to allow Patti's mind to heal properly. If you lived in Europe, you could bring charges against both of them for mental abuse. Unfortunately, the United States is at least ten years behind Europe in this field."

February 8, 2009

I thanked Dr. Andersen for all of his advice, and promised I'd keep him abreast of the situation with Patti.

I decided to drive back to northern California and help my oldest son, Pete, finish producing his independent film, **SPIN OF FABRICATIONS**.

I occasionally tried to call Patti on her mother's home phone, but it became apparent that Muriel and Julie had started screening phone calls and chose not to give Patti my messages. Never before in the previous 15 years did I ever call Margaret's house in Yreka and have my call answered by an answering machine! Now every time I call, I am asked to leave a message. No one ever called me back.

PART FIVE: CONCLUSIONS

February 28, 2009

The end of February, Carol took Patti to Winthrop, Washington to live. That made me feel better, because Muriel and Julie could no longer have influence over Patti. In fact, the joke was on Muriel, because Patti was once again living in the same house as her ex, Mick. Mick was the one person that Muriel would never allow in their house in Yreka. That's how much she despised him.

It dawned on me that Carol must be very happy, because she had her mother, a live-in baby sitter, staying at her house, and she had her mother's disability check!

The one loser was Patti. Of course she would be happy. As Dr. Andersen had mentioned, ignorance is bliss. Patti was the only member of her family to go out into the world by herself, and live, instead of staying in a small town. Even Katy had not moved out of Yreka until I took her to larger cities.

Now Patti would live as if she were "drugged", living under her family's wishes, happy as a pig in the mud, never remembering the amazing woman she used to be, full of life, looking for new experiences and exciting places to visit!

March, 2009

I became very depressed, knowing that Patti's future would never include her zest for life she had once known. I wrote letters to Margaret and to Carol, asking if they could bring me up-to-date regarding how Patti was doing. They completely ignored my requests for information, and never answered my letters.

When I wrote to Carol in Winthrop, asking how Patti was doing, I sent her a picture of the white Shelby Mustang GT 500 Cobra I told her I was thinking of buying for her Mom for her birthday on August 23, 2009, if we ever got back together. We never got the chance to celebrate her birthday in 2008 because of her heart attack.

Since Patti's favorite car was her white 1994 Mustang convertible, I thought she would love the Cobra. Of course, Carol never answered my letter, and I would not be surprised if they have never allowed Patti to drive again since the heart attack. If she knew she could drive, she would also know she could jump in the car and leave them, and allowing Patti to think for herself, and have the ability to leave them, is not in the family's game plan.

Just keep Patti dumb and happy, thinking she must rely on her family for the rest of her life, and Carol will have a free baby sitter for the next fifteen years at least. So, I hope this book is successful and I'll use my first royalty check for the down payment of the Shelby for myself!

I have been so depressed over this whole situation that I asked Dr. Parker for something to help with my depression and he prescribed Lexapro for me. I took one Lexapro and was dizzy within an hour. I called Dr. Parker and told him how I was disoriented after taking a Lexapro. He had me try a Paxil tablet and it seemed to pick up my spirits without the dizziness. I usually hate taking pills, but took the Paxil to reduce my depression about losing Patti.

Dr. Parker had become upset when he heard that Patti no longer wanted to be his patient! He adored her and Patti loved Dr. Parker. Muriel's ability to hurt people had no limitations, so she did not think twice about convincing Patti to stop seeing Dr. Parker, and change doctors. Patti probably never even knew how much she hurt Dr. Parker.

He had just lost one son to suicide, and he lost his wife next when she informed him she wanted a divorce. To think that Patti no longer wanted him as her doctor was almost too much for him to handle!

June 14, 2009

Today, Robert Andrew Baumann, my youngest son, graduated from Pacific Union College in Angwin, California, with a Bachelor's degree in Theology. Family members who attended the graduation ceremony included Margaret, Katy, her daughter Kandi, Kandi's daughter, Kyrra, and her son, Cade, my oldest son, Pete, and myself. Thank God Muriel and Julie had no interest in attending!

Pete had driven down from Ashland, Oregon, with me, the day before. We stayed the night before the ceremony in one of the college dorms. Our room shared a bathroom with another room. In the morning I woke up and walked into our bathroom, to see a naked young lady in the shower! Someone had made a mistake and put five young ladies in the other room, sharing the one bathroom with Pete and me. I knocked on the other bedroom door and announced that the girls might want to put some clothes on because two men were sharing their bathroom with them.

They yelled back through the door that they appreciated the head's up, and promised they would not walk into the bathroom naked anymore..

October, 2009

I emailed Katy at Jim's house in La Jolla, asking if she had any idea how Patti was doing. Her reply:

"Pete, Patti is happy. Move on. Let it go! And by the way, Patti did finally get her disability approved."

I replied, "I'm sure she is happy. Your family has taken her away from me, away from the life she knew. But she is with her family. We both know how she feels about her family. She has her three grandchildren to fuss over, and we both know how much she loves all babies." Only Patti knows how much effort I had put into making sure she could see her grandchildren whenever she wanted over the previous four years.

My question to you, Katy, is will you ever let go? Or are you going to make your sister feel guilty for the rest of her life because she had an affair with your husband a lifetime ago? Are you ever going to recognize and admit that you drove me away with all of your criticism of me and how I ran Probe Golf? Are you ever going to admit that Patti did in 1993 what you would not or could not do, support me in my business?

"Katy, I have another question for you. Patti would never agree to marry me because she still felt guilty about hurting you. If you had forgiven her, and told her that you recognized she and I belonged together, after 15 years, we could have been married. And if we were married, your family could not have stolen her from me after the heart attack. Then I could have taken care of her the way a professional, experienced psychiatrist said she should be cared for. She would not be hidden away from me by your family!"

"My question, Katy, is this: What if you had a heart attack right now, with memory loss, just like Patti did? Since you and Jim are not married, would your family take you away from him? And would Jim fight to keep you with him?"

Katy never answered that question for me! That, in itself, says volumes!

November 16, 2009

Today Bob and I are returning from Klamath Falls, Oregon after playing 18 holes at Arnold Palmer's Running Y Golf Resort. Bob was driving his Saturn Vue and I was writing down some notes regarding my writing this book. I told Bob that I had asked his mother that question: "What if she had a heart attack, with memory loss. Would her family try to take her away from Jim, since they never married, and would Jim fight to get her back?"

Bob's answer shocked me. "Dad, Mom told me two years ago that she wished you and aunt Patti would get married, because just living together was not showing any kind of commitment toward each other."

"Bob, I find that hard to believe. If your Mom felt that way, why wouldn't she tell Patti that's how she felt? Keeping silent has made Patti feel guilty all this time. I don't believe that is how your Mom felt."

"That's what she told me, Dad."

December 24, 2009

It dawned on me this morning that one-third of Americans are obese! One-third of Americans are now one-half of all Americans! I laughed; I made a joke!

I was taking Norco for lower back pain, Paxil for depression, and Ambien to try to get to sleep at night, and hopefully not wake up at 2:00 A.M. thinking of Patti and wonder how she is doing.

I wish I could talk to Patti right now and wish her a Merry Christmas, and a Happy New Year, but her family has hidden her from me. I still wake up in the middle of the night and can't get back to sleep because I wonder if she is all right. I wish I could hear her voice once again.

Carol must be the happiest young mother in the world. She has a free baby sitter in Patti, and receives Patti's disability check every month. I'm willing to bet that Patti is on some kind of drug once again so Carol can keep her Mom "ignorant, but blissful".

Margaret and Katy tell me to move on, that Patti is happy. Of course she is happy. I know that, but that's not the point! She has three grandchildren to care for and she loves children. I wonder if her brain will ever recover sufficiently to remember who she was; the smiling, vibrant woman who went out in the world to discover what was out there. Muriel and Julie were always jealous of Patti because they were stuck in a small town, with no hope to get out and see the world.

Our greatest power is our power to choose! Today, I chose to throw away the Norco, and the Paxil, and the Ambien. I choose to live my life in the future drug-free, and move on to bigger and better things.

January 1, 2010

I am still in Ashland, Oregon, helping my oldest son finish producing his independent film, **SPIN OF FABRICATIONS**. It could have been finished months ago, but my son takes after his Dad, and is a perfectionist. Pete wrote the movie script for a philosophy class at Rogue Community College in Grants Pass, Oregon, in 2004. His professor had instructed the class to write a three to five page paper on the meaning of truth over the weekend. Pete had locked himself in his bedroom for two days, hardly stopping to eat or sleep. He emerged from his bedroom Sunday night with a 52-page movie script.

His Philosophy professor at Southern Oregon University in Ashland, Oregon read the script two years later and told Pete that if he turned it into a movie, he would write a textbook to accompany the DVD and use the two to teach philosophy nationally at institutions of higher learning. Pete came to me in 2006 and asked me to pay to produce the film. I agreed to do it. Now, three years later, it is almost finished.

To say that I am proud of Pete would be an understatement. He not only wrote the script, he directed it, filmed most of it, composed the music used in the film, and edited most of the film himself.

We opened our production company, VERADONIR (see www.veradonir.com) to produce DVDs to sell. Pete is now finally going to finish the last three college classes he needs to graduate from SOU in the spring of 2010.

He will then marry his finance, Talia, who is attending USC's cinema school, in June, and move down to Los Angeles with Talia to pursue a film-making career. I plan to move back to Palm Springs, or possibly near Boulder City, Nevada again, and expand our services and memberships at Reciprocal Golf. I might even talk Pete into directing LOVE WAS NOT ENOUGH, THE MOVIE!

January 5, 2010

My son, Peter Alan Baumann, received today the final 92-minute soundtrack of SPIN OF FABRICATIONS in CD format from the McCoy Studios in Central Point, Oregon. It was delayed because Mr. McCoy had to finish recording the voiceovers of the stars from the newest SPIDERMAN movie before completing my son's soundtrack.

Pete may very well receive an Oscar in the independent film category at the Oscars for SPIN OF FABRICATIONS. At the very least, this film should clinch for Pete a career in the film-making industry.

January 15, 2010

Right now Patti is what Dr. Andersen referred to as "dumb and happy", like a "pig in the mud". Another phrase he used was "ignorance is bliss". I'll bet she is on medication of some kind. Her family has done to Patti exactly what Dr. Andersen said they should not do, keep her away from her life before the heart attack. By doing so, they keep her from remembering her previous life, delay her recovery, and can brainwash her into being what they want her to be, at home with them instead of seeing the world.

Patti would have died on that gurney if anyone else in her family had been with her that night. Either they would have gone to the waiting room when the nurse told them to do so, or they would not have moved swiftly enough or been strong enough to stop Patti's headfirst fall to the hard floor.

I could fill this book with another thousand pages of memories of things Patti and I did together, but what would be the point? She was my best friend, first and foremost, more so than even a lover. How many of us have so many friends that we can simply turn our backs on a single one of them? I can handle Patti living with her daughter and grandsons, nearby or far away, if that is what she decides to do for herself. In this electronic age, we are only as far away as a cell phone, right?

For her family to brainwash her into being someone that they want her to be is criminal in my opinion. To tell her to forget she was my best friend, to tell her not to talk to me, is wrong on so many levels! What I would give just to be able to call her occasionally and talk, and see how she is doing. What would be wrong with that? What I have difficulty with is my not knowing how she is doing.

The Patti I knew and loved died on that gurney at the Emergency Room in Yreka the early morning of August 25, 2008. The Patti I saved from splitting her head open on the Emergency Room floor no longer has the common sense my Patti had. The Patti that was my best friend never would have left me alone the way she did, without being able to talk on the phone once in a while to see how she is doing.

I made a mental note for myself to drive by the Yreka hospital Emergency Room and find out if they ever put movable side railings on their gurneys since August 24, 2008, so someone seizing on a gurney when no one was there to catch them would not fall head first onto the floor! When I went by the hospital, they still had not installed railings on the gurneys!

I hope Patti does what she did after taking the Lexapro for six months after moving to Siskiyou County. I hope she one day gets off the drugs they have her on right now. I do not expect that anyone in Patti's family will ever thank me for saving her life that morning. No one has thanked me yet, so why should I expect it now, more than a year later? Margaret used to thank me for the many things I had done for Patti in the past. The fact that Margaret has never even acknowledged to me that she recognizes and appreciates the fact that I was able to catch Patti's fall is one reason why I am so disappointed in Margaret at this time.

If the Patti that survived for a year so far after the heart attack ever remembers what we shared together for 16 years, she might get off the drugs and give me a call and talk. I would love to hear from her and find out how she is doing. It is doubtful that will happen if she stays near Muriel and Julie, or even her daughter. Their house in Yreka looks like a pharmacy when you walk into their kitchen. Muriel must take at least fifteen different medications every day. At a young age she became obese, while working at McDonald's, yet to this day she thinks McDonald's has some of the best, nutritional food in the country! She has diabetes as a result of her eating habits, as does Julie. I'm afraid Patti will end up a diabetic from being around them, and copying their poor eating habits.

If Patty stays at her daughter's house in Winthrop, WA, she might have a decent chance to survive and thrive in the presence of her three grandchildren. Nolan Wilson saved Carol's life and her future in my opinion, when he was man enough to say he was Gage's father, and married Carol. Unfortunately, no one in that family will recognize that they failed Patti back in December of 2008, and January of 2009 when they refused to allow Patti and me to seek counseling together, as Dr. Andersen said must happen if she was to heal correctly.

January 18, 2010 – 4:30 A.M.

I woke up in the middle of the night, and couldn't get back to sleep. I was in the middle of my typical dream about Patti and me doing something we used to like. In tonight's dream we were on my Bayliner on Lake Havasu, sunbathing nude side by side on the upper deck, with a Celine Dion CD playing. Patti asked me to rub some tanning lotion on her back. I started rubbing the lotion into her skin at her shoulders, then her mid-back. Then I moved lower, rubbing her left cheek, and then her right. Then my hand moved lower, between her legs, and slowly massaged her in a clockwise motion. She moaned, and then opened the gap between her legs. After a minute of her moans she was on top of me and we made love for the next twenty minutes or more. It was almost the very same dream I had five to six times each week for the last year. I decided to get up and work on the book; I'd never get back to sleep after one of those dreams. A million thoughts were going through my head, just like the previous night.

Was I not a good friend to Patti for many, many years? Didn't I help her whenever she needed some help, of any kind? Didn't I help Carol and Mick whenever they asked me for help? I know I helped them every time Patti asked me to give them money, or to drive them someplace. Isn't that what true friends are, someone you can truly count on whenever your back is against the wall?

It's true I did not go to Patti in Boulder City, NV in 1994 when she wanted me to do so. I did not go to her in Palm Springs in 1997, when that is what she wanted. I already explained that it was my concern for my sons that kept me from going to her to live at those two times. My sons are on their way to fantastic careers as a result of my staying with them, and not letting them down.

I just remembered that I was hoping this book would help others to make the right decisions in their futures, especially when it comes to choosing a mate, and raising children.

How many young people really marry the right person today? Why do more than 50% of married couples get divorced? Is there such a person as your soul mate? If you are now divorced, is it because you never found your soul mate to marry? The Cambridge Dictionary defines a soul mate as someone, usually your romantic or sexual partner, who you have a special relationship with, and who you know and love very much. I believe it is much more than that.

I think the relationship between one person and their soul mate is similar to what we have all read about the connection between identical twins. They can almost read each other's minds, and know ahead of time what their soul mate needs or wants, and are perfectly happy giving it to them. Patti seemed to know that about me, and I definitely knew it about her.

I believe most people go through life and never meet their true soul mate. If they did, and they married their soul mate, we would not have so many divorces in our country.

If you are lucky enough to find someone you think may be your soul mate, always encourage them in what they do. Ladies, don't demand that your husband put you and your happiness ahead of everything else, including his career if he is the bread winner in the family. Encourage him in his career, first and foremost, and he will automatically place you first in his life.

Now, what about raising children? My advice, after seeing both sides of the potential successes and failures of raising children, is as follows: First, always raise your kids up when talking to them, and never put them down. Self-esteem can do wonders for children. Secondly, educate them, so they can learn all that is possible for themselves in the future, and tell them they can accomplish anything they put their minds to doing.

And finally, recognize that your greatest power is the power to choose. We can choose our friends, our lovers, and our soul mate. But we cannot choose our family members. Good or bad, we are stuck with our family members!

Therefore, choose which family members you should listen to, and which family members to ignore, if they are a bad influence on you or your children. And positively, without doubt, ignore family members' advice if that family member has no personal experience with the subject at hand!

If your sister is advising you to leave the person you chose to love, the person you chose to have as your best friend, the person you chose to have as your soul mate, make sure that family member has some experience with love, with best friends, with soul mates.

If your sister is obese because she knows nothing about proper nutrition, don't listen to her advice about what to eat. If your sister has never been on one single date with a man, don't listen to her advice about your relationship with your man.

I remember the mental torment I saw on Patti's face the day Bob brought Muriel and Patti to our house the morning of December 21, 2008. I had asked Patti why she was crying, and she said, "You want me to move out!"

Muriel, by trying to convince Patti that was true, is guilty of mental abuse in the worst way possible. When she was in our bedroom, emptying Patti's things out of her dresser and into the plastic tubs she had brought with her, I asked Bob to follow me into the bedroom to confront Muriel. I told Bob I might need a witness to what was happening. But that wasn't what I really wanted. I wanted

Bob there to stop me from wrapping my hands around Muriel's neck and squeezing the life out of her!

So, here I am at 4:30 in the morning, actually thinking of making this book into a motion picture, to better tell my story to the world. Kathy Bates; wouldn't she play a good Muriel? How about Winona Rider playing Carol? Carol always impressed me with her intelligence. She's probably the smartest one in the family at this time. She is married, with three of Patti's grandchildren so far, and has a built-in baby sitter in her Mom, and her Mom's disability check comes to her house in Winthrop. Just what Carol has always wanted! "Merry Belated Christmas, Carol!"

No woman was ever loved more by a man than Patti was by me! To this day, if I learned she was in trouble, and I had to give my life for her, I would do it in a minute. At the very least I'd get to see her one last time, and hear her voice again. She was my soul mate, and we were best friends.

All I thought of during the four years we lived together was how I could make her happy! She can't hate me for that, can she? I saved her life the night of August 24, 2008, only to lose her again. She probably doesn't even know that I saved her life that night, or how I saved her life that night. Her family has probably told her that I was no good for her, and that she is lucky to have survived living with me all those years!

Before Patti's heart attack, we had talked for hours about her hopes and goals for the future. She told me all the sights she hoped to see, from the Hawaiian Islands to the islands of the Bahamas, from a cruise to Alaska to a cruise through the Caribbean Islands. If Patti and I had been able to see a counselor together after the heart attack, like everyone in the medical community said we had to do, we would be making plans for her to reach those goals, so she would see the sites she wanted to see.

By lying to Patti, her family had made sure she will never achieve her goals for the future. Muriel's response to that comment would probably be something like, "If she can't remember what those goals were, what's the harm if she never reaches them?"

That, my friends and readers, is the mentality I have had to put up with for years.

Maybe an attorney experienced in family law will read this book and send me some advice as to my options after all that has occurred in the last 17 months.

I wrote this book so Patti will remember that she was loved, and that she is still loved! Unfortunately, love was not enough!

January 22, 2010

I submitted my "finished" manuscript for this book to several potential publishers online today. Here's keeping my fingers crossed!

I also took a copy to the printer in town here in Ashland, OR, to have five copies printed for five proofreaders to look over this weekend, and see if there are any last-minute changes or corrections to make.

January 26, 2010

I picked up four of the manuscript copies from the printer today. I had left one copy with one of the girls at the print shop, who had asked me Friday if she could read it over the weekend. I got it back from her today, along with the following copy of her opinion of the book. Her comments follow:

> **Mr. Baumann,**
>
> **This was the first book I have read in about a year, and I usually take a week to ten days to read any book. I started reading LOVE WAS NOT ENOUGH Saturday night, January 23, and I could not put it down! I finished it around 4:00 A.M. Sunday morning!**
>
> **My opinion about the whole mess with Patti and her family? You and Dr. Andersen are 100% correct! Muriel, in my opinion, is despicable! To lie to her sister, telling her**

sister that you wanted Patti to move out of your house at Lake Shastina, is beyond description. Muriel should be in jail for mentally abusing Patti. And just because she thinks it was time for Patti to face guilt one more time about an affair that took place ages ago? Anyone with any common sense at all would tell you that you were the best thing that ever happened to Patti.

Katy was not only over the affair, she wanted you and Patti to get married, according to Bob. I agree with Dr. Andersen that the laws in this country (USA) should be changed. The fact that you and Patti chose to live together for four years shows that you should have been able to decide how to care for Patti. You were technically married, but were not only because Patti was worried about how Katy would feel if you married.

Margaret says she was not going to allow Muriel and Julie to influence Patti, but she did anyway. I believe you are right when you say Margaret no longer has the strength to take on Muriel.

Pete, I hope Patti regains her common sense, and realizes she should be with you, for the rest of your lives, and doesn't wait too long before she does something about it. You two deserve each other.

Maybe if that happens, you can write a sequel to this book, and let your readers know how things turned out, OK?

You have my permission to use this statement anywhere in the future.

Shasta

The author's reply:

Shasta,

Thanks for your support, and thanks for your encouragement.

Pete

March 6, 2010

About a month ago I mailed by United States Post Office Certified Mail, Restricted Return Receipt, a copy of the manuscript of LOVE WAS NOT ENOUGH to my best friend and soul mate, the real person under the fictitious name "Patti" in this book, along with the real person known at "Katy" in this book, and the real persons known as "Muriel" and "Margaret" in this book.

I asked each person to read my manuscript, and to let me know in writing no later than by March 5, 2010, if there was anything in the manuscript that they would object to seeing in the final hardback and paperback versions of LOVE WAS NOT ENOUGH. I asked them to call me no later than March 5, 2010 if they did not have time to return their written objections by that day, but if they intended to send them as soon as possible.

As of today, March 6, 2010, I have not received any reply at all from any of those persons.

This morning, March 6, I emailed Katy and asked her why no one in her family had responded to my request that anyone in the family wanting me to make changes do so no later than March 5. She replied by email, and spoke for everyone who had been sent a copy of the manuscript. She basically had two requests:

1. Make sure everyone in her family have fictitious names in the book, and not their real names, and
2. Reduce the number of sexual episodes in the book, and be less explicit in the sexual escapades in the final version.

Why am I not surprised that I did not hear from Patti, Muriel or Carol? I would think that any intelligent person who was about to be depicted in my novel, whether identified with their real name, or a fictitious name, would respond to my certified mailing, one way or the other. When I did not receive any reply at all from Patti, Muriel, or Carol, I concluded that I have been right all along about Patti's family and their apparent drug-induced control of her for the last 18 months.

I think the key word in the previous paragraph is "intelligent". I have researched the different actions and beliefs of Americans when in certain circumstances, with interesting conclusions. For example, polls of the "average" American show that 62% of Americans in general are Christians, and believe in God. But polls of only owners of a Masters Degree show that only eight (8%) percent believe in a God, and that is down from 12% two years ago.

The more intelligent a person, the less likely he or she believes in something that is only based upon faith, and not upon scientific proof.

Another example: I mentioned earlier that we can choose our friends, we can choose our lovers, but we cannot choose our family. Right or wrong, most of us have family. The more intelligent among us will decide if any family member is right or wrong, and act accordingly. The less intelligent among us will follow what our family says is correct, whether it is or not.

The Patti I knew and loved would have responded to my mail. It appears that the signed receipt that I received from the Post Office contains her actual signature. That is further proof in my opinion that she is under the control of her daughter, as I have said all along.

For over sixteen years I tried to lift Patti up, and build her self-esteem, so she would think, and she would know, that she was better than just someone who waited tables at her husband's restaurants, that she was better than just a baby sitter.

Starting in mid-December, 2008, her sister, Muriel, her cousin, Julia, and her daughter, Carol, did their best to convince Patti she was just family and right or wrong, she should follow her family's instructions and suggestions.

Patti's family evidently just pretended to like me when I lived with Patti for four years, and did so much to help her with her self-esteem, with her new teeth, and with her attitude about life. Just when Patti and I should have entered counseling together as a couple, after her heart attack, the family turned on me and ignored my requests and suggestions as to how to best care for Patti. I believe it was their insufficient education that led to that result. Neither of Patti's kids ever graduated high school, and to my knowledge, no one else in the family ever went beyond high school in their education. Patti asked me in 2005 to drive Carol north to her father's house to escape Palm Springs because she was embarrassed she was pregnant and unmarried, and did not know who the father was since she was sexually active with more than one man at the same time. I believe it was the lack of education that put her in that situation.

I wonder what would happen if I hired an attorney, and he (or she) obtained a court order from a Washington State Judge that Carol appear in court with Patti, so the court could determine if Patti is being mentally abused. I am willing to bet that the daughter would fail to show up in court. The entire family is used to hiding their collective heads in the sand, and cannot handle any kind of confrontation.

I mentioned before in this book, and do so again; if any attorney familiar with family law reads this book, and has suggestions for me regarding what can be done to protect Patti from her family, please contact me.

PART SIX: The Free America Party

I lost my best friend and soul mate when disaster struck on the early morning of August 25, 2008 in the form of a heart attack.

If we had been married at the time, I could have given her the best health care possible, and made sure her recovery was based upon modern proven professional medical practices.

Since we were not married, current laws in the United States dictated that her "family", exclusively, could dictate what care she would receive. There was no one to decide if her family was even literate, or if they were completely ignorant of modern medical protocol.

That in my opinion is not only wrong, but is criminally negligent. Today, members of any hillbilly family from Arkansas can choose how they will "care for" a family member who needs modern medical care, and keep that family member from receiving proper care!

To help change these outdated laws, my oldest son and I have founded the FREE AMERICA PARTY, see www.freeamericaparty. org. Please see our Mission Statement at the website. Among other things, we want to correct many of the changes that our liberal modern Supreme Court has brought about in America, and return to the American principles that our fore-fathers brought to this great nation. Changing the laws pertaining to how unmarried couples may decide for themselves how they wish to handle health care issues for each other in the future is one of our top priorities. Whether couples choose to live together and not marry because they are gay, do not have religious beliefs about marriage, or if getting married will hurt their income tax situation, all Americans should have the right to decide for themselves about marriage, and how they want to be able to receive medical treatment if disaster strikes one of them.

If you care about the recent changes in America that have taken our rights away, and want to help us restore America to its original greatness, please go to www.freeamericaparty.org and donate one dollar to our cause. Please donate more if you can.

If you have a PayPal account, you may go to www.paypal.com and send your donation to contact@freeamericaparty.org. We will file your email address for future notices regarding what we are doing to protect your rights and freedoms. We look forward to receiving any help you can send.

A Final word from the author:

I wrote this book in Siskiyou County, California, the northernmost county in California, and in Jackson County, Oregon, the southernmost county in Oregon. I wrote the book during November and December of 2009, and sent it out for proofreading in January and February of 2010. It was a tough time financially due to the recession.

Living in Siskiyou County has never been an easy time for the last 30 years, because very often the residents have to put up with less than quality services offered to them by the local businesses and banks as compared to the rest of the country. When the unemployment figures for the country were in the 5% range, the rate for Siskiyou County was in the 30% range, for over 30 years. The population for Siskiyou County was about 44,000 in 1970, and the population for 2010 is also around 44,000!

Times were exceptionally tough when I was trying to put my two sons through college during the 2009/2010 winter months. Finding a decent bank was crucial to my being able to budget the boys' college expenses, paying their car payments each month as well as car insurance payments, and covering all of the expenses on Pete's film, SPIN OF FABRICATIONS. Pete is a genius when it comes to creating art, whether it is an independent film or a computer game. But like many college students, he never paid much attention to balancing his checkbook. He would often put his checking account balance in the negative, and incur NSF fees. He would use his debit card for small purchases, such as a $3.00 purchase, but because his balance was in the red, the bank would charge him a $33 NSF fee with each purchase. You would think his bank would let him know when he was incurring a $33 charge every time he used his debit card to buy a $2.00 item. I would expect an honest bank to do that for a college student, but unfortunately many banks today are anything but honest.

Money to Pete was not important. He just needed to know I would be able to pay for the production of his film so he could concentrate on creating each detail of the movie. When Washington Mutual Bank was in Yreka, the girls who worked there were personable, and always willing to talk to a customer with a specific problem. It was a good choice for a bank if the residents needed a friendly place to put their savings, or to operate a business in town.

But when Chase Bank took over Washington Mutual in Siskiyou County, especially in Yreka, in October of 2009, the bank lost all of its charm and personalized service. As a customer of the bank, I learned how turning a banking institution from personalized service to working as if the tellers were computers can take its toll on a small business. All common sense went out the window at the Yreka branch of Chase Bank.

For example, when Washington Mutual was my bank, I had overdraft protection on all of my personal and business accounts. All of my credit card sales at Reciprocal Golf were deposited in one business account. Then I would disperse those funds into other business accounts depending upon what my expenses were with each business. Every month my credit card processing company would withdraw funds from one business account to cover their fees from the previous month. I never knew ahead of time what amount would be withdrawn. But if the fees were more than expected in a particular month, I could count on my overdraft protection to cover any shortages, even if it cost me a $33 bank fee. That is called responsible financial planning with your bank's procedures helping me operate several businesses.

But when Chase took over Washington Mutual, everything changed. Chase canceled my overdraft protection without even letting me know they were doing so. That was their rule, no overdraft protection. I guess that letting their customers know about it was too much trouble to bother with.

Over the next three months, they cost me around $1,000 in fees they charged due to their canceling that protection. I had arranged for Pete to use an ATM card on one of my personal accounts, so he could withdraw funds from an ATM as I budgeted how much he could take out each day. One day he was in Los Angeles with his fiancé while doing some work on the campus of USC. I emailed him and told him he had $65.98 in his account, so he could withdraw $60 that morning from the only nearby ATM. He withdrew the $60, but the account was charged $6.95 in ATM fees. That put the balance at ($0.99). Chase immediately charged the account another $33 NSF fee. It cost a college student almost $40 to withdraw his own $60!

I contacted Chase and tried to speak to a human being, if you can call their employees human. They told me to go to their website and request a refund of the $33 fee. I did so, and received a computerized reply two days later in an email, stating they would not refund the fee.

Two weeks later Pete told me he needed about $100 to buy some software for his computer. I made sure Pete had $105 in his ATM account, then called him in L.A. and told him he could withdraw $100 from the ATM. He did so, but Chase charged a $6.00 fee, again putting the balance one dollar in the red. Chase then immediately charged my son another $33 fee, putting his balance at ($34.00).

Many people allow their creditors to charge a debit card or credit card monthly for an ongoing bill, so they don't have to mail a check every month. Don't even think of banking with Chase if you ever do that. Their automated computers will charge your account the $33 fee even if your account becomes even one cent in the red as the result of an automated withdrawal by a creditor!

I am sharing this information with you, the reader, to hopefully help you make good decisions about your choice of banks, especially if you live or expect to live in Siskiyou County, CA. My suggestion to you is, "Have absolutely nothing to do with Chase bank if you value your finances or your peace of mind!" In my opinion, the best bank to use for your personal banking is the Credit Union. They are very friendly, and you will be doing business with real human beings, not with a computerized robot like you would at Chase.

When the manager of the Chase branch in Yreka Learned what I was doing to help my son keep his finances straight, she immediately notified me by email that she was canceling my ATM card on the personal account I was using to help my son! Can you believe that? My own banker, instead of trying to help me solve a problem, interfered with my attempts to help teach my son how to manage his money!

In the present recession, our economy is weak thanks in part to the banking system in this country. With banks like Chase gouging its customers, stealing their money in the form of bank fees so the executives at Chase can receive ridiculously high bonuses at the end of the year, we the populous need to send a message to these bankers; we will not tolerate banks that steal money from their customers!

EPILOGUE

Patti's favorite song was Celine Dion's **BECAUSE YOU LOVED ME:**

You were my strength when I was weak
You were my voice when I couldn't speak
You were my eyes when I couldn't see
You saw the best there was in me
Lifted me up when I couldn't reach
You gave me faith 'coz you believed
I'm everything I am
Because you loved me

Unfortunately Patti, my love was not enough.

Copyright 2009 International Golf Services, Inc., a Nevada Corporation

CLOSURE

From the author: "I published the First Edition of LOVE WAS NOT ENOUGH in March of 2010. Now, in March of 2011, there is an ending to the story of my 17-year-long on and off life with Patti. This section of my book completes that story, together with a look to the future; thus, the 2nd Edition."

April 2, 2010

I received an email today from a company called The Markers Club, asking if I would consider offering our services at Reciprocal Golf to their current and future members. I learned after some investigating online that The Markers Club is one of about ten "Destination Clubs" that operate worldwide offering their members various benefits, including travel, golf, and accommodations in many parts of the world.

The Markers Club at that time owned what was known as the Private Club Network (PCN), a group of about 180 private country clubs that had agreed to allow each of their members the opportunity to play each of the other PCN clubs for just $35. In other words, it was a discount club that let members play at a limited number of other private clubs at a discount.

They also sold various memberships to families for around $25,000 that included a number of opportunities to play golf, visit exotic places and stay in the club's various homes around the world.

I commenced negotiating with the President of The Markers Club to offer our services at Reciprocal Golf of setting up reciprocal play at the approximate 2,000 private country clubs that allow outside play when the proper procedures and protocol are followed.

We originally agreed to finalize an agreement on July 1, 2010, but then the president of Markers Club informed me that Markers Club was going to "go public" and raise millions of dollars to fund their new expansion. I decided to wait for the Markers Club to complete their public offering before continuing our talks.

April 22, 2010

I received a phone call today from my older brother, Scott, informing me that our mother had just passed away at the nursing facility in Riverside, CA where our father had arranged for our parents' care back in 2002. Dad had died on September 2, 2008, and now Mom was gone. Scott said he would be emailing everyone in the family regarding our parents' Last Will and Testament.

May 5, 2010

I received a letter in the mail today from Chase Bank telling me they were going to report me to CHEX SYSTEMS. I had not sent them a payment to cover the bank fees they had charged my bank accounts earlier when they cancelled my overdraft protection without telling me they were going to do that. I wrote back to Chase telling them that their charging me for those bank fees was dishonest. I reminded them that reporting me to CHEX SYSTEMS for a negative balance that was negative due to their improper fees was taking dishonesty to a new level! They never responded to my letter.

May 16, 2010

I received a promotion from Chase Bank in the mail today offering to give me "$100 FREE!" if I opened a checking account with them within the next two weeks! I couldn't believe it! Within the next week I overheard many people at the post office, at Wal-Mart, at the supermarket and elsewhere talking about getting the same promotion in the mail from Chase Bank. I was shocked at how many of these people said they were going to switch to Chase Bank so they could get the free $100!

I wondered how many people received that promotion nationwide from Chase. A million? Ten million? 100 million? If only one million people received that promotion, $100 million dollars would be "created" in our economy by Chase Bank if everyone who received the promotion opened a checking account to take advantage of the promotion, right?

I remembered Abe Lincoln's **Senate Document No. 23** that he presented to Congress before he even ran for President of the United States, wherein he stated: "Money is the creature of law and the creation of the original issue of money should be maintained as an exclusive monopoly of National Government."

More than any other evil, Lincoln warned of the dangers of bankers who would try to create money in the future to control the population if laws were not enacted to prevent such a thing from happening! Rumors have abounded for decades that Lincoln was assassinated on the orders of bankers! Pause reading for a moment and think about that statement.

I thought to myself at the time what Chase's motivation might be to give away free money. I knew from my own experiences with Chase that the more customers they had, the more people they could charge their $33 bank fees for tiny errors that appeared in their customers' bank accounts, even if the customers were not at fault!

Another question on my mind was whether or not Chase could legally create money in today's economy. Or did the $100 they gave each new customer come from their own coffers? Either way, I knew something was wrong. Time would prove me right.

Our own elected officials in Washington gave our banking system $700 Billion to bail them out, only to have banks like Chase give away millions of dollars to get more customers to join their bank so they can have millions of additional customers to charge for NSF fees!

When will someone step up and save our country from our elected officials and banking system? If you care enough to do something about it, please go to www.freeamericaparty.org and donate to our cause!

June 26, 2010

My son, Pete, and his fiancé, Talia got married today. The event took place at the Nunan Estate in Jacksonville, OR. My younger son, Bobby, officiated as a new Seventh Day Adventist minister. Pete and Talia drove up the southern Oregon coast to a beautiful beach hideaway for two weeks for their honeymoon.

Meanwhile I was taking care of Reciprocal Golf business setting up play for my members at private country clubs nationwide.

July 7, 2010

I received an email from my brother Scott today informing me and my brothers and sister that our parents had left us about $220,000, to be split among the five children once Scott took care of all the paperwork. What interested me was the way Scott read one section in particular having to do with me and Patti. It appeared that my parents had thought that Patti and I would be married by that time.

I got busy typing a letter to Patti telling her about the approximate $44,000 I would be receiving from my parents' Will, and I asked her in the letter if she could use any of the $44,000. I mailed the letter via Certified Mail to Patti at her daughter, Carol's, house in Winthrop, WA.

I never received a reply from Patti, although the return receipt seemed to have her signature on it when it came back from the Post Office.

August 2, 2010

I mailed another letter to Patti at Carol's house in Winthrop, WA by Certified Mail, and Registered Mail. This time I informed her that since I had not heard back from her from my first letter, I had used $11,000 of the $44,000 to pay off my son Pete's debts, as a wedding present, and I had paid off Bobby's loan on his 2006 Saturn Vue. I enclosed a check to Patti for the remaining $33,000. I further explained to her that her greatest power was the POWER TO CHOOSE, and that she now had the ability to choose for herself what she wanted for her future.

I knew that her being stuck at Carol's house, with no money and no car, she would be forced to simply babysit Carol's children for the near future at least, with little promise of a nice future. Remember how Patti had been called Cinderella when she was living at Jody's house in Norco, CA in 2004? She was now truly Cinderella because she was stuck at Carol's house in a little town of less than 400 people, taking care of Carol's children for no compensation.

Two weeks later my Certified / Registered letter and check came back to me unclaimed! I called the postmaster in Winthrop and asked why his carriers could not deliver one single package to Patti. He replied that their job was to place a notice in the mail box, which was 100 feet from the house, and the recipient had to pick up the package at the Post Office. I knew for a fact that Carol would not want Patti to know she had a package waiting for her from me.

I decided to try one more time to get in touch with Patti. I mailed one more letter to her via Certified / Registered mail, this time stressing to her that she had options in her life. I wanted to stress to her that if she ever became depressed because she was living with her daughter, babysitting her three grandkids, with no vehicle to escape from Winthrop, WA even if she wanted to do so, she could call me and ask me for assistance. I told her I would be there for her, regardless of whether she wanted to get back with me or if she simply needed the wherewithal to escape Winthrop.

Two weeks later my letter once again came back in the mail unclaimed!

I turned my attention back to business, and took up negotiations once again with the Markers Club. I offered the Markers Club the opportunity to use our services at Reciprocal Golf to sell their new memberships to customers. Their reply to my offer was to offer to buy Reciprocal Golf and Probe Golf, my golf equipment company, from me completely and take them over.

I considered their offer, and compiled a valuation of my two golf companies for them to consider. They in turn sent me a written offer, which was obviously not what I had in mind. When I pushed the issue with them, asking about their recent "Public offering" that had supposedly been concluded weeks previously, I learned they had misrepresented the facts.

They referred me to their new website to show me all of their plans for the future. When I went to their website, it became obvious to me that they were making promises to their new customers / members that they could not possibly deliver! More importantly, they were making promises to new potential members that they could get their members onto more than 4,000 private country clubs, and "at a discount" to boot!

I knew they were expecting me to make their promises come true, even though I had told them their promises were not doable.

I decided then and there that I was going to keep Reciprocal Golf and continue to expand its membership. I also decided I was going to keep Probe Golf and introduce a new putter style for the upcoming 2011 PGA Merchandise Show in Orlando, FL.

I had decided a few weeks earlier that I was going to retire on my birthday the next year, June 1, 2011. I'd get a nice boat around 30 feet in length and pull it to different lakes around the southwest where I could fish, play golf, and write another book or two; try to share my experiences in life with millions of Americans so they would (hopefully) not make the same mistakes I had made during my lifetime!

That would be perfect timing! Introduce my new putter in January, start to build up some inventory, and then turn Probe Golf over to another golf company that needed a unique niche in the golf industry to succeed. Take a little money in front for the sale, but take their company stock for most of the sale, help them succeed, and make money off of their stock while I help them make money! My putter is much more beneficial to the average golfer, and has much more potential than virtually any other putter on the market.

It would be a crime to walk away from Probe Golf without someone else to carry the inverted-shafted putter concept to the next level. Heck, Callaway bought Odyssey Golf for over $100 million, and that putter can't hold a candle to what my putter can do! I would have convinced Phil Michelson to switch from his Odyssey putter back in May of 2010, and finally show him how to make a three to five foot breaking putt, if his attorney had not threatened me to stay away from Phil! Phil Michelson should have made it to the world's number one position years ago, but his contract with Callaway has kept him from using better golf equipment and becoming Number One!

Regarding the Markers Club, I also realized I had not followed one of my business rules I had implemented clear back in 1987 when I started Probe Golf, when I promised myself I would not consider signing up any golfer as an exclusive Probe Golf Distributor until I played 18 holes of golf with any applicant. Playing golf with someone for the first time is like hooking them up to a lie-detector machine! I'll learn more about them and their character, or lack of character, in four hours playing golf with them than I will negotiating over a conference table for six months!

Had I taken one day to meet the Markers Club President and play golf with him I would have seen right through their plan, and would not have wasted months talking to them on the phone!

October 2, 2010

Today was a life-changing experience! I learned that Patti had died! I learned that as a result of a letter I received in the mail from Patti herself. In the letter the person sending me the letter said things that made it perfectly clear to me that it was not the Patti I had known who had written the letter. The writer was obviously a child, writing childish things and making childish comments. My Patti was no longer intelligent, no longer had any common sense, and her personality and zest for life were gone!

I wondered if Patti had also lost her sex drive as a result of her not going through the proper counseling with me as Dr. Andersen had indicated was necessary for her brain to heal properly. Patti had been the sexiest woman I had ever known, and it was the fun we had together in sexual situations that helped make us soul mates.

I was both shocked and relieved at the same time after receiving Patti's letter. Shocked to learn what had happened to Patti's mind. At the same time I was relieved to know that my Patti was truly gone! It had been two years since Patti's heart attack, and many months of trying to educate her family of the importance of getting her proper counseling, to no avail! I was worn out mentally. I could now move on with my life.

January, 1961 (GOING BACK IN TIME)

When I was 13 years old, my dad took me out on the golf course for the first time to learn the game, a game I came to know as the greatest game mankind has ever invented!

After my first 18 holes, on the way home in the car, my dad asked me, "Pete, what do you want to be when you grow up?"

"I want to be an astronaut, and then I want to be the President of the United States."

"Why an astronaut?"

"I want to explore what is new and unknown, so we can learn what is out there, and what our future will hold."

"And why do you want to be the President of the United States?"

"Because our country needs honest men leading it, and I want the best for our country."

Well, my dad is gone. My dad was the most honest person I have ever known. Heck, he was the most honest man I have ever even heard of! My dad was much more than simply "honest". If my dad heard of any wrongdoing anywhere in the world, he had to try to do something about it. Anywhere, even if he did not know any of the people involved in the wrongdoing!

Our country is presently run by politicians. And I know of no honest politician. Yes, there are people who run for office who have good intentions, but they quickly become corrupted by incumbents. Who was it that said, "The road to Hell is paved with those who had very good intentions."?

I intend to do what I can together with my son, Pete, with the FREE AMERICA PARTY, to return honesty and integrity to politics in this country. One of my favorite quotes is by Sir Edmond Burke: *"All that is necessary for evil to triumph is for good men to do nothing."*

I mentioned earlier why I wrote LOVE WAS NOT ENOUGH. One of our goals is to educate the population about medical advances, so uneducated back hills families might make better decisions in the future about how to care for a loved one.

Another goal of ours at the FREE AMERICA PARTY is to return America to its original values that made our country great, values relating to our freedoms that have been taken away from us by politicians in the last thirty years.

In my own short lifetime I have personally witnessed injustices by local court judges, by local and statewide police officers, and by statewide politicians who were elected by the American people who thought their candidate was honest.

Have you ever personally witnessed an injustice and wished you could do something about it? How about receiving something as simple as a traffic violation from a police officer who was wrong, and you knew you received it because the officer was trying to reach his quota for writing tickets rather than doing his job of being honest and fair with the automobile drivers in his territory?

Our country is based on laws, and if our law enforcement officers get away with such injustices, our country that we love so much is doomed!

HAVE YOU BEEN WRONGED?

Have you ever lost money to your bank in the form of NSF fees? Was the charge unfair? Have you ever been stopped by a law enforcement officer and given a violation that you felt was unfair?

If so, I hope you will join with me and become a member of the FREE AMERICA PARTY by going to <u>www.freeamericaparty.org</u>. It is time the American public stood up and complained as a group, in force, about dishonest banks and dishonest law enforcement officials in our country! In my opinion these are two cancers in our country that will end our freedoms as we know them if we don't do something about it now! If we allow banks and local law enforcement to continue their corruption, our freedoms will be lost forever. No American can afford to "***do nothing***" any longer.

Presently my own personal pet peeve is the law enforcement personnel in the small town of Ashland, Oregon, home of the world-famous Shakespeare Festival. While I lived in Siskiyou County, CA, just 30 minutes south of the city of Ashland, I visited my son, Pete, at Southern Oregon University in Ashland a number of times. I have never had an accident in my 45 years of driving an automobile.

I had not received a traffic violation in over ten years. One day in September of 2008 I visited Pete in Ashland, and received a "speeding ticket" in a school zone where the posted speed limit was 20 MPH.

The school in question was not only closed, it was boarded up by an 8-foot fence for reconstruction! Four months later I visited Pete again, and received another speeding ticket at the same intersection, by the same school, which was still boarded up! I was following a local vehicle, with Oregon license plates, through the same intersection, but I was stopped with my California license plates and given a ticket.

Five months later I received another speeding ticket in Ashland, this time driving from a 55 MPH zone into Ashland, where the legal speed dropped from 55 to 45 to 35 to 25 MPH in less than half a mile distance. I did some research and learned that Ashland was famous for being the "most pedestrian friendly city in America". Pedestrians are exalted as "gods" in Ashland, Oregon. If a pedestrian steps off a curb onto a road in Ashland, anywhere, not just at a crosswalk, all traffic must immediately stop. Rear-end accidents happen all the time in Ashland due to this local law favoring pedestrians.

But what is more troublesome to me than a few police officers making sure they reach their "quota" of writing speeding tickets to out-of-state drivers is the city managers who encourage such activities. The local judges are no better!

It reminds me of the famous stories about drivers who used to drive across the southern states in the Hollywood movies, and then not only get stopped by the local police officers, but also thrown in jail for petty ridiculous laws and working on a chain gang for the rest of their lives unless they are saved by the hero in the movie!

One other personal example I experienced with law enforcement will help make my point even further. In 2000 I was driving north on Interstate 5 in northern California one day, and noticed I was almost out of gas. I slowed down to conserve fuel and looked for the nearest gas station. I was barely coasting when I crested a hill in Mt. Shasta and coasted down the other side. I saw that a California Highway Patrolman (CHP) had stopped another vehicle for speeding.

As I coasted by the CHP car the driver pulled out right away and turned on his red lights, basically instructing me to pull over. The officer, Officer Mehl, walked up to my window and demanded to see my license and proof of insurance. I tried to ask why he was stopping me, but he cut me off and demanded my paperwork. I gave it to him, and he immediately started writing a speeding ticket. I asked him why he thought I was speeding, and started explaining that I was slowing down to conserve fuel because I was almost out of gas, but he did not want to hear it.

Officer Mehl handed me the ticket, and then ran back to his cruiser, jumped into it, pulled out and immediately stopped the next car that was driving by! He ended up giving three vehicles three speeding tickets as fast as was physically possible.

I was so mad at the officer's rudeness that I ended up filing a complaint with the local CHP office against Officer Mehl. But that is not the end of my story. Not even close!

Eight months later I was entertaining a client on the Lake Shastina Golf Resort, trying to sell the golf course to my client for over $5,000,000. My client had had too much to drink, and got in an argument with one of the club's local drunks. My client got into my Ford Probe, license plate PROBE07, and we drove to Mt. Shasta. My client had evidently announced out loud to his golfing buddy that we were driving to Michael's Restaurant in Mt. Shasta for dinner. The local drunk, I learned the next day, called 911 and told them that two drunks were leaving Lake Shastina in a Ford Probe, license plate PROBE07, and heading to Michael's Restaurant in Mt. Shasta, and that "they are going to kill someone if they aren't stopped!"

When we arrived at Michael's Restaurant in Mt. Shasta, we noticed two CHP cruisers were parked across the street. We spent two hours in the restaurant having dinner and discussing the purchase of the golf course. During that two hours the four of us shared one bottle of red wine, total. When we left the restaurant, my three clients took their car back to Redding, CA to the south while I started driving north back to Lake Shastina.

As I pulled out of the parking lot, the two CHP cruisers pulled out close behind me and followed me to the freeway. They were driving too close behind me, violating the rules of the road. Then each cruiser took turns pulling up close behind me, then falling back almost out of sight, then repeating the process. I decided they were trying to startle me into doing something stupid. Finally one of the cruisers pulled behind me and turned on his red light. I pulled over and stopped. An "Officer Rogers" walked up to my window and asked for my paperwork. I handed it to him, then he asked me to step out of the car. I asked why he had stopped me, and he replied, "You were driving recklessly!"

I replied, "Why were you and the other officer (who had pulled in behind Officer Rogers' cruiser) driving recklessly behind me?"

Rogers said they were not driving recklessly. I told him that I knew why he had stopped me. He asked why. I replied, "Because eight months ago I was rudely stopped by an Officer Mehl for speeding, and due to his rudeness, I filed a complaint with the CHP. It's obvious to me that you two officers are trying to get even."

"I don't know of any Officer Mehl in the CHP."

Then I heard, "I know Officer Mehl." from the other officer in the dark behind us.

Officer Rogers then asked me to perform some walking maneuvers to see if I was drunk. I told him that I had shared one bottle of wine with three others at Michael's Restaurant over two hours previously, and was fine to drive.

Long story short, Officer Rogers made me go with him to the local hospital where they could draw blood and test my blood-alcohol level. They claimed I was marginal, and held me overnight, for about six hours, before releasing me. I called my attorney the next morning, told him the story, and he said he would investigate.

My attorney called me back an hour later and told me that the second officer that had stopped me, the one in the dark parked behind Officer Rogers' cruiser, WAS OFFICER MEHL!

Both officers had lied to me!

My attorney spoke to the local District Attorney over the next week and was successful in getting me out of a DUI. I spent months after that filing complaints against both Officer Rogers and Officer Mehl, and took my complaint all the way up the line to the highest ranking CHP officer in the State of California. Did those officers' superiors ever reprimand the two officers who harassed me that night? Of course not.

Do you remember when you were young and believed that your local police officer was your friend? Do you remember ever telling your children that if they are ever afraid and alone that they can find a policeman and he will help them?

Today, both of my sons do not have any faith in policemen to do the right thing. My sons do not trust police officers to be honest, to have any integrity. That is not only sad, it is dangerous to our way of life. When our military is overseas protecting our way of life, can this country afford to have its laws here at home jeopardized by dishonest law enforcement officials and street police?

Bringing back honesty and integrity in law enforcement in this country has to start at the local, small town level, and branch out to the national government.

From July, 2010 through December 31, 2010 my office conducted a poll of Americans who Drive extensivelu up and down the Interstate-5 corridor from southern California to northern Washington to find out which towns the majority of those drivers think have the most dishonest law enforcement officers.

My associates came up with ten cities that were reported by those taking part in the poll as the most dishonest law enforcement officers, with traffic courts backing up their dishonesty.

At the end of January 2011, we emailed the city officials in those ten cities and told them what we were doing, that their city was in the top ten, and that we would reduce those ten cities to the top three cities with the most dishonest law enforcement officers on the west coast. We asked each of the ten to reply back to our office if they disagreed with our assessment of their city.

After two weeks, we have received no replies! Do these city officials not care what the driving public thinks of their dishonest law enforcement officers? Do the law enforcement officers in these cities think they themselves are above the law?

HERE ARE THE RESULTS OF THAT POLL:

The three cities along the Interstate-5 corridor with the most dishonest law-enforcement officers, according to our poll, are as follows:

Ashland, Oregon – This town boasts the world-famous Shakespeare Festival, which is the "hook" that brings people from all over the world to Ashland. Watch out for the town's police department, especially if you have out-of-state license plates! They will get you for parking incorrectly and speeding if you fail to notice the descending speed limits posted all over town. One stretch on Pacific Highway going north to south through town changes from 55 MPH to 45 to 35 to 25, and they expect you to reduce your speed before you reach each posted sign! Also, this town boasts it is the most pedestrian-friendly town in America. Pedestrians step off the curb "everywhere", and cause traffic to stop everywhere, so rear-ender accidents are plentiful. Drive cautiously in town.

Mt. Shasta, CA – As already mentioned in this book, the California Highway Patrol working out of Mt. Shasta cannot be trusted to be honest with travelers driving up and down Interstate-5. They are out to make money giving tickets, period. My own experience in this book showed the extent to which these officers will lie and cheat to hand out tickets. Set your cruise control to 60 MPH before you reach Mt. Shasta, and do not turn it off until you are miles past this town!

Newhall, Santa Clarita, CA – As you drive south on Interstate-5 approaching the north end of Los Angeles, the interstate goes from two lanes to five lanes in this mountainous town, and the locals increase their speed to over 90 MPH from the posted 65 MPH! If you stay at that 90 MPH speed, like the locals, you may get through this town without being stopped. Otherwise, slow down and get in the right lanes early, before you get caught up with the speeders. But don't get surprised too late, and find yourself speeding along with the rest of traffic, because it is not easy to signal to the right and slow down as you merge to the right-hand lanes. The traffic will pass you on the right doing over 90 MPH, and make changing lanes dangerous! The CHP will be looking for out-of-state vehicles to stop and ticket, not expecting those drivers to come back to town to fight the court system. And the tickets handed out in this town exceed $350!

At www.freeamericaparty.org, we want to hear from Americans who have been wronged by dishonest local governments. Send us your story by email, and we will see what can be done to right the wrong you experienced.

October 15, 2010

I played golf and met a man on the first tee today who has been another life-changing experience for me. His name is Bill, and he is part of a medical research team that has been instrumental in learning the secrets of how and why the human body ages. His research included how human cells can be intentionally instructed to regenerate themselves to slow down the aging process in the body, and prolong and lengthen the lifespan in human beings! I learned from Bill that his research became not only believable but downright probable since 2003 after his group learned the secrets of gene regeneration from DNA research.

Imagine being able to lengthen the average lifetime of human beings from 65 or 70 years to over 150 years, and longer in the future! Bill told me during the 18 holes we played that day that medical science will be able to prolong human life longer than 200 years within the next 50 years.

Readers of LOVE WAS NOT ENOUGH are invited to email me at contact@lovewasnotenough.com in the future and ask for updates on such research. I for one will stay in touch with Bill and will follow his lead in using future products that will extend my life and the lives of my friends and associates. I hope to hear from you on this subject.

October 19, 2010

This morning, a Tuesday, I informed my son, Bobby, that I had entered us in a two-man Scramble golf tournament, the Civil War, at Centennial Golf Club in Medford, Oregon that coming Saturday, October 23. Bobby was excited about entering the tournament, and suggested we go practice.

We called the club about a tee-time that morning and learned the course was closed until 2:00 P.M. because there was a senior event going on. They suggested we go play Quail Point Golf Club in Medford, their other club owned by the same people, Pacific Retirement Services, Inc.

We called Quail Point to make sure they had a tee-time for us, and then headed up Interstate 5 to play. Bobby informed me he had to work at the Sports Authority in the Medford Mall at 2:00 P.M., and could only play nine holes. We met his buddy, Sione Saenz, who also worked at Sports Authority, on the first tee. Sione had time to play 18 holes.

After nine holes, Bobby headed off to work, and Sione and I headed to the tenth tee. As we were teeing off, the two assistant pros from the club drove up in their golf cart and asked if they could join us.

"Of course", replied Sione and I simultaneously.

Brent Santoni was a big boy, husky with a big smile on his face. Bobby had introduced me to Brent about three weeks earlier when we were teeing off on the first hole at Centennial. Brent had his young son with him in his cart that day, and could only play four holes with us before he took his son home for an important event. Brent was a player, and just as long as Bob off the tee.

Anthony Ulloa was smaller and more reserved than Brent. I had met Anthony in the pro shop at Centennial but had never seen him swing a golf club before.

The pros teed off, and I was impressed with their drives. They were both long and down the middle. I made a mental note not to get into any kind of bet with them since I was no longer a +2-handicap! Not unless I got some strokes from them.

We played the first three holes, and then drove up to the 4th tee. Number 4 at Quail Point is a short, downhill Par-3 with residences running down the hill on the left side of the hole. After the four of us teed off, I hopped in my cart and started down the hill on the cart path. Sione was walking, so he headed straight down the hill, while I drove on the winding cart path. It wound down the hill rather than staying straight because of the steep slope, and it was easier on the brakes to take a less inclined path.

As I approached the green, I slowed my cart at the point in the cart path that was nearest the green. Just as I stopped, I heard the sound of screeching tires behind me, and then felt my cart lurch forward. I realized my cart had been struck from behind by Brent's cart! I looked back and saw that Brent was driving and Anthony was sitting in the right seat.

As I got out of my cart, I heard Sione yelling, "Pete, are you all right?" I stood there, looking up the hill as I saw Sione running down the hill with his golf bag on his shoulder, and vaguely remember seeing people coming out of the residences to the left of the hole to see what had made all the noise.

Then I looked to my left as Brent asked if I was OK.

"Yeah, I think so." I moved my arms and felt my neck with one hand, and everything seemed to be fine.

Brent and Sione seemed concerned about me, but I said again that I was fine. Strangely, Anthony was quiet and showed no emotion that I could see at the time. He's kind of a strange duck! We continued playing the hole, and then moved on to the next hole. We didn't mention the accident for the rest of the round.

October 20, 2010

The next morning I woke up with a sore neck. I knew it was from the cart collision the day before, but I was not concerned. I knew from reading about whiplash injuries that soreness for a few days was common in such cases. I just hoped the soreness would clear up by the weekend so I could play with Bobby as my partner in the Civil War tournament.

By Thursday night my neck was still sore. Since I had played golf for years with one pain or another, I knew I would play in the weekend's tournament unless I couldn't swing at all.

Come Saturday morning Bobby and I drove to the golf course. The weather that day was terrible, with wind blowing about 30 MPH out of the north, and rain was falling diagonally. Bobby asked me what I thought about the weather, and I told him, sore neck or not, that I felt our chances were good because I had played in cold, wet, windy weather for years while at Lake Shastina Golf Resort. I told Bob we had the advantage over the rest of the field for that very reason!

I told him the story about the year when I was playing in our Men's Club Championship at Lake Shastina and the south wind was blowing over 40 MPH. I shot even par that day, a 72, and no one else broke 80! It was a walk in the park for me the next day with such a lead. I won that year's Men's Club Championship by ten shots!

Bobby and I shot a one-under 71 that day in the Civil War scramble format at Centennial Golf Club, the low gross score for our flight!

I continued playing golf with Bobby once or twice per week for the next three weeks, even though my neck and shoulders were still sore from the cart collision. I was used to playing with pain over the previous four years with a pinched nerve in my lower back, so playing with a new pain in my neck and shoulders would not stop me from playing.

November 5, 2010

My son, Pete, emailed me today and asked me to help him advertise his Premier screening of his independent film, SPIN OF FABRICATIONS, to take place the weekend of December 17, 18, and 19, 2010. I told him I was looking forward to helping him spread the word about his film.

We agreed that after the screening that weekend we would discuss entering his film in about 150 film festivals around the world. Information about Pete's film can be found at our production company's websites, www.veradonir.com, and www. spinoffabrications.com.

November 13, 2010

I watched the Monday Night NFL game this evening between the Washington Redskins and the Philadelphia Eagles; 28 to nothing Eagles after the first quarter! I had noticed that Bob had finished the gallon of milk in the refrigerator before heading off to work, so I drove down to Wal-Mart at halftime to replace it, mostly thinking about having milk for my coffee the next morning.

As I walked out of Wal-Mart with my gallon of milk, I noticed something strange out of the corner of my eye as I approached my car in the parking lot. A shopping cart next to my car had a woman's purse in the top section of the cart. I noticed the purse was open at the top and had a wallet sitting on top. I grabbed the purse and walked back to the entrance of the store.

As I entered, the woman responsible for watching for returns saw me enter and said, "You just walked out with that milk, are you returning it already?"

I said, "No, I found a purse in the parking lot. Where should I turn it in?"

"At the counter there", she said, pointing to the return counter to my left. I walked up to the counter, where two employees were waiting on four ladies with returned items.

I waited for a few minutes while the employees were helping the shoppers. Finally, one of the ladies behind the counter asked me what I needed.

"I found this purse in a shopping cart out in the parking lot."

Her eyes lit up and she exclaimed, "Wow, twice this week someone turned in a lost item!"

Then I heard clapping from the group of shoppers standing in line at the counter. I was shocked.

"Hurray!" I looked up to see four women clapping their hands as they stared at me.

"Good for you! An honest man in this day and age!"

I blushed as I looked at the women for a few minutes, and saw amazement in their eyes. I was blushing because I was amazed that the women were so excited about my actions.

Then I saw something else in their eyes. I saw HOPE! A feeling of warmth came over me, as if these women were feeling something they had not known for a long time, and I had something to do with it.

Then I envisioned tens of millions of Americans all at once showing that look of hope in their eyes, as if I had opened a window to the future, and the future looked great!

A feeling of humbleness came over me, and tears almost developed in my own eyes.

As I walked out of Wal-Mart that night, a feeling of hope came over me as well. Hope that we can return America to the feeling of greatness that I had felt many years earlier as an American. I vowed then and there to do what I could do with our FREE AMERICA PARTY to return our country to the greatness it had once enjoyed worldwide!

THE GREATEST GAME EVER PLAYED

There are over 25 million golfers in the United States. Most of them know what is so great about the game of golf. We've all seen the TV commercials, how golf teaches our kids honesty, integrity, perseverance, how to overcome adversity, the importance of following the rules, not only in the game of golf but also in life.

I have played golf since I was 13 years old. I have learned how golf can help anyone achieve their goals in life through networking on the golf course with people you meet during 18 holes. I have also learned how golf is better than a lie-detector to learn about the people with whom you are playing!

Two weeks out of college in 1970 I met two potato farmers from Idaho on a golf course in San Diego. During our 18 holes, I showed each of them how to correct their slice(s) off the tee. They learned to like me, how I conducted myself on the golf course, and we became friends immediately. Over lunch I told them I was starting a company called Intertel, Inc., and that we were going to manufacture and market the world's first cordless telephone. They asked if they could invest in Intertel, Inc., and I told them I would love to have them as investors. A week later they brought two other potato farmers from Idaho into the company as investors

Intertel, Inc. was the first small business I started out of college. Over the years I met new friends on the golf course, and my attitude and personality on the course showed through to those new friends. By playing golf with someone I knew who was honest, who was intelligent, who I could trust as a future partner, and who I would ultimately work with in each new business I started. I could play 18 holes, or less, with a stranger, and knew if they were "partner" material. Or, their faults or lack of character would show through to me and I knew they would never be partner material.

I remember when Arnold Palmer was in his prime in the 1960's, and he was loved by millions of Americans. I even remember having discussions with friends when we all thought Arnie would make a great President! We thought he would make a great President because of how he conducted himself on the golf course! The game of golf is all about character! I can learn about a man's (or woman's) character, or lack thereof, during one round of golf with them.

In 1964 my dad took my brother and me to the San Diego Open, and we posed with 15 or more junior golfers and with Arnie for a picture to appear on the cover of Sports Illustrated that month. In that issue was not only our picture with Arnie, but there was also a quote by Mr. Palmer that I have memorized for decades:

"GOOD GOLF IS A STATE OF MIND!"

"Golf is deceptively simple and endlessly complicated. A child can play it well and a grown man can never master it. Any single round of it is full of unexpected triumphs and seemingly perfect shots that end in disaster. It is almost a science, yet it is a puzzle without an answer. It is gratifying and tantalizing, precise and unpredictable. It requires complete concentration and total relaxation.

It satisfies the soul and frustrates the intellect. It is at the same time rewarding and maddening. And it is without doubt the greatest game mankind has ever invented."

Arnold Palmer 1964

To this day, Arnie, at 80 years of age, earns about $22 million per year endorsing products on television, because everyone trusts what he has to say! That is how powerful the game of golf has been to him in his life's goals. Only seven professional golfers, all much younger, earn more than Arnie each year.

I also remember similar discussions we had in the 1960's about John Wayne running for President. The "Duke" was a great American; he wasn't a great actor. He simply played himself in all of his films, and people liked what they saw. They knew he had character. Can you imagine "President" John Wayne telling his colleagues to go out and find Osama bin Laden after 9/11 in 2001 and bring him to justice? Who would dare come back without bin Laden?

I believe our country needs a shot in the arm when it comes to our future leaders, because our country has no leaders when it comes to honesty and integrity within our law enforcement officers on patrol in our towns and cities; our country has no one who will step up and require that banks treat their customers honestly.

Wouldn't it be nice if together we could find a way to make banks in the United States more honest? I have told you what Chase Bank did from September 2009 through January, 2010 to hurt my own small business' banking efforts to run my business properly. Their refusal to acknowledge that fraudulent ACH requests to take money out of my business account was causing overdraft problems and is the reason they referred my account to Chex Systems!

I changed banks, switching to Bank of America in February of 2010, and ran into a different problem. I switched to Bank of

America because the bank manager with whom I first spoke told me how "special" their internet website was supposed to be! I had told him that I used my business account debit card a lot so I could more easily keep track of my account balance. He explained that the bank's accounting always listed an accurate "available balance" because their procedures told each customer what was pending, and already taken off the apparent balance, so that the listed "available balance" was current and accurate. That made sense to me, providing it was true. It took me five months to learn that his explanation was not the truth!

I learned after running hundreds of transactions through Bank of America that their website accounting procedures had a flaw. Their so-called "available balance" at their website was misleading. Any purchases with my debit card that were "pending" were listed as stating they were already calculated in the "available balance". Then, on November 12, 2010, Bank of America charged my business account four NSF charges of $35 each! I lost $140 to the bank that day! I was furious. I went to the bank branch in Ashland, Oregon with my records and told the woman at the bank I wanted an explanation. She looked through my records, and the printout from their website I had brought in, and she was confused. She said she did not understand why my account had been charged for the four NSF charges.

Then she noticed my account was opened in California, and she looked relieved. She told me that her branch was not responsible because I had a California account. I asked what difference that made, and she said that Oregon accounts were treated differently from California accounts! She said she would have to connect me with a California agent on the phone. She did so, then handed me the phone. I talked to that young lady, who informed me that the bank had already reversed two NSF charges before on my business account, and that they could not reverse any more!

I asked her what that had to do with proper accounting reporting at their website. She gave me some double-talk that made no sense, so I told her I would have to take my complaint to her supervisor. A few weeks later I drove to Yreka, CA and stopped in at the Bank of America office there. I told them my story about my phone conversation from their Ashland, OR branch with the California bank representative. The Yreka bank manager immediately reversed the four NSF fee charges I had incurred. Why did I have to drive to the next state to get the bank to do the right thing?

Bottom line; I never got a satisfactory explanation as to why their customers could not believe what the bank told them was their "available balance"!

I have come to the conclusion that banks in the United States can afford to pay their top executives tens of millions of dollars in bonuses each year because they fool their customers into believing their accounting procedures, which at the very best is confusing, if not fraudulent!

Why else would Chase give away hundreds of millions of dollars to get people to open an account with them?

Our Congress gave away $700 Billion in 2009 and 2010 to bail out banks in the United States! That money came from you and from me, hardworking Americans who try to get by each day, and who depend on our banks to properly report our balances so we don't incur a $35 NSF fee every time they fool us with their accounting procedures!

I don't know about you, but **I am fed up!**

The question is, "**Are you fed up?** Are you fed up with banks in this country that take advantage of their customers? Are you fed up with law enforcement that gives hard working Americans driving violations to fill their city's quotas to pay the salaries of city officials? Are you fed up with dishonest politicians who make promises just to get into office, and then fail to do what they promised?

That may be the most important question you ever answer for your own future, and for the future of your children, so let me ask you again. **IF YOU KNEW FOR A FACT THAT BIG BANKS AND MAJOR CORPORATIONS ARE PLANNING TO TAKE OVER CONTROL OF OUR NATION'S FUTURE, AND TAKE AWAY MOST OF OUR FREEDOMS AND LIBERTIES, DO YOU INTEND TO LET THEM DO SO, OR ARE YOU WILLING TO HELP ME KEEP THAT FROM HAPPENING?**

I hope your answer is to help me keep it from happening!

Assume for a moment that the following facts are 100% correct:

1. Every politician running for President in this country knows for a fact that it will take a lot of money for him or her to be elected. Television commercials are not cheap!
2. Every politician running for President knows that the politician whose name is in front of the millions of American voters the most will be elected.
3. Every politician knows that the big banks and the major corporations have the most money to buy television advertising.
4. Therefore, it stands to reason that if you want to get elected President of the United States, YOU MUST give in to the demands of those big banks and major corporations.

It is a never-ending circle that cannot be stopped by traditional politics in this country!

I want to do something to help save our country, save our freedoms, before it is too late! I can't run for President like I told my dad I wanted to do when I was 13 years old, forty-nine years ago. Why not? Because all politicians who run for President must comply with the future goals of the big banks and big corporations, because those are the people who buy the millions of dollars in television advertising to get them elected.

So, what can we as concerned Americans do to get our freedoms back? As a small business owner, I always approached any problem with this rule: **Set a specific goal**, **make a plan to reach that goal**, and then **follow the plan.**

Our country is in serious trouble thanks to the politicians we have elected in the past, mostly attorneys. Attorneys make terrible businessmen! We need more businessmen to run for office in this country. I for one hope that Donald Trump runs for President in 2012 or 2016. He knows what kind of trouble our country is in, and in my opinion would make a great President, the kind of businessman I could get behind and support.

Join me at www.freeamericaparty.org and help me show Donald Trump that we can help him get elected if he runs! I need the help of every American who is fed up with losing his or her freedoms, with losing his or her country to politicians who have a different agenda, the same agenda the big banks and major corporations have for your future. Together with millions of other Americans we can get started on the right path to return the United States to the greatness it once enjoyed!

You can help us achieve that goal by going to www. freeamericaparty.org and CONTACT US as an individual interested in joining our cause. Allow me to show the major political parties in this country that collectively we have the votes to bring about positive change. While you are at the website, donate one dollar, more if you can.

Imagine! If we can get 25,000,000 golfers in this country together with the millions of John Wayne fans behind our cause, we can take our country back from the politicians who have allowed the banks to take over control of our country!

Abraham Lincoln warned that this country was doomed if we allowed the bankers to control the future of this country, and it has already begun. It started with the creation of the Federal Reserve in 1913. When the United States political leaders in this country made the decision back then to require that the country borrow money from an outside agency, the Federal Reserve, instead of print its own money, they put the country on the road to financial doom. As Lincoln said in 1839, only a country should be able to create money to support its economy. A country having to borrow money from bankers leads to financial disaster. If we do not take our country back from the bankers, and from the law enforcement officials who may have good intentions, but have been corrupted without even knowing it, we may as well give up hoping for a good future!

Can a hard-working, honest American ever hope to become the President of the United States, or are those days long gone? I have watched elections of politicians who hoped to become President for many years, and one thing has amazed me. The American public seems to expect their President to be multiple people all at once! They expect their President to be a peacemaker, a negotiator, an economist, an accountant, a foreseer, a mind reader, and basically the smartest person on the planet all in one! The Americans who believe abortion is bad want their President to believe the same. Americans who believe a woman has the right to choose   want their President to be in favor of abortion. The best candidate for President may or may not believe in abortion, and it should not matter when choosing our President.

The government of the United States is nothing more than a very big business. It will take a businessman to properly run our national government, no more and no less. Any businessman worth his salt can run the government with the proper business plan that was the secret of Mr. Andrew Carnegie. Carnegie built up his personal fortune by following one simple rule; **"surround yourself with the best minds in each field of endeavor, then follow their advice"**.

Our Presidential candidates should not be fielding questions from the press about what he or she will do about our economy if he or she is elected President! They are not economists! Whoever wins the Presidency in 2012 hopefully will be an honest leader who has the intelligence to hire the best economists to advise them in the future!

I am not a multimillionaire, and I have heard the many comments that only a multimillionaire can run for President. I don't believe that. The American public, together, is stronger than any one man with millions of dollars of his own money. At the same time, a wealthy businessman like Donald Trump would have an edge over most other experienced businessmen if he also has millions of FREE AMERICA PARTY members helping with the cost of getting elected.

Heck, there are 25 million golfers in the country. Maybe we should hold a golf tournament between Presidential candidates in the 2012 and 2016 Presidential elections instead of holding debates, so the voters can watch the "real" candidates come through! Let each candidate put up his own money into the purse, and let each candidate post his or her own handicap, and play for the "Net" lowest score. (I for one would like to see if each candidate's handicap is legitimate, or if he is a sandbagger!)

After watching such an event, we all will learn which candidates are honest, which candidates have integrity. We will learn who can handle stress, and who cannot! We will find out who handles adversity with calm and dignity, and which candidates have a temper. Let me watch such an event, maybe even compete in it myself, and the whole world will learn who should become the President of the United States. Let me watch such an event, and I'll tell you who we want as our President! You will know for yourself as well!

President Eisenhower entertained VIPs and diplomats on the golf course in Washington D.C., and I would like to think he analyzed those people just as I have outlined here. Perhaps, if we can help get Donald Trump elected President, he would recognize why he should select me as his Vice Presidential running mate once he makes it to the ballot. With millions of concerned Americans behind me at www.freeamericaparty.org, we would be able to make a difference!

Most Vice Presidents are delegated to entertaining diplomats from other countries. I would love the opportunity to entertain visiting diplomats to Washington D.C. on one of our country clubs, or meet them on a golf course in their respective countries. Believe me; I would then be able to report to the President **exactly** what he could expect from that diplomat in the future!

I am a businessman who has started and run six small businesses since my college days majoring in Business Management, from creating and selling the world's first cordless telephone in 1970, to new innovations in golf equipment, to the first and only service company that offers millions of golfers help in setting up play on private country clubs in the U.S.

America is strong because of the millions of small business owners who employ tens of millions of other Americans, and they deserve better from their federal government than they have been receiving the last few years. I think the most people I ever employed in any one business was 55 employees. But I know what this country needs to be profitable, so we no longer need to borrow billions of dollars from the banks, who at this rate will own our future, and our freedoms and our childrens' freedoms will die as a result! This country needs a businessman, not another politician, as our President.

I have shared with you some of my personal experiences with banks and with local law enforcement in this book. One of my proofreaders of this book asked me if I wasn't being a little bit petty in my complaints" about Chase Bank and Bank of America.

Sure, I could have done what most Americans do when they are charged an NSF fee by their bank; they just suck it up and let their bank take their money! But as a small business owner many times over I know the importance of having a bank that works with you and your employees, not against them!

A small business needs much more from its bank than simply having a checking account and a savings account. A small business needs a merchant account so it can allow customers to use credit cards to make purchases. A small business needs a line of credit so it can "finance" its sales to its customers, such as "2% ten, Net 30 days".

Banks in this country must change their ways if this country is to return to its pervious grandeur! Banks in this country MUST support small businesses, not hurt them with petty, tricky fees! Without small businesses in America there will be no America that we can be proud of in the future!

November 26, 2010

November 26, 2010 - (3:00 A.M.): I woke up with pain in my left hand. My whole left arm was numb, and the right side of my face was numb. I sat up and massaged my left arm while swinging it over my head to relieve the pinched nerve in my neck that had to be causing the problems. I tried to get back to sleep, and was successful around 5:00 A.M.

November 27, 2010

The right side of face is still numb from the top right side of my head to the lower right jaw.

November 28, 2010

I have the same symptoms as the day before.

November 29, 2010

I typed up an accident report about the golf cart accident I experienced on October 19, when I played golf with the two assistant pros at Quail Point Golf Course in Medford, Oregon. I took a copy of my Accident Report to Brent in the Quail Point pro shop and told Brent about the symptoms I was experiencing. I asked him if he could confirm when the Civil War tournament occurred so we could estimate when the cart accident happened. He checked his computer and confirmed the tournament was on the 23rd of October, and the accident happened on the 19th. I asked Brent to talk to his superiors to see what we should do regarding helping me get my neck checked.

Next, I called my doctor, Dr. Guthrie, in Mt. Shasta, CA to make an appointment to see him regarding my neck. His secretary told me I could not see him until the 9th of December at Noon.

November 30, 2010

I have the same symptoms. I had trouble sleeping again just like before.

December 1, 2010

I went to see Brent again at Quail Point pro shop to see if he had talked with his superiors. He said he had talked to Vince Domenzain, the General Manager at the club, and that Vince said he would send the incident "up to legal". I gave Brent a copy of the Accident Report I had typed up, and asked for his assistance in completing the Accident Report since we had not made such a report at the time of the accident. He said he would talk to Vince about my request. I took my typed Accident Report by several of the residences on the 4th hole to see if anyone remembered hearing the accident on October 19. One resident called Security, complaining I was not supposed to be knocking on doors. One security officer drove up, I explained to him what I was doing, and he suggested we go to his office for some assistance. I followed his car to his office at the Rogue Valley Manor.

I met Gary Elkinton, Security Supervisor. I told him why I was there, to get an Accident Report completed by all parties, and he responded, "Brent was driving the cart that ran into the back of your cart? Then you have nothing to worry about!" Gary had a Mr. Jim Van Horn come in and introduced us. Mr. Van Horn had me follow him while he called a Kristi Scales, their insurance agent, on the phone to see what they could do about helping analyze my neck then and there. He could not reach Kristi at the time, so he gave me a card with his number and her number on it. They said they would have Kristi call me about my neck. When I got home I emailed Gary and thanked him for his help. He replied to my email with a "Thanks."

I found it interesting that he not only said he'd help me get an accident report completed, but he also gave me his card with Kristi's phone number on it. He and a Jim Van Horn said they would have Kristi call me about helping with an analysis of my neck.

About an hour later I received an email from a Beth Lori, assistant general counsel for Pacific Retirement Services, Inc., telling me not to contact anyone at the Rogue Valley Manor any further. I was especially not to contact Gary Elkinton again. In her letter she stated the Mr. Santoni is not their employee, that they are under no legal obligation for Mr. Santoni's actions, and that "they will not be paying me for any injuries I allege I am experiencing as a result of the "alleged" accident."

I replied to her email with my email of December 1, asking if golfers playing their golf course are protected by any liability insurance if they get hurt while playing the course, at no fault of their own. She never replied back to me.

December 2, 2010

My son, Bobby, asked me if I wanted to try playing golf, but I told him I didn't want to risk it. But I did say I'd drive the cart for him. We went to Centennial, and it was raining. Bob still wanted to play, so we got our rain gear on and headed out on the course, with me driving and him playing. We had fun, but the right side of my face and neck were getting sore. At one point I cringed, and Bob asked me what happened. I told him I had just had a pain like a hot poker stabbing me in the right side of my neck. It lasted about 30 seconds.

December 3, 2010

My neck was getting worse, so I drove to the Ashland Hospital Emergency to see if they could help. There were four people ahead of me, and it looked like it would take hours to see someone, so I drove home.

December 4, 2010

I woke up with added problems with my neck! My right eye socket hurt, and hurt to touch when I tried to massage it. I had to drive to Yreka for my prescriptions. First I emailed this message to

Gary Elkinton, the chief security officer at Rogue Valley Manor who had tried to help me:

Gary,

We appear to have a failure to communicate regarding my request for your help filling out an Accident Report on the cart collision on October 19, on the Quail Point Golf Course.

The Medford Police Department told me your security office should help complete such a report. That is all I need from your office. I never asked for anything else.

I received an email from an attorney the other day representing Pacific Retirement Services, Inc. stating Brent Santoni is not your employee. I know that.

Please request an accident statement from Brent and from Anthony Ulloa regarding what happened on the course on October 19, 2010.

Thank you,

Pete Baumann

I never heard back from him. I asked Bobby if he had talked to Sione Saenz about signing a statement about the accident. Bob informed me that Sione told him that Brent had cautioned Sione about what he said in any such statement. **Brent was telling Sione what to say in an accident statement?**

December 5, 2010

I bought a new shower head with massage options to try to reduce the pain in my neck. Symptoms that continued as before include numbness from the top right side of my head down to my lower right jaw. Also my right eye socket throbs at times, on and off. I am still having no luck getting in to see a doctor before my appointment December 9 with Dr. Guthrie. I took a chance and drove 35 minutes to Yreka to see if Emergency could get me in, but they were swamped with patients, and told me it would be hours before they could see if I stayed.

I asked, "How many hours?"

The nurse replied, "Hours!"

Other, new symptoms include short-term memory loss (I can think of something I need to do, and get up to go to my table to write it down, before I forget what I needed to do! When I get the note pad in my hands, I have forgotten what I wanted to remember.)

December 5, 2010

At 4:00 P.M., I drove to the Sports Authority in Medford where Bob and Sione work, and presented Sione with another written request that he email me with his statement about what happened on the golf course on October 19, since he was the only other witness. I gave Bob a copy of that request so he could witness the exchange. Sione said he would email it tonight.

His email was on my computer when I got home:

From: Sione <sionesaenz@gmail.com>
Date: December 2, 2010 8:17:24 PM PST
To: "bsantoni@quailpointgolf.com"
<bsantoni@quailpointgolf.com>
Subject: Incident report

On October 19, 2010 Brent Santoni, Anthony Ulla, Peter Baumann and I were all playing a quick round of golf at Quail Point golf course. As I started walking down from the T-box

on 4 to the green I heard a noise by the bathroom down the side walk. As I arrived everyone was getting out of their carts, reassuring each other that one another were okay. I asked Peter if he was okay, he replied he was fine. We then proceeded to the green to finish out.

Sione A Saenz

The first thing that was obvious to me was that Sione had sent his "statement" to Brent, the pro who had run into me, three days earlier! He had told me he had not talked to Brent about what was in his statement, yet it was obvious from his email to me that he had done just that on December 2!

His statement: **He "heard a noise!"**

I replied to his email with my comment that he had lied to me about not talking to Brent about his statement. Sione called me on his phone just a few minutes after I had sent him my email. **He said he would agree to change his statement, saying "I heard a screech, and I heard a crash, but that is all I will say."** I told him just to tell the truth, and all of the truth. Then I ended the phone call. I was tired of talking to him.

At 7:00 P.M., I am trying to take care of my weekly bookkeeping for www.reciprocalgolf.com, processing credit card sales, and I can't concentrate! Major headache!

December 6, 2010

Bob drove me to Dr. Guthrie's office in Mt. Shasta. He had a cancelation, so I could see him sooner than December 9. He took an X-ray of my neck, and reported it showed no bone breakage. He ordered an MRI, and told me to wait to hear when it could be done. The same symptoms were still going on going on for about a week now.

December 7, 2010

Bob wanted to play golf today, and I wanted to support him. So I went to Centennial Golf Club with him and drove the cart while he played. I put my golf clubs in storage after he played. **After three years of not being able to play golf due to surgeries, I was able to start playing again in September, 2010. Now I can't play due to Brent Santoni driving his golf cart into mine.**

At 6:00 P.M., I received an email from Sione ranting on about his being upset that I was "forcing him" to tell the truth, or else! I printed it out and gave it to Bobby, to show him what kind of people he had as friends. He apologized for his "friend", but said I needed to be more tactful with Sione. I told Bob to be tactful with Sione if he wanted to, but that I was disappointed he had such "low-character" friends, and that I no longer wanted to see or talk with Sione any further.

I got in a big fight with Bobby over that issue! I lost my temper, something I had never done with him before. Bob went to his fiancé's house for the night. I knew I was wrong to argue with Bob, and promised I would apologize to him when I saw him the next morning. I felt like I was changing into another person due to the constant headache I was suffering as a result of the neck injury, and did not like the person I was becoming.

December 8, 2010

The Yreka hospital called me and said they could schedule my MRI in about a week. I asked why so long, and she said it would take time for Dr. Guthrie's office to mail the X-rays to me. I told her I needed help sooner than that, because I felt like I was losing my mind due to the injury. It felt like my head was swollen, and pressure on my brain was causing me to forget almost everything, and I couldn't get any work done.

I offered to drive to Mt. Shasta the next day and bring back whatever they needed to the Yreka hospital. They called back an hour later saying they could schedule my MRI for Friday, the 10th, if I did that. I agreed.

My eyes are starting to hurt more and more. My eyesight is getting worse! I have always had 20/20 vision, but have used reading glasses for up close. Now things are blurry, bouncing around.

Bobby came home from meeting with Brent Santoni, hoping to convince Brent to give me an honest written statement about what happened on the 19th of October. Brent informed Bob that he was instructed by O B Sports not to talk to anyone about what happened on that date regarding the cart collision.

I was reminded that Vince Domenzain had informed me by phone a few days ago that the accident statements by Brent and Anthony were forwarded to O B Sports to go into their employee files, and were not available to anyone else.

December 10, 2010

I drove the 30 minutes down to the Yreka hospital for the MRI. The girl doing the test asked me if I was claustrophobic, and I told her I had had two MRI's before, one for more than an hour, with no problems.

She had me lie on my back and the table entered the unit. Within 30 seconds I panicked! I had noticed my personality changing in the last week, and I was getting more and more emotional, losing my temper, and becoming argumentative. I was going nuts in the MRI unit! I tried to think of something I could concentrate on so I could calm down. I thought of how badly I felt about arguing with Bobby previously. I started thinking about what I could do for Bob to show how sorry I was. Thinking about anything other than being stuck in that MRI unit would help.

I started planning how I would contact Arnold Palmer and ask him if he could play a round of golf with Bobby the next time Arnie came out to Klamath Falls to check on his Running Y Golf Club. Klamath Falls was only an hour drive from Talent, OR. I knew Bobby would be ecstatic about playing with Arnie, and would have a ton of fun telling his golfing buddies about it!

Putting that plan into action in my mind at that time kept me from thinking about the MRI unit, and before I knew it, I was out of there! Driving back to Talent I kept thinking about my plan and it helped me make it back without falling asleep. For years I had commuted between Yreka, CA and Palm Springs, driving the 752 miles each way in 10.5 hours, including two gas stops. Now I couldn't drive 30 minutes without dozing off, and getting headaches at the same time. I'm having difficulty with my eyesight as well. I had to get some help from the cart accident! I kept thinking of all the things I had to do in the next six months before I retired, and was worried my mind would be gone long before I could make it all happen! I have always been sharp, in command, and I do not like what I am feeling right now.

I also thought about the article I had read online about how X-rays, MRI's and CAT scans did not detect "soft-tissue" neck and brain injuries in whiplash cases, so I wondered why I was wasting my time. The article also said many doctors did not even know about that subject, or who they should refer a patient to who was having such symptoms. I started getting concerned that I would never be able to convince anyone that I had suffered injuries from the cart accident, and without such proof I would not be able to afford the medical help I needed to (hopefully) get better.

December 11, 2010

I was supposed to drive to Los Angeles this week to pick up my son, Pete, with his computer and other stuff he needs to put on his movie screening on the 17th, but I was afraid to drive that far due to my neck and head injuries. Instead, I bought him a train ticket for a 23 hour-train ride to Klamath Falls, OR. I figured I could drive the hour and a half to pick him up in K. Falls Sunday morning. This evening my eyesight was getting worse, and my eyes hurt. I was afraid I should not try to drive to Klamath Falls in the morning to pick up Pete from the train station, so I called Pete's friend Shabo and asked if he could drive over in the morning to pick up Pete. He said he could, so that took a load off my mind!

December 12, 2010

I decided to take it easy today and watch golf and football all day. Symptoms are getting consistent and steady; headache, dizziness, eyesight fuzzy, and eyes hurt all day, the right eye worse than the left. After November 26, I started using Ambien again to sleep at night. Today, for the first time, I took another Ambien at 3:00 P.M. to try to sleep during the day to get away from the headache and dizziness!

December 16, 2010

I received a phone call from Dr. Guthrie today with the results of my MRI. He confirmed I had had **recent injuries to my neck, from the C3-4 vertebrae to the C7-T1 vertebrae, indicated the injuries were serious, and that I would need surgery, possible fusion, etc. Technically, the report stated I had "severe central**

and mild bilateral foraminal stenosis". The report listed other details that are confusing to me; too technical! I notified Phil Green, President of O.B. Sports, of the findings by email. He never replied to my email.

December 19, 2010

My son's premier of his independent film, SPIN OF FABRICATIONS, which I produced for him over the last four years, was today. I operated the projector at the Meese Auditorium at the SOU campus for the approximate 110 viewers who attended. Halfway through the 80 minute viewing I felt sick and almost passed out in the projection booth. I sat down and rotated my head while massaging my neck and started feeling better in a few minutes. After the movie finished, there was a Champagne celebration party, but I missed it and went home early to sit in my massage chair. My neck and head were killing me!

O.B. Sports Management has been emailing me, stating they will do whatever is necessary to help me with my neck injuries since November 30, 2010. I would have been able to get help sooner if Pacific Retirement Services, Inc.'s attorney had not interfered with my attempts to get a written accident report from those involved in the accident, and the one other witness who was playing with us.

I do not understand how Pacific Retirement Services, Inc. can get away with covering up the fact that the accident happened by having their attorney interfere with my getting an accident report when it happened on their property!

The people in the golf industry were trying to do the right thing, while the people in the medical and retirement profession were covering up what had happened! As things turned out two months later, I was wrong about O.B. Sports! The appearance that they wanted to help was just that, appearances.

The incident regarding my neck injury is an example of what is wrong with our politicians in Washington D.C. Have you ever noticed that most of our United States Senators and Representatives are attorneys, or were attorneys before they ran for office? The same is true of state governors. Most of our Presidents were attorneys before being elected, with a few exceptions. Ronald Reagan was an actor, as was Arnold Schwarzenegger. One state governor, Jesse Ventura, was a retired professional wrestler.

What is your opinion of most attorneys? Give that some thought. Now, what is your opinion of our elected representatives in Washington, knowing that most of them are or were attorneys? Are you starting to see where I am going with this?

In 1975, I met a man named George Romero, who specialized in advising wealthy clients how to shelter most of their taxable income to reduce the amount of income taxes they had to pay. George was amazing in that he had invented a new way to shelter income for his clients earning more than $500,000 per year!

George taught me how to do the same thing for people I knew in that kind of tax bracket. In most cases, I brought fairly wealthy people that I knew to George, and together we would show the client how we would save him from $100,000 or more in income taxes for the year.

George had one rule that I had to follow. He told me never to bring him an attorney or a doctor for help with their tax problems!

Why wouldn't George help attorneys or doctors with their income tax problems? As George explained it to me, "Attorneys and doctors earn a lot of money per hour for what they do, but they are the worst when it comes to understanding what I can do for them. If I save an attorney or a doctor $100,000 in taxes, and then charge them a $2,500 consultation fee for my help, they scream!! They ask how I can charge them so much for one hour's worth of work?"

George explained to me that was why attorneys and doctors make the worse businessmen. They live in a totally different world than the rest of us. They feel their time is worth hundreds, even thousands of dollars per hour, but no one else's time is worth very much.

Now are you beginning to understand why our elected politicians are not doing a good job in Washington D.C.?

Our Federal Government is a big business, and the American people need businessmen to run the government, not attorneys!

February 3, 2011

I learned today that O.B. Sports Management has been pretending for months to be concerned about my neck! They had been delaying my attempts to obtain a written accident statement since November 28, 2010, so it would be more difficult for me to prove what had happened on October 19, 2010. I had no accident report, and had not been able to get details on the condition of the golf carts after the collision.

O.B. Sports' insurance company, Travelers Insurance, notified me today that they were taking the following position regarding the cart incident:

1. "I had not been injured because I continued playing golf for another three weeks after the incident."

2. "My problems with my neck and head were the progression of previous problems with my spine that were evident in a previous MRI three years earlier."

3. "There was no evidence of any damage to the carts involved in the 9/19/10 incident." (They had the date of the accident wrong, but that is minor) I had not been able to examine the carts involved

because no one would cooperate with my requests for a written accident statement.

I immediately emailed Dr. Guthrie's office and asked my doctor to send me a follow-up letter further clarifying that I had new, more recent and serious injuries that occurred long after the MRI of 2008. In anticipation of getting such a letter, I made an appointment with a personal injury attorney in Medford, OR.

My hopes of O.B. Sports Management doing the right thing so I would not have to go to court are gone. It seemed that my rule that the game of golf taught people honesty and integrity only applied to one-on-one experience playing with an individual. It did not mean that people in the golf business made them automatically an honest company!

FINAL THOUGHTS

I hope you have enjoyed reading LOVE WAS NOT ENOUGH as much as I have enjoyed writing it. My story about my love affair with Patti for over 17 years is true. The end of that story is sad. No, the end of that story is criminal! The end should have been a happy one, and would have been a happy one if it were not for two uneducated family members of Patti's. I intend to do something about that situation for others in the future through our work at the FREE AMERICA PARTY.

My story about my golf businesses is also true. Over the last 17 years I have learned a lot about marriage, about raising children, about conducting business, about politics, about life in general.

I hope my suggestions to young couples about maintaining a happy marriage make sense to you. Ladies, if your husband is the breadwinner in the union, especially if he owns his own business, allow him to put his career first, and then he will put you first in his list of priorities. If you insist he put you first, ahead of his career, your marriage will not last.

When raising your children, encourage them to seek their dreams. Never discourage them in that quest. On November 24, 2010, the day before Thanksgiving, I spent much of my time helping my oldest son, Pete (Director's professional name, Rio Veradonir), prepare his Premier Screening of his independent film, **SPIN OF FABRICATIONS**, scheduled for December 17, 18, and 19 at Southern Oregon University in Ashland, OR. Pete had been working on editing the film in Los Angeles since May of 2010. I received the following email from Pete on November 24:

Dad,

Mike and I are making great progress on the film. It's amazing. You're going to be so proud of me. What an endeavor. The cinematography is beautiful. The special effects are astounding. The music is very artistic. Even the sound effects are coming together. We're finishing a great work of art.

As the deadline approaches, I'm getting nervous, though. We still have a lot to do. I know we can finish it in time, but I'd like to increase Mike's hours from 20 to 30 hours per week, and take him through Dec. 7th.

Also, I need to bring my computer and keyboard with me when I come north (for the purpose of burning DVDs, and allowing the musician Robbie to play piano at the reception). Robbie is an Ashland celebrity, and he's playing for us for free. Pretty cool. Anyway, since I need to bring these things, is there any way you can drive down and pick me up Dec. 8th? Or can I rent a car? I think it would be cheaper for you to pick me up, but it's your call. If you'd prefer, I can fly, but I'm nervous about flying with my computer.

Thanks, Dad. I love you very much. I know you're stressed out, and I'm sorry about that. I can't tell you enough how much your support has meant to me through this whole process. Very few parents would be as supportive as you've been of my film. Very, very few indeed. Almost none. I'm aware of how lucky I am to have such an amazing father, and I hope never to take it for granted.

Love,

Your son.

Receiving that email makes all the years supporting Pete's dream of being a movie director worthwhile!

I hope that my sharing my experiences in this book will help you be more successful in your own marriage, in raising your own children, in your own career, in your own life.

Please join with me by joining the FREE AMERICA PARTY at www.freeamericaparty.org. I cannot become your Vice President the traditional way because only the candidates selected by the Republican Party or the Demographic Party can and will be elected.

So, **here is my plan, our plan**: My goal is to be selected as the Vice-Presidential running mate of either the Republican or Democratic final candidate. I want and need your help in getting Donald Trump selected as the candidate for one of those major parties. With tens of millions of Americans behind me as FREE AMERICA PARTY members, one or both of those candidates would (should) choose me as their running mate if they want to win the election!

After the Presidential election, as your Vice President I can start from within the system to push for the changes we have discussed in this book. Together, we will bring about real change, not the changes that politicians have promised us for decades!

Won't it be nice when we all can live healthier, happier, longer lives in the future by sharing our life's ambitions and knowledge with friends and family? I especially encourage you to email me at contact@lovewasnotenough.com about the health aspects of the anti-aging products I learned about from "Bill", the medical researcher I played golf with on October 15, 2010. In all my years as a small business owner, I can't remember any opportunity that can match the health and financial opportunities this new product offers!

If you care about your freedoms, and the future freedoms your children can and will enjoy if we are successful in changing Washington, please go to www.freeamericaparty.org and join our cause. Together we can make America a better place to live. Heck, together we can make our entire planet a better place to live and flourish!

I look forward to hearing from you.

Peter Edward Baumann

President – www.probegolf.com

www.reciprocalgolf.com

www.veradonir.com

www.spinoffabrications.com

www.freeamericaparty.org

Author: – www.lovewasnotenough.com

Email addresses: – contact@reciprocalgolf.com

contact@lovewasnotenough.com

contact@freeamericaparty.org

contact@probegolf.com

POSTSCRIPT

The author hopes that readers of LOVE WAS NOT ENOUGH will send him their comments and opinions about the true story depicted in the book. Do you believe the author is correct in his opinion about Patti's family, or do you think her family was correct when they took over caring for Patti, and took her away from the author?

Readers are invited to send their comments and opinions to the author at contact@lovewasnotenough.com. If and when you submit your comments, please give us your permission to use your comments in any sequel or motion picture that may follow this book. Your contact information (email) will not be made public. Thank you!

The very first feedback I received from this book was from another proofreader, as follows:

> **Mr. Baumann,**
>
> **You made the right decision in choosing your sons over any other person & no one can blame you for that......& that is not the reason that you & Patti are not together now. If it had not been for her memory loss after her heart attack, you two would probably be married & living happily ever after. You can't blame anyone for that happening. I know Carol has it made with a built in babysitter & the extra money coming in for her mom, but that will get old when Patti is no longer needed as a babysitter & becomes a burden around the house. It will happen; no matter how much Carol loves her mom....parents are not meant to stay with their grown children...it doesn't work! I am shocked Mick still lives with her! Is Carol collecting his retirement money as well?**
>
> **I know it's been over a year, but maybe you can start emailing Patti. Do they "allow" her to use a computer? Maybe she would like to correspond with you & you can begin to make her understand what she means to you. She is your life & needs to know it. You have spent your entire**

grown up life trying to help everyone but yourself & now it's come back to "bite" you....& that has to hurt. Just don't give up on being happy again. It will happen!

You have my permission to use this statement anywhere in the future.

Toni

The author's reply:

Toni,

Thanks for your input. I believe it will be a miracle if Patti gets the chance to get away from her family, and contact me. She no longer has the common sense to know when a member of her family is full of it!

Pete

Two days later an email came in from another proofreader, as follows:

Mr. Baumann,

I finished proofreading your book last night, and mailed it back to you this morning with a few typos marked, and a couple of suggestions for rewriting several places. Call me if you have any questions about my notes. May I offer my opinion about the situation with Patti?

First of all, my best friend's father is a professional counselor. He has counseled couples for over 25 years, and is mostly familiar with couples wherein either the husband or wife suffers a trauma. I discussed your situation with him, and he told me that it is mandatory that both parties in a couple be counseled together after the trauma, to allow them to move forward from their previous relationship to a continued relationship together. Separating Patti from you was the worst thing her family could have done to her. He told me that it is unfortunate that you and Patti never signed a POWER OF ATTORNEY for each other, each stating he/she wanted the other person to care for them if

incapacitated in any way. That would have given you the right to care for Patti after the heart attack.

You obviously were already taking care of Patti for the last four years. From what I read, you were also helping her kids with all of their problems. You had, and still have, Patti listed as your beneficiary in your life insurance policy, wherein she will receive $100,000 if anything happens to you. Now that her family has kidnapped her from you, I recommend you talk to an attorney, to make sure her family does not have a chance to acquire that $100,000 if something should happen to you while Patti is under medication, and living with any of her family. It sounds to me that her daughter would jump all over your $100,000 in life insurance if she ever got the chance!

It is also obvious that no one in her family has more than a standard high school education, if that. For that reason I am not surprised to see them make the mistakes they made after Patti's heart attack. Maybe some time in the future the laws in the United States will recognize that couples who choose to live together come under the same laws as married couples. You two lived together for four years, and many marriages do not last for four years.

If Patti regains her previous level of common sense in the near future, perhaps she will read your book, be reminded of all the things the two of you shared for 16 years, and call you to talk. It sounds to me like she is too intelligent to settle for living with her family for the rest of her life. I believe she will want to get back to the exciting and loving life she shared with you before the heart attack. By the way, I assume you never were given the opportunity to take her to Hawaii as you wanted to do for her Christmas present in 2008, due to her family's interference?

One final comment: The night you drove Patti to the hospital, you promised her during the ride that you would never let anything bad happen to her. She answered, "I know that, Pete. You are my best friend. I love you." Then you were able to save her life when you stayed with her, instead of going to the waiting room as the nurse told you to do. By staying by her side, you were able to keep your promise that you made to her in the car, and did not let her falling from the gurney split her head open.

My question to you is, "Does Patti even remember that promise you made to her that night, and does she even know that she is alive today only because of your actions that night? From what you said in the book, her family has never even once thanked you for saving Patti's life that night. Am I correct in assuming that they would not want Patti to know what you did that night to save her life?

I wish you both the very best.

You have my permission to use this statement anywhere in the future.

Donna

The author's reply:

Donna, you assume correctly. Patti will probably never see Hawaii, because it won't be in her family's interests for her to enjoy a Hawaiian trip. The family might take her to Hawaii some day, but they won't let her out of their sight. They can't afford to let Patti think for herself, or experience anything exciting on her own! If she does, she might gain her common sense back and leave them.

And don't worry about Carol getting her hands on my $100,000. She is greedy, but not smart enough to do that!

You are also correct in assuming that her family would not want Patti to know what I did that night to save her life. And they would never want her to find out how I saved her life. Maybe if she did find out, she might call me to talk. If she does ever call me, maybe I'll get the opportunity to remind her of the goals and dreams she shared with me, and I'll be able to convince her to follow through with those dreams, with me as her friend, lover, soul mate, and guide to reaching her dreams and goals.

Pete

February 2, 2010 – A fourth proofreader sent me her comments along with her proofed copy:

Mr. Baumann, I'm sorry, but I do not believe Patti ever loved you! She just said she did all those years so she could use you to give her and her kids money, and to get you to spend money on her. You would have been better off if you had just had a prostitute on the side for sex when you wanted it. You wasted your money and years of your life on a woman who never loved you, and never appreciated what you did for her and her children, including saving her life!

Your son was right; you can do much better. Forget her and her hillbilly family and find a good woman who will love you the way you deserve to be loved.

You have my permission to use this statement anywhere in the future.

Shelley,

The author's reply to Shelley:

You may just be right, but I choose to believe she did love me. We were best friends. I believe her younger sister just confused her by lying to her, telling her that I wanted her to move out of our house, telling her that her relationship with me was based on alcohol. I believe that telling Patti that I wanted her to move out of our house at Lake Shastina when I wanted to spend the rest of my life with her was the cruelest thing anyone could have done to her, especially her own sister! It didn't do me much good either. Thanks for your comments, Shelley.

Pete Baumann

On February 25, a fifth proofreader returned her copy of the manuscript, and her own comments about the book. I think this proofreader hit the nail right on the head, and solved the question of why my best friend and soul mate would leave me after all the things we shared for 16 years.:

> **Mr. Baumann, there is an aspect of your story that you may not have figured out yet. Patti probably did not become confused and allow her family to lie to her just because of her brain damage from the heart attack. If that was true, she would not have had the common sense to call you around October 27, 2008 from her daughter's house in Winthrop, WA and ask you to come and get her. Therefore, she was thinking clearly enough two months after the heart attack. Her mind became confused long after the heart attack, and because of her sister and cousin lying to her in December of 2008, telling her things such as, "You wanted her to move out, or her relationship with you was based on alcohol, or it was time for her to finally recognize her guilt for having an affair with you "a million years ago". (What a joke.)**
>
> **So, I do not believe the heart attack caused her to leave you at all. It is obvious it was the lies told to her by her family that caused her to become confused, and ultimately leave you. I hope that someday she figures that out for herself, and leaves her family completely. They do not deserve to have her in the family. The younger sister, the cousin, and the daughter are especially guilty of telling lies to Patti to get control over her. I hope Patti becomes strong again on her own in the future and realizes she owes everything to you over the 16 years, including the fact that she lived that night at the Emergency Room instead of dying from splitting her head open.**
>
> **You two definitely belong together. I hope Patti realizes that some day and calls you to get back together. You deserve her. Not only that, but if they ever give someone a Nobel Prize for persistence and perseverance, you should**

win it hands down. No one deserves to have to put up with her family for all those years.

You are welcome to use my comments any way you wish in the future.

Sincerely,

Emme

The author's reply to Emme:

Emme, you are amazing! I think you just won the grand prize!

You answered the question that has puzzled me for over a year; why did Patti, the love of my life, my best friend, decide to leave me in December, 2008, after I thought we would spend the rest of our lives together?

Patti had already showed signs of improving after the heart attack. That was obvious on October 27, 2008, when she asked me over the phone if I would drive north to her daughter's house and bring her home.

That was two months after the heart attack, and was exactly what I had predicted she would do six weeks earlier in Yreka, before she went north with Carol. I knew that she would not be able to stand living in the same house with her ex.

Four months after the heart attack is when she and I should have started therapy, and counseling together as a couple, as Dr. Andersen told me we had to do if her mind was going to heal properly. But that is when both Muriel and Carol called Patti (at the 800 number I had set up for Patti on her cell) and started telling her not to trust my decisions.

That is exactly when Patti started showing signs of heartache and confusion about everything that was going on at that time.

When we could not proceed with proper counseling due to Muriel's, Carol's and Julie's interference and lying to her, her intelligence started to slip. Once again here is proof that I was right all along, and Patti's family was wrong. Dr. Andersen was right in his diagnosis, but what chance did Patti have to do the right thing when she believed Muriel, the know-it-all in the family?

That is further proof that what Dr. Andersen said would happen did happen. Going through any kind of counseling by herself months later would be pointless, as further explained by Dr. Andersen. The family has seen to it that Patti will never recover "properly" as explained by the American Psychological Association. To recover properly, she had to continue her life, with counseling, as she had lived just prior to the heart attack, with (in her case) the man she chose to live with for four years. She was kept from doing that by Muriel, Julie, and Carol, with Margaret not wanting that to happen, but unable to stop it.

Patti was my life, and I hoped to spend the rest of my life making her happy. She does not deserve to have family members who hurt her as much as they hurt her psychologically. As I already said in the book, they should be in jail for the mental abuse they have put Patti through.

I am hoping that someday Patti's common sense will come back to her, and when a family member tells her something that is obviously wrong, she will tell them that they are full of shit, like she used to do.

Pete

Beginning February 19, 2010, I started receiving emails from people who read the rough draft of my book before it was released in hardback by the publisher. Here is one from my own son:

> **"Dad, please change the names of characters in the (original copy of the) book and take out the pictures of Patti and her family. They are not a selling point, anyway. It makes your book look like it's about white trash, since much of mom's family is, including Patti. Mom (Katy) and Nona (Margaret) are the only classy ones of the bunch. Anyway, please don't use this book as "revenge." Bobby feels the same way."**

> **You may use this statement any way you choose in the future.**

> **Pete (Alan) Baumann**

Reply to Pete's email:

Pete, I agree with one of my proofreaders who called the family hillbillies, but to call them white trash? That's a little harsh. I'm sorry you put Patti in that same category. I know she was no rocket scientist, but she had more common sense than most five people put together before her heart attack. Most importantly she was my best friend, and she was my soul mate. That makes her very special, if only to me. I loved her with all my heart.

I remember the day that Muriel drove out to our house to pick up some (free stuff) I was giving away before moving out of the house, and she brought Patti with her. Patti walked up to me and said, "Pete, here is the cell phone you gave me. I don't want to be indebted to you anymore, so I want you to take this back. We are finished."

Pete, the first thought that went through my mind at that moment was that Patti's statement, or skit, was obviously rehearsed. I asked myself who could have given her that line to repeat to me. The next day I learned it was you!

You said you went by Nona's house the night before, and told Patti that she would be doing me a favor if she told me, in no uncertain terms, that we were finished, and to return the cell phone to make that point.

I know you didn't think much of Patti, mostly because you think she caused the divorce between your Mom and me, but that is not true. I would have divorced your Mom anyway, due to the reasons I state in this book. Secondly, you keep telling me, "Dad, you can do better than Patti." Pete, that might be true if I was looking for my intellectual match, but my best friend's and my soul mate's intelligence had nothing to do with what I wanted in a woman. Patti and I had a connection that cannot be described in words. Believe me when I tell you that you did not do me a favor when you told Patti she would be doing me a favor if she broke off our relationship. She was my life, and my life almost ended when she left me. It took all my strength and intelligence to carry on when I did not wish to live without her.

At a time when her sister, her cousin, and her daughter were filling her mind with a bunch of lies, it did not help when you told her another (white) lie. I know you did what you thought was good for me, but it was not. If I am ever lucky enough to get Patti back, please do me a favor and let us be happy together.

    Dad

The author

The author with Arnold Palmer
at the 1992 GTE Western Classic
in Seattle, WA

The author states in LOVE WAS NOT ENOUGH why America needs an experienced businessman in the White House, and not another politician (attorney)! He hopes Donald Trump will run for the Presidency, and the author will endorse "The Donald" if he does run.

Shawn Beasley,
one of the stars of SPIN OF FABRICATIONS

Sophia Palosaari, star of SPIN OF FABRICATIONS

The author's son, Pete, directing a scene from SPIN OF
FABRICATIONS at Mossbrae Falls, Dunsmuir, CA

The author and his son, Bobby,
at Lake Shastina Golf Resort, 2000

The author's son, Pete (professional name Rio Veradonir), and
Pete's fiancé, Talia, at recording studio for
SPIN OF FABRICATIONS

The author's son, Pete (Rio), with Sophia Palosaari at a
recording session for SPIN OF FABRICATIONS

Patti in the wig the author bought for her, near the
Lake Havasu Golf Course, March, 1998.

The author and Patti at his parents' 60th Anniversary Party in
Riverside, CA, April, 2006.

Patti on the author's 27' Bayliner on Lake
Havasu, 1998.

Trump National Golf Club entrance. The author endorses Donald Trump for President if "The Donald" decides to run. The author argues why America needs an experienced businessman in the White House, not another politician, and not more attorneys!